fishes of the northern gulf of mexico

t.f.h.

jerry g. walls

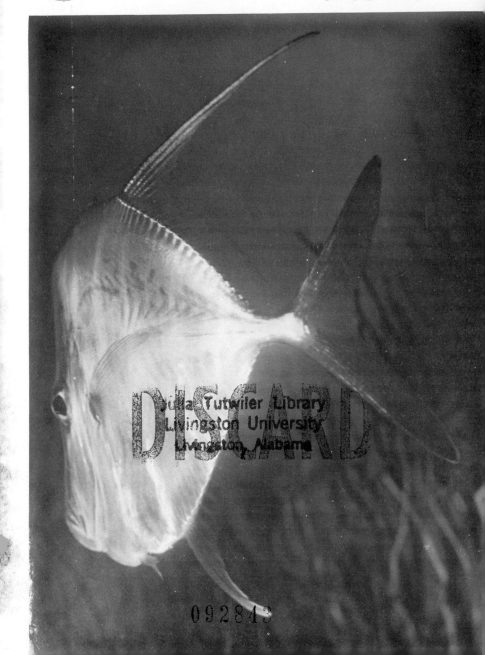

Frontis: *Selene vomer*. Photo by G. Marcuse.

ISBN 0-87666-445-1

Distributed in the U.S.A. by T.F.H. Publications, Inc., 211 West Sylvania Avenue, P.O. Box 27, Neptune City, N.J. 07753; in England by T.F.H. (Gt. Britain) Ltd., 13 Nutley Lane, Reigate, Surrey; in Canada to the book store and library trade by Clarke, Irwin & Company, Clarwin House, 721 St. Clair Avenue West, Toronto 10, Ontario; in Canada to the pet trade by Rolf C. Hagen Ltd., 3225 Sartelon Street, Montreal 382, Quebec; in Southeast Asia by Y.W. Ong, 9 Lorong 36 Geylang, Singapore 14; in Australia and the south Pacific by Pet Imports Pty. Ltd., P.O. Box 149, Brookvale 2100, N.S.W., Australia. Published by T.F.H. Publications Inc., Ltd., The British Crown Colony of Hong Kong.

To my mother

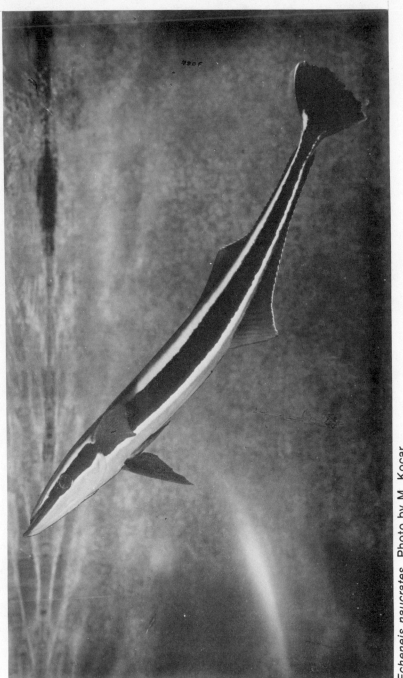

Echeneis naucrates. Photo by M. Kocar.

CONTENTS

ACKNOWLEDGMENTS 9
MAP OF AREA 10
INTRODUCTION 11
THE FISH FAUNA OF THE NORTHERN GULF . 16
IMPORTANT TERMS AND STRUCTURES 21
LITERATURE 35
FAMILY AND SPECIES ACCOUNTS 38
ORDER SQUALIFORMES 39
Orectolobidae 39
Rhincodontidae 40
Odontaspididae 41
Alopiidae 42
Lamnidae 43
Carcharhinidae 45
Sphyrnidae 54
Squatinidae 57
ORDER RAJIFORMES 58
Pristidae 58
Rhinobatidae 59
Torpedinidae 60
Rajidae 61
Dasyatidae 64
Myliobatidae 68
Mobulidae 70
ORDER ACIPENSERIFORMES 72
Acipenseridae 72
ORDER SEMIONOTIFORMES 73
Lepisosteidae 73
ORDER ELOPIFORMES 74
Elopidae 74
Albulidae 76

ORDER ANGUILLIFORMES 76
Anguillidae 78
Moringuidae 78
Muraenidae.........79
Muraenesocidae 80
Congridae 81
Ophichthidae 84
Dysommidae 91
ORDER CLUPEIFORMES....................92
Clupeidae...........92
Engraulidae 99
ORDER MYCTOPHIFORMES 102
Synodontidae 102
ORDER SILURIFORMES 107
Ariidae 108
ORDER BATRACHOIDIFORMES 109
Batrachoididae 109
ORDER GOBIESOCIFORMES................111
Gobiesocidae 111
ORDER LOPHIIFORMES 112
Antennariidae 112
Ogcocephalidae.....115
ORDER GADIFORMES 121
Bregmacerotidae ...122
Gadidae 122
Ophidiidae..........125
Carapidae 131
ORDER ATHERINIFORMES.................132
Exocoetidae 132
Belonidae...........139
Cyprinodontidae 142
Poeciliidae 147
Atherinidae.........149
ORDER BERYCIFORMES 150
Holocentridae.......150
ORDER ZEIFORMES 152
Caproidae 152

ORDER LAMPRIDIFORMES 153
Regalecidae 153
ORDER GASTEROSTEIFORMES 154
Aulostomidae 154
Fistulariidae 155
Syngnathidae 155
ORDER PERCIFORMES 163
Centropomidae 163
Percichthyidae 164
Serranidae 165
Grammistidae 185
Priacanthidae 185
Apogonidae 187
Branchiostegidae . . . 190
Pomatomidae 191
Rachycentridae 192
Echeneidae 192
Carangidae 195
Coryphaenidae 213
Lutjanidae 214
Lobotidae 222
Gerreidae 223
Pomadasyidae 225
Sparidae 230
Sciaenidae 237
Mullidae 246
Kyphosidae 248
Ephippidae 249
Chaetodontidae 250
Pomacanthidae 255
Pomacentridae 261
Labridae 269
Scaridae 277
Mugilidae 284
Sphyraenidae 288
Polynemidae 292
Opistognathidae 292

Dactyloscopidae 296
Uranoscopidae 297
Clinidae 304
Blenniidae 308
Callionymidae 317
Gobiidae 320
Microdesmidae 333
Acanthuridae 335
Trichiuridae 337
Scombridae 338
Xiphiidae 347
Istiophoridae 348
Ariommidae 351
Centrolophidae 352
Nomeidae 353
Stromateidae 355
Scorpaenidae 357
Triglidae 360
Dactylopteridae 370
ORDER PLEURONECTIFORMES............. 370
Bothidae 371
Soleidae 387
Cynoglossidae 390
ORDER TETRAODONTIFORMES............. 394
Triacanthodidae ....,394
Balistidae 395
Ostraciidae 406
Tetraodontidae 408
Diodontidae 413
Molidae 414
INDEX 417

COLOR ILLUSTRATIONS FOLLOW PAGE 257.
The illustration numbers correspond to the species
numbers in the text.

ACKNOWLEDGMENTS

The compilation of a book of this type depends on many people, most of whom died long ago—the original describers of the fishes concerned. The work of Issac Ginsburg, although commonly ignored or deprecated, was of immense importance, and this book would not have been possible without his basic researches into the taxonomy of Gulf fishes.

I am especially grateful to Warren Burgess for the loan of important literature and numerous discussions on taxonomic philosophy and the best approach to a guide book to fishes. Little unpublished information is contained herein, although the discussions of three groups—the cusk-eels, amberjacks, and batfishes—are based to a large extent on information supplied by Dr. C. Richard Robins, Miami, Dr. Frank J. Mather III, Woods Hole, and Dr. Margaret Bradbury, San Francisco, respectively. Any errors in interpretation of their information are of course exclusively mine.

Finally, to my wife, Maleta, I say thanks for putting up with three years of literature and drawings scattered throughout the house, long silent hours while drawing, and occasional long interludes during which nothing was done. Without her encouragement this book would have never been finished.

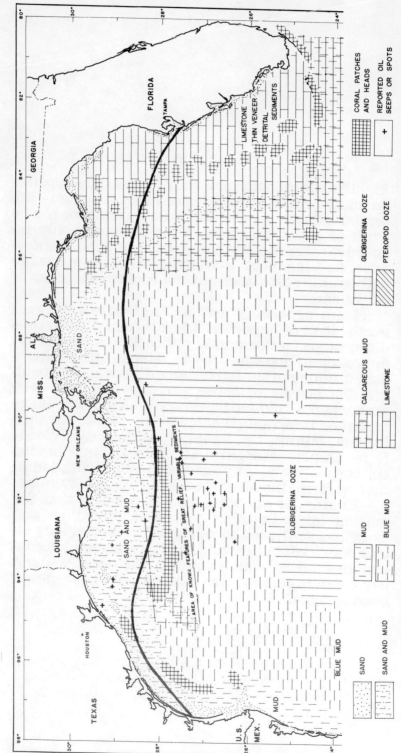

Part of the Gulf of Mexico, showing the area included by the 69° F. February isotherm. From P.S. Galtsoff, ed., *Gulf of Mexico*.

INTRODUCTION

Biologists working in the area of the Gulf of Mexico have always faced the difficult and often impossible task of trying to identify the fishes collected in both freshwater and marine habitats. The last twenty years have seen the publication of several state guides to freshwater fishes as well as more general guides to the fishes of the entire inland United States. Unfortunately, the marine fishes have not fared so well. Ichthyologists, both professionals and students, have had to rely on such excellent but greatly outdated works as Jordan and Evermann (1896-1900), Hildebrand and Schroeder's *Fishes of Chesapeake Bay* (1928), and Longley and Hildebrand's Tortugas paper (1941). Many species were described from Gulf material, but these papers are scattered in many different journals and hard to compile into a working library. The northern Caribbean has recently been well covered by such volumes as Bohlke and Chaplin's *Fishes of the Bahamas* (1968) and Randall's *Caribbean Reef Fishes* (1968), both of which contain many Gulf species, especially the tropical stragglers.

Unfortunately, even these diverse and not always adequate sources have seldom been available to general students and to fishery biologists, who have been forced to resort to Breder's *Field Book of Marine Fishes* (1929 and later editions), even though this work is over forty-five years old and was never adequate for the Gulf of Mexico to begin with. The nomenclatural and taxonomic changes which have occurred since 1929 are legion and affect the names of even some of the most common species in the Gulf of Mexico.

With the publication in 1960 and 1972 of *A List of Common and Scientific Names of Fishes* by the American Fisheries Society (called the AFS *Checklist* throughout this book), it became possible to compile a reasonably complete list of the marine fishes of the northern Gulf of Mexico and use up-to-date taxonomic concepts. Using this list as a basis, I have tried to compile short descriptions and illustrations of all the marine fishes likely to be encountered in the northern Gulf of Mexico between Pensacola, Florida and Brownsville, Texas. The depth range has been from estuaries to about twenty-five fathoms, excluding typically freshwater species adequately covered by the standard freshwater manuals.

One of the major problems in assembling this book has been in deciding which species to include and which to leave out. It was finally determined to include all species which have been listed from the northern Gulf, even when the records have never been authenticated but it seems likely that the species will eventually be found in our area. In addition, no book would be complete without including the stragglers, both from deeper water and from the warmer Caribbean. The inclusion of a species in this guide should not be taken as proof that a species actually occurs in the northern Gulf. Some of the larger snappers and groupers, for instance, have not been recorded from our area in as little as twenty-five fathoms, but it is likely that they do sometimes venture inshore. Some of the tropical species, such as the wrasses and angelfishes, almost certainly occur regularly on the poorly known coral patches off our shores or are attracted to the favorable habitats of the offshore oil rigs. I believe that most, if not all, of the fishes in this book will eventually be found in the northern Gulf. Just as certainly, many unexpected species not included here will also be found in our area. This probability should always be remembered when attempting to identify any fish.

Pelagic and other offshore species have also been included when they are of commercial or sporting interest. Thus the tunas and billfishes are illustrated here. It has been my experience that fishermen need all the help they can get when it comes to naming a fish—even most of the experienced charter boat captains and commercial trawlers cannot be relied upon to accurately identify even the most common species. This is not really their fault, but simply due to a lack of correct information.

Whether to include the reef fishes of southern Florida has been another difficult decision. It was finally decided that a compromise was in order. The fauna of the coral reefs of southern Florida is a more-or-less distinct unit comprised of many species that probably never stray into the colder waters of the northern Gulf. Their inclusion here would have been both unnecessary and confusing to the fishery biologist trying to identify a fish collected in an estuary in Louisiana, for instance. Yet some of the species found on the reefs are wide ranging and possibly occur on the southern edges of our range at least occasionally. For this reason a secondary coverage was added to this guide, including the coast of Florida between Pensacola and Tampa Bay. This western coast of Florida is home for several species which are adaptable enough to withstand occasional cold winters and not require a living coral reef to sustain life. This coast is also probably the true home of many species described by Jordan and his co-workers from the snapper banks off Pensacola. With very few exceptions, the coral-restricted gobies, blennies, and small eels found from the Tampa Bay area south have been omitted. Their place is in a book dealing with the reef fauna of southern Florida.

We are thus left with a total of 502 species illustrated and described in this guide, plus another dozen or two mentioned briefly in the text. This number includes all the species which I believe deserve a place on the list of fishes of the northern Gulf of Mexico plus a few which have been dubiously recorded from our area. The coverage is as complete as possible for the area between Brownsville, Texas, and Pensacola, Florida, and is at least ninety percent complete for the area between Pensacola and Tampa. It includes all species described or recorded in the literature before the end of 1973. The phrases "our area" or "our shores" of course refer to the northern Gulf between Brownsville and Tampa.

In any identification guide, one of the most important parts is the illustrations. I am not an artist nor have I had the funds or time to hire an artist. Perhaps a later worker will be able to do much better—which would not be too hard to do—but I have done my best. All the illustrations should be considered more as diagrammatic sketches than accurate portraits. The only criteria have been that the body shape and basic identification features show in each illustration. Color patterns are indicated, though usually much simplified. Diagnostic features are sometimes exaggerated for ease of comparison. I have tended to ignore or play down, whenever possible, the use of tooth characters, internal anatomy, and similar complicated identification characters in both the illustrations and discussions. Keys have been kept to a minimum and made as simple as possible. It is my experience that most people will not use a key under any circumstances.

It has fortunately been possible to include numerous plates of photos in this book, a feature which will be of much use to the biologist or other user trying to verify an identification. Please remember, however, that any photo or drawing has its limits—all fishes are variable and individual species may not fit either the photo or the drawing exactly.

No effort has been made to include information on breeding cycles, food habits, or detailed distribution of the species. This book has already grown far too large for the simple task it undertakes—identification of fishes. For the vast majority of our species what little natural history information is available is even more widely scattered than the taxonomic information. Most of the notes given here are based on the literature or on my limited observations on the coasts of Louisiana and Mississippi. Species said to be rare generally are so everywhere, but exceptional areas where they may be common can be expected. The same applies to species said to be common—no guide of this type can give detailed information for every area. Also, all the distributional notes given in this manual refer only to the northern Gulf of Mexico. Extralimital ranges are generally not given; most of our species have wide ranges.

Finally, I must admit that this work is in no way intended as a definitive work on the fishes of the northern Gulf. It has many weak spots of which I am already aware—the uneven quality of the illustrations, the often too brief descriptions, and the sometimes probably over-simplified statements of range and abundance. I believe that it will make it much easier for any biologist or other interested person to identify almost any fish he is likely to catch, see at the dock, find in the waste of shrimp trawls, or find dead on the beach. If I am right in this belief, then this book will have served its purpose.

Carapus bermudensis. Photo by W. Starck.

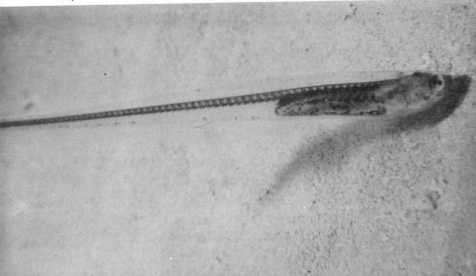

THE FISH FAUNA OF THE NORTHERN GULF

Although there is not room here for a detailed discussion of the various environments in the northern Gulf, a brief review of the major areas and types of environments available is necessary.

As used here, the northern Gulf of Mexico comprises the non-tropical waters of the United States coast from Florida to Texas. This area is in part characterized by the low surface temperatures, the February average being 69° F. or less. There are few areas of living coral reefs, although some small areas do occur on the southern edges of the area off Texas and Florida. These coral reefs are very poorly known and little published information exists on their fauna, especially off the Texas coast.

Our shores are characterized mostly by the great abundance of shallow brackish to fully saline bays and marshes. These estuarine areas are of major importance in the life cycles of numerous marine fishes and invertebrates, but are generally poorly known. The same applies to the shallow bay fauna. Several species of fish seem to either be restricted to estuarine areas and shallow bays or at least prefer such areas to such an extent that they are rare in other environments. Many of our gobies are found only here, as are some blennies, clupeids, drums, and the young stages of more typically deeper water species.

Unfortunately the estuarine habitat is poorly collected and much of it is inaccessible to the average collector lacking shallow-draft boats and small trawls. Thus the apparently restricted distribution and rarity of such estuarine fishes as the gold brotula and emerald goby, both of which can be relatively common in shallow, low salinity water. I would not be greatly surprised to find that there are undescribed species and perhaps genera of such shallow estuarine fishes yet to be discovered in our area. A careful study of estuarine fishes would certainly be worthwhile from both the taxonomic and ecological viewpoints.

Because the Gulf of Mexico is a relatively shallow enclosed basin with a very gradually sloping continental shelf over most of its northern edge, Gulf bottoms in the zero to ten fathom depth range tend to be muddy with silts from the numerous coastal rivers. There are also large areas with a mixture of mud and sand, but generally the shallow to moderately deep (ten fathoms) fauna must be able to survive in silty waters subject to a good bit of seasonal temperature change. Thus most of the tropical reef species which reach our shores cannot survive in the available environments. These fishes are adapted to relatively silt-free water which does not vary greatly in temperature with the seasons. Most of our shallow to moderate depth fauna is composed of wide ranging northern species such as the croakers and some sparids and grunts, plus large numbers of clupeids, gobies, and similar species which are commonly shared with the Atlantic seaboard of the southeastern United States. A few species in this depth range have become somewhat differentiated from their more northern counterparts, but the relationship is close and obviously differentiation only occurred recently.

The great delta of the Mississippi River has over the years deposited a gigantic layer of silt and at the same time dug deeply into the continental shelf. The delta marks a somewhat obscure division of some of our fauna into an eastern Gulf and western Gulf fauna. Whether this division actually exists or not is still subject to debate, but there is little doubt that some species occur mainly east of the delta while others are found generally to the west. Good examples of this are seen in the naked soles (*Gymnachirus*), the *Chasmodes* blennies, and the *Sphoeroides* puffers, each of which has a pair of closely related species generally distributed to the east or west of the delta and narrowly overlapping in the Mississippi-Alabama coastal area.

Very poorly known is the hard-bottom fauna of the northern Gulf, especially that part of the fauna not composed of the "tropical stragglers" which occur in our area during the summer, usually in the form of juveniles. The fishes which occur in resident populations on the offshore snapper banks, coral and rubble reefs, and the oil rigs are all poorly known, even if they seem to be relatively common in their habitat. Included in this category are such fishes as many of the eels, the pygmy sea bass, some of the flounders, the dogfishes, and many other species. The reader has only to look through the distribution notes in this book and see how many read "poorly known, seemingly most common on hard offshore bottoms." These hard bottoms are difficult to sample because nets are easily torn or lost completely; commercial fishermen looking for shrimp or trash fish for pet foods avoid such areas. Sportsfishermen, however, long ago learned that the hard "snapper banks" provide good fishing for many species of groupers, snappers, and other fishes.

A significant portion of our fauna is comprised of deeper water species generally found only beyond the ten to fifteen fathom depth level. Many of these are merely truly deepwater species which range to the edge of the continental shelf and are present in our area only as stragglers or juveniles, much as are the shallower water tropical stragglers. A few species, such as the ragged goby, seem to be restricted to an intermediate depth zone in the thirty fathom, more-or-less, level.

The fauna of the western coast of Florida and the southern portion of Texas differs considerably from that of the remaining area in the more common presence of such forms as butterflyfishes, pomacentrids, parrotfishes, cardinalfishes, and other more typically tropical species. In some cases these species almost certainly occur in our area in the form of small resident populations on offshore hard bottoms with clear water, numerous encrusting invertebrates for food, and relatively stable, though not necessarily warm, temperature. It is perhaps these resident populations which serve as the source for the rare tropical stragglers over the rest of our shores, not the recruitment of fishes from the reefs of the Caribbean. Systematic collecting with SCUBA on the offshore coral heads will probably add many species to our resident fauna.

Finally, there are a large number of offshore fishes which could be truthfully called pelagic (more properly epipelagic). Such fishes as the tunas, many sharks, the manta, headfishes, billfishes, and others probably never come near shore unless disabled or dead. They are a true part of our fauna, however, even if they never occur in as little as twenty-five fathoms. This is easily proved by visiting any commercial dock out of which fishing boats operate and noting the many small tunnies, billfishes, and various sharks brought in from offshore.

The above discussion makes it very clear that our fauna is still very poorly known, even after one hundred years of sporadic study. It is perhaps instructive that the past studies of the Gulf fauna have always been sporadic ones, usually by government or privately employed biologists stationed on the Atlantic seaboard for most of their time. Even the extensive trawling and exploratory fishing by the *R.V. Oregon* and other government fishery vessels virtually ignored the area under consideration here, working either in more southerly waters along the Central American and West Indian coasts or in deep water near the edge of the continental shelf. Presumably shallower waters should be well known and not in need of exploration.

Let us hope that it will not take another one hundred years before more detailed and extensive studies are made of the shallow water and moderate depths of the northern Gulf of Mexico. Proper utilization of shallow water resources requires an in-depth knowledge of their identification and distribution, knowledge which does not exist at the moment.

Thalassoma bifasciatum, supermale. Photo by G. Marcuse.

IMPORTANT TERMS AND STRUCTURES

Although technical terminology has been kept at a minimum, a certain amount has of necessity crept in. The following discussion and a good dictionary should make most puzzles clearer.

Measurements

Standard length (*SL*): the length of the body of a fish, taken from the middle of the tip of the upper jaw to the base of the caudal fin. The base of the caudal fin is most easily found by folding the fin back; a crease is formed at the hypural bone, the end of the vertebral column. The caudal fin is not included in this measurement.

Total length (*TL*): the greatest possible length of a fish, from the tip of the longest jaw to the longest caudal ray. Seldom used in scientific work. Most of the sizes given in this book are a compromise between total and standard length, as the figures represent the rough **body length** (longest jaw to base of caudal fin). This compromise measurement is often used in commercial fishery work.

Disk width: greatest width between the lateral corners of the disk of skates and rays.

Depth: usually the greatest body depth from the dorsal profile to the ventral profile, excluding the height of the dorsal fin. In eels and other very elongate fishes the depth is usually taken just anterior to the anus.

Head length: distance from tip of upper jaw to the upper edge of the operculum, usually including any flaps or spines at the upper edge. In eels the measurement is to the upper edge of the gill slit, while in sharks and rays it is to the upper edge of the last (fifth) gill slit.

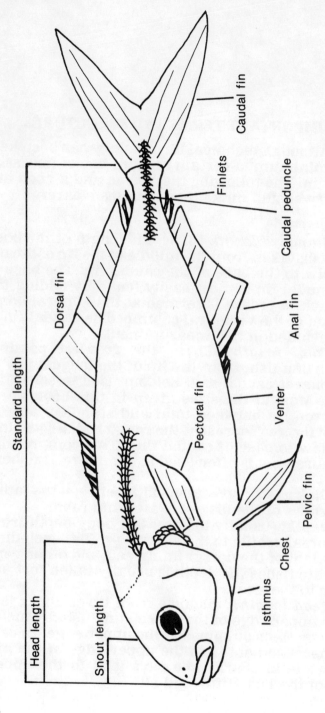

Important parts and measurements of a hypothetical fish. The lateral line is interrupted and there is a large humeral scale.

22

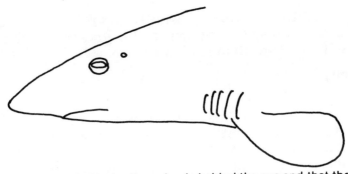

Head of a shark. Notice the spiracle behind the eye and that the last gill slit is located over the base of the pectoral.

Snout length: distance from the middle of the tip of the upper jaw to the anterior edge of the eye socket (not the eye proper).

Eye length: the horizontal length from the anterior to posterior edge of the bony socket of the eye. In most forms this is equivalent to the actual width of the eye, but not in all.

Predorsal length: distance from the first dorsal fin element (spine or ray) to the middle of the tip of the snout. This measurement is taken along the dorsal midline of the head. The **nape** or **occiput** of many fishes is well defined by a sudden change in scalation or the density of the skin, and in some fishes the distance from the nape to the dorsal fin is measured.

Fin measurements: pectoral, caudal and pelvic fin lengths are measured along the longest ray, from its base to its tip; be careful of broken fin rays. Dorsal or anal element height is measured from the exposed base of the spine or ray to its tip. Dorsal and anal fin lengths are measured along the base of the fin from the base of the first element to the base of the last element, not the tip of the last element.

Caudal peduncle: the length of the caudal peduncle is measured along the lateral midline from a vertical through the base of the last dorsal or anal element (whichever is most posterior) and the base of the caudal fin. The least depth of the peduncle is exactly that—the narrowest height of the peduncle, usually near its middle. Peduncle thickness refers to the greatest thickness (from side to side).

Counts

Fins: in most fishes the fins are made of elements which are either segmented and often, but not necessarily, branched (**rays**) and elements which are without visible segments at any point between the base and the tip (**spines**). In most counts spines are indicated by Roman numerals and rays by Arabic numbers. When the spines and rays are continuous, a comma is used to separate their numbers; a hyphen is used when the spinous fin is separated completely from the rayed fin.

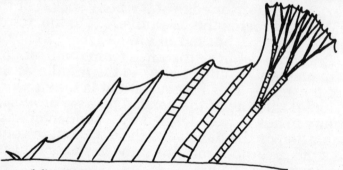

Types of fin elements. A small antrorse spine followed by three spines, an unbranched and partially spinous segmented ray, a normal but unbranched segmented ray, and a branched segmented ray.

The dorsal fin is abbreviated by D., the anal by A., the pectoral sometimes called pect. or P1, the pelvics P2. Thus dorsal fin formulas: D. 12 (twelve rays only); D. III,12 (three spines and twelve rays, connected); D. III-I,12 (three spines in the first dorsal fin, one spine and twelve rays in the second); D. 12 + 1 (twelve rays followed by a separate single ray, called a **finlet**). Rays are counted at their base—if two rays have a common base, they are counted as only one.

Lateral scales: in fishes the **lateral line** (Ll.) is usually visible as a series of scales with distinct

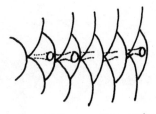

Lateral line scales are counted from behind the opercular margin.

Five lateral line scales, only three with pores.

pores or canals. Lateral line counts generally start at the first pored scale at the upper edge of the operculum where the flap of the opercle is anchored to the body; the count usually includes all scales in the series, whether pored or not, and stops near the caudal base where the scales become small and irregular. Where a lateral line is absent, one counts scales in a **lateral series**, meaning a horizontal row from the upper edge of the operculum to the base of the caudal. When the scales fall off easily (deciduous) one must sometimes count the scale pockets, usually a dark reticulation, for an approximate lateral series count.

In some fishes the lateral line is distinctly **interrupted** or consists of two discontinuous sections, usually one under the anterior part of the dorsal fin and the other on the caudal peduncle; in such cases the two lateral lines are counted separately, Ll. 14 + 8.

In fishes with small or crowded lateral scales, it sometimes helps to rub on a very small amount of India ink, which helps outline the scales and indicate their pores.

Gill rakers (GR): the gill rakers are hard, simple projections, sometimes bearing spines or plates, but never branched, on the anterior surface of each gill; the longer thin gill filaments occupy the posterior surface. Only the rakers on the first or most anterior arch are counted, usually by folding or cutting back the operculum. Every raker which is higher than wide is generally counted. Counts are expressed as rakers on the

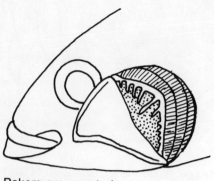

Rakers are counted
on the first or most
anterior gill arch.

Four rakers on upper limb,
one at angle, eight on
lower limb, plus a
rudiment.

upper arch plus those on the lower, with the raker
at the angle either counted separately or com-
bined with the ones on the lower arch. Thus, GR. 3
+ 1 + 8. Rudiments, or small knobs wider than
high, are usually not included.

Teeth: Teeth are seldom counted except in
sharks, where only those with exposed, usable
cutting edges in the outer row are included.

Structures

The following discussion is not intended to be
complete, and is supplemented by the illustrations.

The upper and lower jaws are usually obvious
and separated from the rest of the head by deep
labial folds. The "chin" where the left and right
lower jaws or **mandibles** join is referred to as the
symphysis. The upper jaw is composed of the bones
at the front margin, the **premaxillaries**, and those
along the sides, the **maxillaries**. There is usually a
distinct lobe on the posterior upper edge of the
maxillary, which may or may not be visible externally when the mouth is closed. If the lobe disappears under the bones near the eye, it is said to
be hidden or to slip under the **preorbital** (or suborbital).

Teeth in the lower jaw are for our purposes
composed of those on the jaw itself (**mandibular**

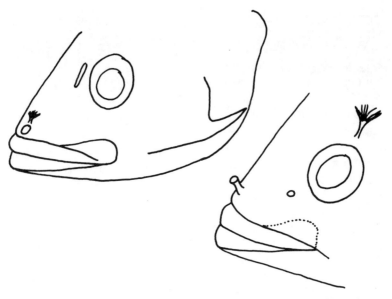

Heads. At left, the maxillary is visible posteriorly, there is a strong preopercular spine, the posterior nostril is a slit anterior to the eye, and there is a group of cirri over the anterior, non-tubular nostril. The head at right has the maxillary slipping under the preorbital, the anterior nostril tubular, and a group of supraorbital cirri.

teeth) and those on the tongue (**lingual**). The upper teeth are more complex. They are the **premaxillary** teeth on the premaxillary bones (usually a patch or row across the very anterior edge), the **maxillary** teeth on the sides of the jaw, **vomerine** teeth which usually form a patch or wide row at the middle of the roof of the mouth, and the **palatine** teeth which are generally two patches, one on each side of the midline of the roof. In eels any teeth on the roof of the mouth are simply **palatal** teeth. To find out if teeth are present, use a fine needle and pass it along the area to be examined.

Tooth types in fishes are many, but only a few terms·are used here. Simple **conical** teeth seem to be the basic type; if some are much longer and stronger than the others they are called **canines** or **fangs** (eels). If the tooth is flattened with a horizontal free edge, the tooth is an **incisor**; it may or may not be notched. **Molar** teeth are usually heavy, flat

Molariform teeth, preceded by four conical teeth, the second a canine.

Incisorform teeth, variously notched and simple.

teeth used for grinding. Shark teeth usually consist of a high, triangular **main cusp** and low ridges on each side near the base known as **lateral cusps**. Tooth shape in all but the smallest fishes can usually be determined with a 10X hand lens. Such a lens is also adequate for most identification work.

Most fishes have two **nostrils**, often widely separated and called the anterior (most near the tip of the upper jaw) and posterior nostrils. In many eels one or both nostrils may have a fleshy tube (**tubular**) or have a flap. Nostrils may be oval pores or elongated slits.

The gill cover or **operculum** is for our purposes composed of two important bones, the thin and moveable posterior operculum, which sometimes bears spines at its upper edge, and the immoveable **preoperculum**. The preoperculum has an upright or vertical edge or limb and a lower or horizontal limb. Either limb may have small spines, usually called serrations, larger spines, or be smooth. Usually the larger spines are at the lower corner of the preopercle as in the angelfishes or at the upper end of the vertical limb as in the scorpionfishes. Some fishes have **antrorse**, or forwardly

Types of preopercles: a, plain; b, weak serrations on vertical limb; c, strong spines on both limbs; d, long spine at lower angle, few weak spines above; e, group of antrorse spines at angle; f, strong spine at upper angle accompanied by supplemental preopercular spine, also antrorse spine at lower angle.

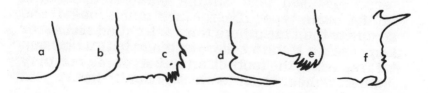

directed, spines on the lower limb. Spines which point backward are said to be **retrorse**.

The **mouth** may be said to be terminal, dorsal or oblique, or inferior. If it is **inferior**, it is usually either overhung by the snout or said to be **included** by the longer upper jaw. There are often **barbels**, usually small simple or branched filaments, on the lower jaw—an especially large single or paired barbel is often present at the symphysis.

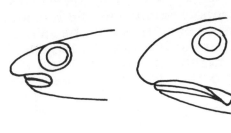 

Inferior mouths.

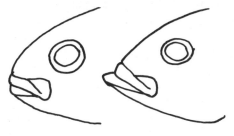

Dorsal mouth.

Terminal mouths.

Lower jaw showing a large barbel
at symphysis, a row of smaller
barbels at the edges of the jaw,
and a pair of reduced
filamentous pelvic fins.

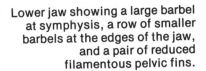 

On the ventral surface of the head the opercula may be said to be **free** from each other or separate, **fused** to each other, or even fused to the chest. The area between the ventral part of the

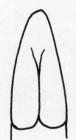

Gill membranes separate from each other and free from chest.

Gill membranes*
fused to chest.

gill covers is more properly known as the **isthmus**, so the gill membranes or opening would be said to be fused to or free from the isthmus. As the chest is the larger area between the opercles and the pelvics, it is also said that the membranes are fused to the chest.

Scales are of several types. These are seldom used in our descriptions, but sometimes it is useful to be able to tell a **ctenoid** scale (the free edge possesses numerous small spines or points and is rough to the touch) from the smooth or nearly smooth **cycloid** scale. Small, very distinctive **pla-**

Placoid scale, dorsal and lateral view.

Ganoid scale

Cycloid scale

Ctenoid scale

Normal overlapping scalation

Imbricated scales with long free margin

Embedded scales

30

coid scales occur on the sharks and rays, while heavy, bony scales, called **ganoid** scales, occur on the gar. In some of the jacks the scales along the lateral line are heavy and enlarged into bony **scutes**, usually bearing sharp ridges. Many fishes lack scales over at least part of the body or have them **embedded** in the skin. In the tunas the scales near the pectoral fin are commonly enlarged and partially fused to form what is called the **corselet**.

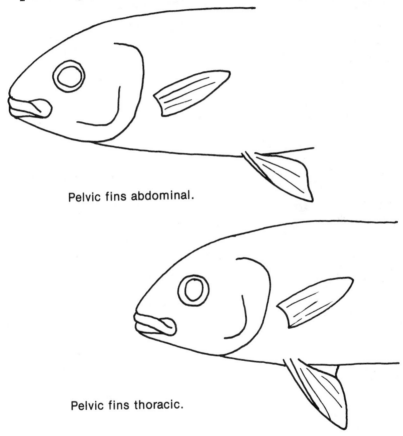

Pelvic fins abdominal.

Pelvic fins thoracic.

The position of the **pelvic** (or ventral) fins is very important in identification. If the fins are about under the base of the pectoral fin they are called **thoracic**. If they begin or are inserted posterior to the region of the pectorals, they are **ab-**

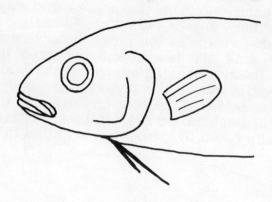

Pelvics jugular, on the
isthmus.

dominal. All gradations between these insertions
exist. If the fins are inserted on the isthmus or
more anteriorly, they are **jugular**; such fins are especially characteristic of the cods and cusk-eels,
where the fins are often reduced to **filaments**. The
pelvic fins are rarely absent except in the eels, the
swordfish, and a few genera of other families.

Sometimes the anterior dorsal or anal rays
are longer than the others and form a **lobe**. This
lobe may be low and rounded or very long and
pointed (**falcate**). The **caudal rays** are especially
variable in length, resulting in several distinct
types, some of which are illustrated. If the caudal
rays extend onto the upper and lower edges of the
caudal peduncle, usually as simple short spines,
they are said to be **excurrent** rays. These are especially characteristic of the genus *Chromis* in the
Pomacentridae and the genus *Erotelis* of the Gobiidae.

In the catfishes and lizardfishes there is a
small, rayless fin between the dorsal fin and the
caudal fin. Since this little fin is usually composed
of fatty tissue, it is called the **adipose** fin. Only
these two families of our marine fishes have an
adipose fin.

Caudal fin types.

Lanceolate

Rounded

Truncate; adipose fin present

Biconcave

Convex, edges slightly produced

Strongly lunate

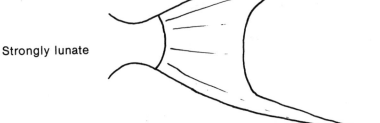

33

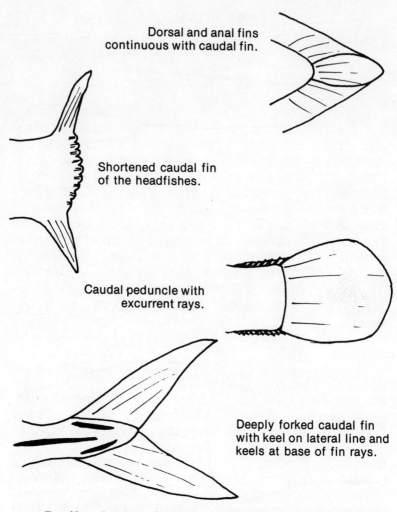

Dorsal and anal fins
continuous with caudal fin.

Shortened caudal fin
of the headfishes.

Caudal peduncle with
excurrent rays.

Deeply forked caudal fin
with keel on lateral line and
keels at base of fin rays.

In the jacks, tunas, billfishes, some sharks
and a few other groups, there are low fleshy **keels**
present along the middle sides of the caudal peduncle. These are sometimes distinctly colored and
sometimes not, but can always be seen by looking
down at the peduncle from above. In the jacks
there are also two or more small keels placed
obliquely at the bases of the caudal lobes.

Any terms used in this book should be simple
enough to interpret from the above discussion, the
dictionary, and a little thought.

LITERATURE

No attempt has been made to list all the literature consulted during research for this book. Instead, only the most important major references, which should be available at any good college library or fishery laboratory, are listed here. A few more specialized works of particular interest are also included with the family discussions. The worker interested in checking identifications should additionally have access to sets of two important journals, *Copeia* and *Bulletin of Marine Science* (Miami, Florida), which contain numerous large and small papers dealing with our fauna.

GENERAL MARINE REFERENCES

American Fisheries Society. 1970. *A list of common and scientific names of fishes*. Third edition. American Fisheries Society, Washington, D.C. The AFS *Checklist*.

Bohlke, J.E. and C.C.G. Chaplin. 1968. *Fishes of the Bahamas*. Livingston Publ. Co., Wynnewood, Pa. (available through the Academy of Natural Sciences, Philadelphia, Pa.). This massive (771 pages) volume contains many tropical species which stray into our area. Unfortunately it is too large for easy use and too expensive for most individuals.

Breder, C.M., Jr. 1929 (and later reprintings). *Field book of marine fishes of the Atlantic coast*. G.P. Putnam's Sons, N.Y. Too outdated to be of much use in the northern Gulf, but generally the only easily available guide.

Galtsoff, P.S. (editor). 1954. *Gulf of Mexico: Its origin, waters, and marine life. Bull. U.S. Fish*

& Wildlife Serv., Fish Bull. #55. This extremely interesting and useful work contains a wealth of information on the oceanography and fauna of the Gulf, with emphasis on the invertebrates. It is usually available through used book dealers at a reasonable price.

Herald, E.S. 1961. *Living fishes of the world.* Doubleday & Co., Garden City, N.Y. A useful general account of the natural history and major species of the fish families of the world.

Hildebrand, H.H. 1954. *A study of the fauna of the brown shrimp grounds in the western Gulf of Mexico. Publ. Inst. Mar. Sci.* (Univ. Texas, Port Aransas), 3(2):231-366. A useful general study of the offshore fauna of the western Gulf.

Hildebrand, S.F. and W.C. Schroeder. 1928. *Fishes of Chesapeake Bay. Bull. U.S. Bur. Fish.*, 43(1). A useful but outdated work which contains much general information on our most common fishes. Recently reprinted by the TFH fund and for sale by the Smithsonian Institution Press, Washington, D.C. 20560.

Jordan, D.S. and B.W. Evermann. 1896-1900. *Fishes of North and Middle America. Bull. U.S. Nat. Mus., #47.* The classic work on all American fishes. Although old, it remains the most useful general work on our fauna. Technical. Formerly very expensive to obtain, but now available as a TFH reprint through the Smithsonian Institution Press, Washington, D.C. 20560. Should be in the library of every fishery biologist.

Longley, W.H. and S.F. Hildebrand. 1941. *Systematic catalogue of the fishes of Tortugas, Florida. Papers Tortugas Laboratory, #34.* Useful for some of the tropical and deep reef fauna, but outdated and no longer available.

Miller, D.J. and R.N. Lea. 1972. *Guide to the coastal marine fishes of California. Calif. Fish and Game Dept., Fish. Bull. #157.* Although covering a different ocean, the many drawings and useful information on the larger or cosmopolitan fishes make it very useful.

Randall, J.E. 1968. *Caribbean Reef Fishes*. T.F.H. Publ. Inc., Neptune City, N.J. A useful, very well illustrated (color and black-and-white photos) book on tropical species, many of which occur in our fauna.

GENERAL FRESHWATER BOOKS

Blair, W.F., et. al. 1957 (and later editions). *Vertebrates of the United States*. McGraw-Hill Book Co., N.Y. The fish portion is by G.A. Moore. The most complete set of keys to American freshwater fishes, but of course hard to use because of its complexity. This book also contains a good treatment of the whales and dolphins in the section on mammals by W.F. Blair.

Carr, A. and C.J. Goin. 1959. *Guide to the reptiles, amphibians and freshwater fishes of Florida*. University of Florida Press, Gainesville, Fla. Useful guide. Contains some brackish water species found mostly in southern Florida and not treated in this book.

Eddy, S. 1957 (and later editions). *How to know the freshwater fishes*. Wm. C. Brown Co., Dubuque, Iowa. A "pictured key" covering almost all American freshwater fishes and relatively easy to use. Each species is illustrated.

Hubbs, C.L. and K.F. Lagler. 1947 (and later editions). *Fishes of the Great Lakes region. Cranbrook Inst. Sci., Bull. #26*. Bloomfield Hills, Michigan. The standard work on freshwater fishes of the northern Mississippi Valley and Great Lakes. Contains much basic information on making counts, measurements, etc. Very useful in both fresh and salt water.

FAMILY AND SPECIES ACCOUNTS

Although it is almost impossible to construct a usable key to separate our 107 families and 502 species of marine fishes, most of the families and species are easily recognizable by general body form, fin counts, color pattern, and occasionally teeth or more complicated characters. Familiarization with the illustrations will soon allow the recognition of most of our fishes on sight. The purpose of these accounts is to provide concise descriptions of the families and species of the northern Gulf, with brief comments on range, rarity, and occasional other information as needed. The order of discussion generally follows the AFS *Checklist*, but it should be pointed out that this sequence is really a compromise between several different systems currently in vogue among ichthyologists; family relationships have always been doubtful and are no more certain now than 200 years ago. The genera and species are listed in alphabetical order after the family and not in order of natural relationship.

As usual in manuals covering limited geographic areas, the distinguishing characters used may not apply outside the northern Gulf of Mexico; this is especially true of ordinal and family characters, which have generally been limited to features seen in our species. Caution should be used with specimens from the southern edges of the northern Gulf and from water deeper than twenty-five fathoms. Although this manual has been made as comprehensive as possible, it cannot cover all possible strays from warmer or deeper water, especially the latter. This would be mainly true when trying to identify commercially taken material from off the mouth of the Mississippi, Pensacola, and the Mexican shrimping grounds.

SHARKS AND RAYS
CLASS CHONDRICHTHYES

Easily recognized fishes which lack the larger, flat scales of bony fishes, having instead the small, keeled placoid scales which impart a rough or shagreened surface to the skin. In our families the operculum is absent and all five gill slits open externally and separately. The body is generally cartilaginous and lacking "true" bone, but this is not really a usable character to separate the class. Two orders, fifteen families, forty-six species.

ORDER SQUALIFORMES — the sharks and angel sharks

Generally round-bodied fishes with large gill slits which open laterally and not ventrally. The pectoral fins are moveable and are not fused to the sides of the head anteriorly. Even in the flattened angel sharks the mouth is more-or-less terminal or overhung by a heavy snout and contains separate, usually sharply pointed, teeth, not rows of grinding plates. The rays, order Rajiformes, have the gill slits ventrally placed, the pectoral fins firmly joined to the sides of the head, and rows of grinding tooth plates in a usually small and ventral mouth. Eight families, twenty-nine species, many common.

Family ORECTOLOBIDAE — carpet sharks

A single species in our area, with the characters of the family.

1. NURSE SHARK
Ginglymostoma cirratum (Bonnaterre)

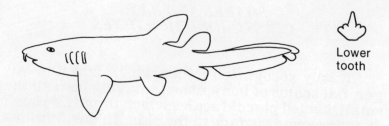

Lower
tooth

Our only shark with the first dorsal fin located far posteriorly, its origin about over the pelvic fin origin. The second dorsal is nearly as large as the first and is situated close to the first dorsal. The caudal is long and low, with the lower lobe weakly defined. There are long nasal barbels. Teeth with a high central cusp and four small lateral cusps. Yellowish to grayish, sometimes with small scattered spots. Generally small, under five feet, but attains about twelve feet.

A casual visitor to shallow Gulf waters from warmer climates; usually seen during the summer.

Family RHINCODONTIDAE — whale shark

Only one species in our area.

2. WHALE SHARK
Rhincodon typus Smith

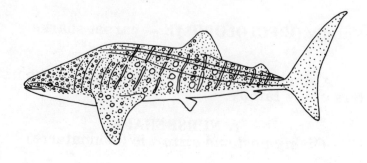

A pelagic shark of gigantic size, perhaps exceeding forty feet in length. The small head slopes strongly upward to the dorsal profile. The first dorsal fin is set behind the pectorals and is much larger than the second dorsal. There are prominent longitudinal ridges on each side of the trunk running from the dorsal hump to the caudal base. The caudal fin is very high (upper lobe to about six feet long) and nearly lunate, the lower lobe perpendicular to the upper and over half its length. The teeth are very small; the gill slits are large but do not meet ventrally. Color pattern distinctive, consisting of regular white spots and stripes on a grayish background.

Living examples are very rare in the northern Gulf and are most likely to be seen basking many miles offshore. Stranded specimens always draw much interest.

Family **ODONTASPIDIDAE** — sand tigers

Represented by only one species in the northern Gulf.

3. SAND TIGER
Odontaspis taurus (Rafinesque)

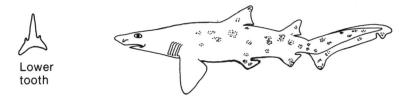

Lower
tooth

The first dorsal fin is located over the pelvic fins but anterior to their origin and behind the pectorals. The second dorsal is somewhat similar in size to the first but set well posteriorly to it. There is a distinct lower caudal lobe. All the gill slits open anterior to the pectoral fin. The teeth have a large erect central cusp and two similar but much smaller lateral cusps. Light grayish-brown above, lighter below. Young and some adults sometimes with irregular yellowish spots or blotches. Reaches nine feet in length, usually much smaller.

An uncommon shark on the western coast of Florida in about one to five fathoms. It probably occasionally ranges further west but must be very rare in the northern Gulf.

Formerly known as *Carcharias taurus* of the family Carchariidae.

Family ALOPIIDAE — thresher sharks

Large (13-20 feet) offshore sharks instantly recognizable by the very long upper caudal lobe which is equal in length to the rest of the body. The pectoral fin is very long and the eye large. This family is sometimes included in the Lamnidae (below). One species definitely in our area, another probably so. Many shark species are called threshers by anglers, but few sportsmen in the northern Gulf are acquainted with the true threshers.

4. BIGEYE THRESHER
Alopias superciliosus (Lowe)

Lower
tooth

An offshore species not definitely recorded from our area but probably confused with the species below. The first dorsal base is only slightly anterior to the insertion of the pelvics. There are only ten or eleven teeth on each side of the upper jaw.

5. THRESHER SHARK
Alopias vulpinus (Bonnaterre)

Lower
tooth

A large, stout-bodied shark with the characteristic long pectorals, large eye, and rounded short snout of the genus. The base of the first dorsal is situated far anterior to the pelvics. There are twenty-one or twenty-two smooth teeth in each side of the upper jaw. Slatey-blue above, lighter below. Mottling is often present near the pectorals and on the pelvics and caudal. Reaches at least twenty feet, perhaps more; specimens under ten feet are rare.

This blue-water species is apparently rare in the northern Gulf, the numerous anglers' records usually referring to offshore species of *Carcharhinus*, which have the upper caudal lobe much less than half the body length (equal to the body length in threshers) and the upper teeth serrated (smooth in threshers).

Family **LAMNIDAE** — mackerel sharks

Large open-water sharks with the caudal fin distinctly lunate, the lower lobe nearly as large as the upper. All gill slits are situated anterior to the pectoral fins. The caudal peduncle bears a distinct lateral keel. The teeth are large and triangular. Two species in our area.

6. WHITE SHARK
Carcharodon carcharias (Linnaeus)

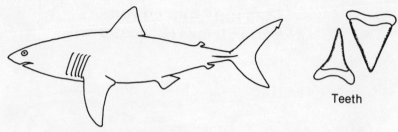

Teeth

A large, deep-bodied shark with the first dorsal concave posteriorly, its origin over the rear edge of the pectorals. The anal fin is behind the second dorsal. A short lateral keel on the caudal peduncle begins near the level of the anal. The large, coarsely serrated teeth in the upper jaw are broadly triangular. Slatey, with dark fin edgings and a black spot in the pectoral axilla. Large specimens are nearly uniform whitish. Six to sixteen feet in length.

This is a pelagic species which sometimes comes into very shallow water. It is definitely a man-eater and is greatly feared. Generally tropical in distribution, but a great wanderer and to be expected in our area; recorded from the western coast of Florida.

7. SHORTFIN MAKO
Isurus oxyrinchus Rafinesque

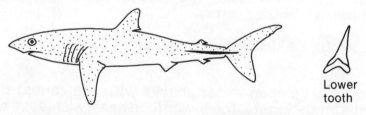

Lower
tooth

A smaller shark with a fusiforme body and the posterior edge of the first dorsal fin nearly straight. The first dorsal is placed entirely behind the pectorals, and the second dorsal is about over the anal fin. The keel on the peduncle is long, extending to about the second dorsal. The teeth of both jaws are smooth-edged and slender, forming tall triangles. Deep gray-blue above, white below. Six to twelve feet long.

A common pelagic species well known for its high jumps when hooked.

Family **CARCHARHINIDAE** — requiem sharks

A large family of "typical" sharks containing several different body and tooth forms. The caudal fin has the lower lobe short, less than half the length of the upper lobe; the upper lobe is much shorter than the body length, usually less than half the length of the body or one-third of the total length. There are one or more gill slits located over the pectoral base. The head is not expanded laterally as in the hammerheads (family Sphyrnidae). Fin positions and proportions variable. Sixteen species in the northern Gulf of Mexico, many very common.

The species in our area can be divided for convenience into three groups:

  I. A distinct spiracle behind the eye (species 18, 19, 20);

 II. No spiracle; main cusp of upper teeth smooth (species 8, 21, 23);

III. No spiracle; main cusp of upper teeth serrated, although the serrations sometimes small and irregular (species 9-17, 22).

8. FINETOOTH SHARK
Aprionodon isodon (Valenciennes)

Lower
tooth

Group II. A small shark with the first dorsal fin over the pectoral base; the second dorsal is small and located over the anal. The snout is long. Teeth slender, simple cusps without accessory cusps; this tooth shape is unique in our requiem sharks. Slate above, white below. Pelvics and anal whitish. A small species, usually one-and-a-half to three feet in total length.

This species and the Atlantic sharpnose are often the two most common small sharks on the coast of the northern Gulf. Although the finetooth is uncommon in more than five fathoms, it is also uncommon in estuarine situations.

Genus CARCHARHINUS — this complex genus of often common sharks contains several species which are hard to identify. A check of the teeth, however, should allow easy assignment to the genus. In all our species the upper teeth bear at least some serrations, usually large; the blue shark has the serrations small and irregular and in addition has a small first dorsal set far back behind the pectorals—in *Carcharhinus* the first dorsal is large and usually begins near the posterior edge of the pectoral. The tiger shark has doubly-serrated upper teeth but also has a small spiracle. The very common Atlantic sharpnose has smooth upper teeth.

A preliminary division of the genus can be made by checking for a low fleshy ridge on the dorsal midline between the first and second dorsal fins. This ridge is present in species 10, 13, 15, and 16, but absent in species 9, 11, 12, 14, and 17.

9. BLACKNOSE SHARK
Carcharhinus acronotus (Poey)

Teeth

Smooth-backed. First dorsal fin behind posterior corner of pectoral; second dorsal origin over anal origin. Upper teeth notched, asymmetrical, serrations larger at base than at tip. Lower teeth straight, pointed, with low lateral cusps. Brownish to cream colored. Three to six feet long.

A tropical species poorly known in our area, with most records from offshore.

10. SILKY SHARK
Carcharhinus falciformis (Bibron)

Teeth

Ridge-backed. First dorsal entirely behind pectoral fin. The free posterior portion of both second dorsal and anal long, pointed, equal. Tip of first dorsal acute. Snout long. Upper teeth asymmetrical, notched, coarsely serrated. Lower teeth symmetrical, pointed, with low lateral cusps. Grayish above, whitish below. Large, six to ten feet.

A common offshore species usually found in over ten fathoms.

Carcharhinus floridanus is a synonym.

11. BULL SHARK
Carcharhinus leucas (Valenciennes)

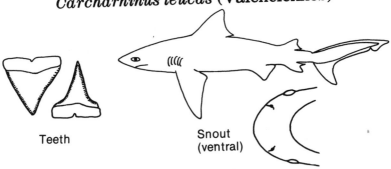

Teeth

Snout
(ventral)

Smooth-backed. First dorsal over posterior base of pectoral. Second dorsal and anal with short free tips. Snout short, the portion anterior to the nostrils half or less distance between nostrils.

47

Upper and lower teeth similar, symmetrical, slender, without lateral cusps. Gray above, white below. Seven to ten feet, but smaller specimens common.

Young specimens under five feet long are common inshore and sometimes ascend rivers for many miles. Adults are most common offshore.

12. BLACKTIP SHARK
Carcharhinus limbatus (Valenciennes)

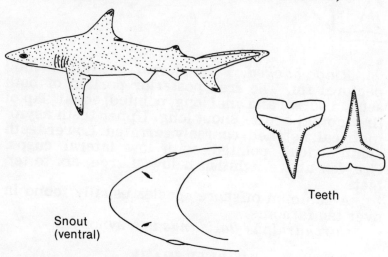

Snout
(ventral)

Teeth

Smooth-backed. First dorsal originates over pectoral base. Second dorsal and anal with long free corners. The snout is long, the area anterior to the nostrils two-thirds or more of the distance between the nostrils. Upper and lower teeth symmetrical, slender, without lateral cusps. Grayish and white, the fins with black tips. Reaches about six feet in length.

Often confused with the bull shark, but the snout is longer and the corners of the second dorsal and anal longer. Also, the first dorsal of the blacktip is higher and more concave with a longer free posterior corner.

Common in shallow water, the young seldom found in fresh water but often common in brackish water.

48

13. OCEANIC WHITETIP SHARK
Carcharhinus longimanus (Poey)

Teeth

Snout
(ventral)

Ridge-backed. First dorsal fin broadly round-ed, located over the posterior corner of the pectoral. The pectoral fin is noticeably long. Anal fin with a long free corner extending almost to the caudal base, longer than corner of second dorsal. Upper teeth symmetrical, broadly triangular. Lower teeth pointed, with low lateral cusps. Gray-ish above, dirty white below. Six to twelve feet in length.

A common offshore species.

14. SPINNER SHARK
Carcharhinus maculipinnis (Poey)

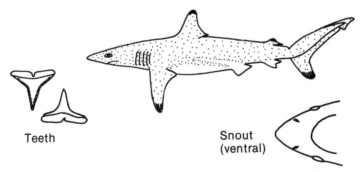

Teeth

Snout
(ventral)

Smooth-backed. Similar in most respects to the blacktip shark. Lower teeth generally smooth, not serrated as in blacktip. Distance from the tip of snout to the nostrils 1.2 to 1.5 times the distance from the front edge of nostrils to the front of the mouth, this distance only 0.7 to 1.1 times in the blacktip.

A moderately common species in offshore waters.

15. SANDBAR SHARK
Carcharhinus milberti (Valenciennes)

Teeth

Ridge-backed. First dorsal origin over axilla of pectoral, higher than distance from eye to first gill opening. Second dorsal normal, its free corner not elongated and its origin behind anal origin. Upper teeth notched, asymmetrical, finely serrated. Lower teeth symmetrical, pointed, with low lateral cusps. Gray above, white below. Adults about seven feet long.

A rare species in the northern Gulf, generally recorded from deeper offshore waters.

16. DUSKY SHARK
Carcharhinus obscurus (Lesueur)

Teeth

Ridge-backed. First dorsal fin originates over outer corner of pectoral, its height less than the distance from eye to first gill opening. Second dorsal originates over or slightly before anal, its corner short; anal free corner short. Upper teeth notched, serrations coarse. Lower teeth straight, with low lateral cusps. Gray and white. A large species, eight to twelve feet long.

An apparently rare species of our offshore waters.

17. SMALLTAIL SHARK
Carcharhinus porosus (Ranzani)

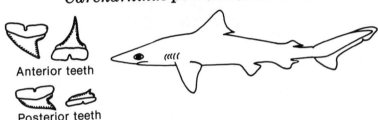

Anterior teeth

Posterior teeth

Smooth-backed. First dorsal over posterior part of pectoral; second dorsal originates over middle or posterior half of anal fin. Upper teeth notched, asymmetrical. Teeth in lower jaw straight anteriorly, without lateral cusps, becoming low, notched and asymmetrical posteriorly. Upper caudal lobe distinctly short. Slatey above, whitish below. A small species, probably not greatly exceeding four feet in length.

Another poorly known shark in our area, the few records coming from offshore waters.

18. TIGER SHARK
Galeocerdo cuvieri (Peron & Lesueur)

Tooth and detail of serration

Group I. A very distinctive shark. First dorsal fin over pectoral, much larger than second dorsal. Small spiracle behind eye, inconspicuous. A low keel on the caudal peduncle and another between the dorsals on midline of back. Teeth asymmetrical and deeply notched, strongly serrated, large serrations at notch bearing smaller serrations. Snout short. Grayish to leaden blue above, belly white. Young with brown blotches usually arranged in vertical rows. Six to fourteen feet in length.

This large pelagic species is considered to be a good sportsfish. A regular summer visitor to the northern Gulf of Mexico.

19. SMOOTH DOGFISH
Mustelus canis (Mitchill)

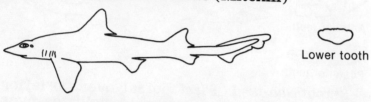

Lower tooth

Group I. Prominent spiracle behind eye. First dorsal rounded, over posterior edge of pectoral fin. Second dorsal large, rounded, placed before anal origin. Lower caudal lobe low and rounded. Teeth small, rounded, without serrations. Grayish to brownish, lighter below. Three or four feet long.

The smooth dogfish is a species of moderate depth, seldom being found in less than fifteen fathoms. It forms large colonies which seem to be associated with snapper banks and other hard offshore bottoms, and is generally absent elsewhere. Records from brackish water are probably founded on misidentifications.

20. FLORIDA SMOOTHHOUND
Mustelus norrisi Springer

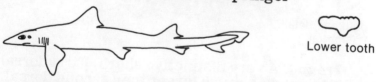

Lower tooth

Group I. Very similar to the smooth dogfish. First dorsal somewhat more posteriorly located; pectoral fin smaller. Major difference is the distinct and pointed lower caudal lobe, indistinct and rounded in the smooth dogfish.

Maximum size under four feet.

A species characteristic of the west coast of Florida, but apparently occurring occasionally, though rarely, further west at least to the Mississippi delta.

21. LEMON SHARK
Negaprion brevirostris (Poey)

Teeth

Group II. Snout short, blunt; body form stout. First dorsal fin behind the pectoral. Second dorsal fin larger than anal, only slightly smaller than first dorsal. The teeth are straight, symmetrical, the main cusp smooth. Lateral cusps of upper teeth wavy or coarsely serrated. Yellowish-brown above, belly often yellowish. Seven to eleven feet long.

This is an inshore species which is often common near wharves. It seems to be a sporadic summer visitor along the northern Gulf, most records being from Texas and Florida.

22. BLUE SHARK
Prionace glauca (Linnaeus)

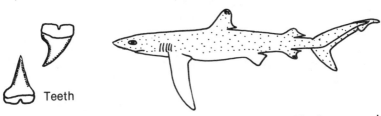

Teeth

Group III. First dorsal fin small, low, set more than one dorsal fin-base length behind the pectoral fin. Pectoral fin comparatively long and slender. Upper teeth with slender main cusp bearing weak and irregular serrations. Color above distinctly deep blue, whitish below. Reaches more than twelve feet.

A wide-ranging pelagic species which is rarely recorded from the northern Gulf in deep water.

23. ATLANTIC SHARPNOSE SHARK
Rhizoprionodon terraenovae (Richardson)

Teeth

Group II. First dorsal fin over or slightly behind the posterior edge of the pectoral fin base. Second dorsal small, its origin behind anal origin. Snout long, pointed. Teeth notched, asymmetrical, smooth-edged. Grayish above, whitish below; fins sometimes dark-edged. Small, maximum size about three feet.

An abundant inshore species in the northern Gulf, but also common out to at least fifteen fathoms.

Family SPHYRNIDAE — hammerhead sharks

Instantly recognizable by the laterally extended sides of the head, bearing the eyes; head spade-like to hammer-like. Otherwise very similar to the Carcharhinidae. Five species in our area, four of them very similar. The species names used here follow C.R. Gilbert, 1967 (*Proc. U.S.N.M.*, 119(3539):1-88) and differ considerably from those in the older literature, especially *Fishes of the Western North Atlantic, Volume I.*

Present work	Fishes WNA
S. *tiburo*	S. *tiburo*
S. *tudes*	S. *bigelowi*
S. *lewini*	S. *diplana*
S. *mokarran*	S. *tudes*
S. *zygaena*	S. *zygaena*

24. SCALLOPED HAMMERHEAD
Sphyrna lewini (Griffith & Smith)

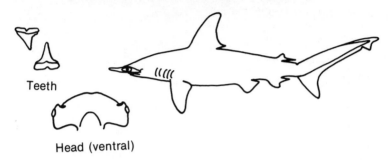

Teeth

Head (ventral)

Head hammer-like, with a median notch. Eyes about on level with or posterior to anterior edge of mouth. Teeth smooth. Free rear corner of second dorsal fin longer than fin base. Gray above, white below. Adults six to ten feet long.

This is apparently the most common typical hammerhead in shallow inshore Gulf waters, but it is also common in waters of moderate depth.

25. GREAT HAMMERHEAD
Sphyrna mokarran (Ruppel)

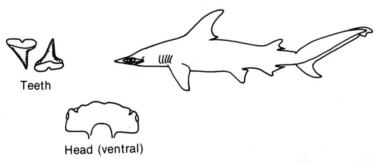

Teeth

Head (ventral)

Head hammer-like, with a median notch. Eyes on level with anterior corner of mouth. Free rear corner of second dorsal shorter than base of fin. Teeth distinctly serrated at all sizes. Gray and white. Reaches about fourteen feet.

Exact status in our waters unknown because of confusion with other species, but probably common offshore.

26. BONNETHEAD
Sphyrna tiburo (Linnaeus)

Teeth

Head (ventral)

Head oval, shovel-shaped, without a median notch. Free corner of second dorsal long. Teeth all smooth. Grayish above, white below. Reaches about five feet in length, but usually much smaller.

A common shark from shallow inshore waters to at least twenty-five fathoms.

27. SMALLEYE HAMMERHEAD
Sphyrna tudes (Valenciennes)

Teeth

Head (ventral)

Head hammer-like but with rounded edges, with a distinct anterior median notch. Eyes small and anteriorly placed, on a level anterior to the anterior edge of the mouth. The free posterior corner of the second dorsal fin is shorter than the fin base. Teeth smooth. Grayish and white. Four to six feet long.

Another little known shark previously confused with the scalloped and great hammerheads. Possibly common.

28. SMOOTH HAMMERHEAD
Sphyrna zygaena (Linnaeus)

Teeth

Head (ventral)

Head hammer-like, lacking a median anterior notch. Eyes small and placed on a level with the anterior edge of the mouth. Free posterior corner of second dorsal fin much longer than base of that fin. Teeth usually smooth, but may be weakly serrated in larger individuals. Gray and white. Reaches twelve or thirteen feet.

A species with a typically northern distribution. Has apparently not been recorded from the Gulf, but it should be looked for.

Family SQUATINIDAE — angel sharks

Flattened sharks greatly resembling skates. Mouth large, terminal, with large and pointed teeth. Pectoral fins free anteriorly. One species.

29. ATLANTIC ANGEL SHARK
Squatina dumerili Lesueur

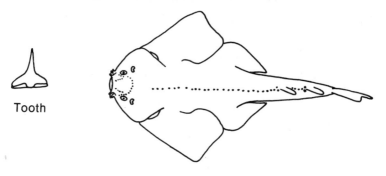

Tooth

Mouth with variable barbels and flaps. Median rows of prickles on back. Two large dorsal fins on stout tail. Grayish-brown above, often with reddish-brown fin margins. Lighter below. Reaches three to five feet in length.

A bottom-dwelling shark usually found in moderate depths of twenty to forty fathoms; rare in shallower water. Not common in the northern Gulf.

References: The best general work on North Atlantic sharks is Bigelow and Schroeder, 1948 (*Fishes of the Western North Atlantic, Volume I.* Memoirs Sears Foundation Marine Research), but this has become somewhat outdated. Clark and von Schmidt, 1965 (*Bull. Marine Science,* 15(1):13-83) have a great deal of natural history information on our common species.

ORDER RAJIFORMES — sawfishes, rays, and skates

Generally flattened elasmobranchs with ventral gill slits and large spiracles behind the dorsally located eyes. The mouth is ventral, with rows of small pebble-like teeth. The pectoral fins are fused to the sides of the head. Seven families, seventeen species, few common.

Family PRISTIDAE — sawfishes

Easily recognized by the combination of the shark-like body with typical skate features and a long, flat rostrum bearing more-or-less paired teeth on the lateral margins. Two species.

30. SMALLTOOTH SAWFISH
Pristis pectinata Latham

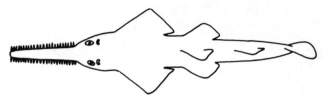

First dorsal fin originates over the pelvic fin origin. Lower caudal lobe rounded. There are about twenty-four teeth on each side of the saw, for a total count of forty-eight or more teeth. Grayish to chocolate above, whitish below. Adults commonly more than ten feet long, sometimes to eighteen feet.

This is the sawfish commonly found throughout our area in shallow water, especially near river mouths and in large bays.

31. LARGETOOTH SAWFISH
Pristis perotteti Muller & Henle

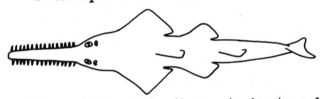

First dorsal fin originating anterior to pelvic fins. Lower caudal lobe distinctly pointed. The teeth of the saw are large, totalling less than forty. Grayish to brown above, whitish below. Twelve to twenty feet long.

This is a tropical species, found along the western shores of the Gulf east to the southwestern corner of Louisiana. Apparently rare.

Family **RHINOBATIDAE** — guitarfishes

Only one species in the northern Gulf of Mexico.

32. ATLANTIC GUITARFISH
Rhinobatos lentiginosus (Garman)

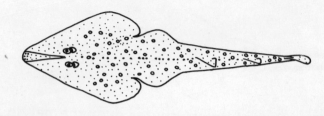

Greatly flattened, elongated skates with a longish snout and thick tail with two large dorsal fins. The pelvic fins are inserted posterior to the pectorals, not under them. Snout acutely rounded in this species, with about six prickles dorsally near the tip. There is a middorsal rows of prickles from the eyes to the first dorsal fin. Grayish to brown above, with numerous close-set white spots over the entire trunk. Specimens from the Texas coast may be mostly uniform brown, but this unicolor pattern may be found in other localities as well. One to two-and-a-half feet.

Locally common in shallow to moderate water. A bottom-dweller often taken in commercial trawls at two or more fathoms. Rare in over ten fathoms.

Family **TORPEDINIDAE** — electric rays

One shallow water species is common in our area.

33. LESSER ELECTRIC RAY
Narcine brasiliensis (Olfers)

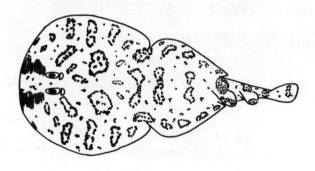

Disk broadly rounded anteriorly. Tail stout, with two dorsal fins, the first over the rear edge of the pelvics. The spiracles are close to the posterior edge of the eyes and are tuberculate on the anterior margins. There are large kidney-shaped electric organs posterio-lateral to the eyes, covered with a granular skin different from the remainder of the disk. Color very variable. Background light brown or grayish, usually with many kidney-shaped dark blotches, often reddish, which may be absent or present in outline only; sometimes unicolor. Usually nine to eighteen inches in length.

Common in shallow water, especially on sand or hard bottoms. Seldom found in more than ten fathoms.

Family **RAJIDAE** — skates

Typical skates with long, thin tails bearing two dorsal fins of similar shape near the end. A distinct caudal fin is present. All our species have one or more rows of prickles on the tail. Four species.

34. CLEARNOSE SKATE
Raja eglanteria Bosc

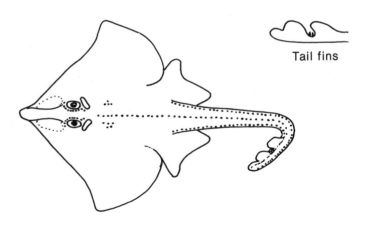

Tail fins

Dorsal fins close together, separated by less than the width of one fin base. Pectoral fins distinctly angled anteriorly. Rows of prickles continuous from behind eyes to tail; only one row above pelvics. Brown, with numerous darker spots and bars and irregular pale areas. One-and-a-half to three feet in total length.

A species which has been identified as the clearnose skate is uncommon in the shallow waters of the northern Gulf. Whether it is really that species remains uncertain.

35. FRECKLED SKATE
Raja lentiginosa Bigelow & Schroeder

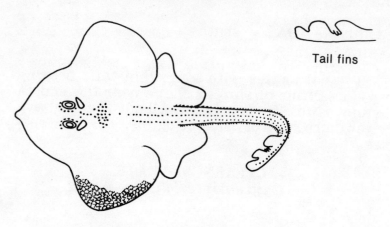

Tail fins

Dorsal fins close together. Pectorals broadly rounded anteriorly. Dorsal prickles in three or more rows, the rows discontinuous at mid-disk. Brown, with many dark and light brown freckles mixed with small white freckles. One to two feet long.

A borderline deep water species generally found in more than thirty fathoms but recorded occasionally in less than twenty.

36. SPREADFIN SKATE
Raja olseni Bigelow & Schroeder

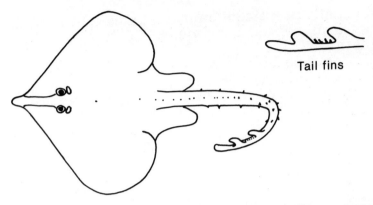

Tail fins

A rounded skate with the dorsal fins separated by at least the width of one fin base. No indentation between the head and the pectoral fins. Prickles usually absent on the midline of the disk and present as about three irregular rows on the tail. Brown above with darker spotting. Black ventrally. One to two feet.

Another normally deep water species rarely recorded from less than thirty fathoms.

37. ROUNDEL SKATE
Raja texana Chandler

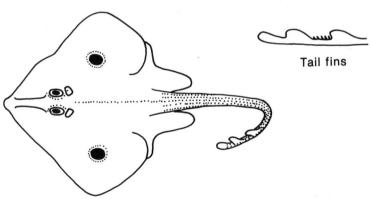

Tail fins

Dorsal fins separated by at least the width of one fin base. Definite indentation between the head and the pectorals. A single line of prickles on the middorsal line, continuous. Brown, light below. A dark brown ocellated spot on each pectoral, usually prominent but sometimes rubbed off in poorly preserved specimens. Up to two feet in length.

Common in waters of ten to thirty fathoms, but rare in shallower or deeper water. Not as common east of the Mississippi delta as west of the delta. Our only really common skate.

Family DASYATIDAE — stingrays

The most common family of rays in our area, but hard to define because of variability among the contained genera. They are best defined by negative characters: absence of paired dorsal fins, cephalic area not raised to produce a distinct forehead, and no cephalic fins. Mouth ventral. Caudal fin present or absent. Low ridges may be present on the tail, probably equivalent to dorsal and anal fins but greatly reduced in size. Large barbed spine or sting usually present. Tail generally long and thin; may be long and stout or short and thin, however. Five species.

38. SOUTHERN STINGRAY
Dasyatis americana Hildebrand & Schroeder

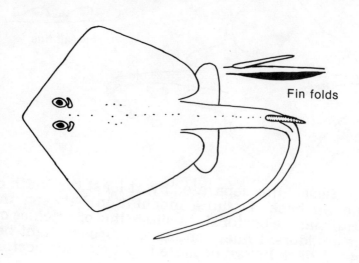

Fin folds

Dorsal fin a low keel or fold posterior to spine, not distinct. Anal fin about as high as tail is high. Disk with outer corners narrowly rounded, producing a distinct angle. Anterior edges of disk straight, not concave. Brownish above, white below. One-and-a-half to five feet in width.

This is a common ray in shallow waters out to at least fifteen fathoms. It is not normally common in bays.

39. ATLANTIC STINGRAY
Dasyatis sabina (Lesueur)

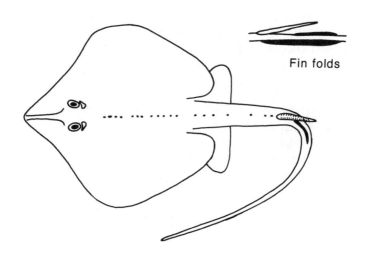

Fin folds

Dorsal fin a membrane about half of tail height. Anal fin about equal to tail height. Corners of disk broadly rounded. Anterior edges of disk concave, distinctly setting off comparatively long snout. Brownish above, white below. Up to about sixteen inches wide.

This is the common inshore stingray of the northern Gulf coast. It is seldom found in more than a few fathoms and is common in bays.

40. BLUNTNOSE STINGRAY
Dasyatis sayi (Lesueur)

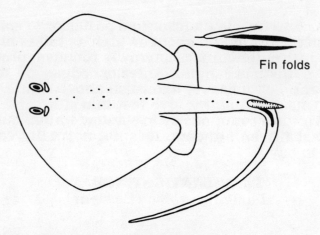

Fin folds

Dorsal fin a membrane half or more of tail height. Anal fin usually higher than tail height. Disk with outer corners broadly rounded. Anterior margins of disk straight or slightly convex, continuous with very short snout. Brown above, white below. Up to three feet wide.

The bluntnose stingray is apparently the least common stingray in our area. It is mostly a shallow water species, but does occur out to at least two fathoms. Reports of five-foot wide rays from twenty or more fathoms apparently refer to the southern stingray, not this species.

41. SMOOTH BUTTERFLY RAY
Gymnura micrura (Bloch & Schneider)

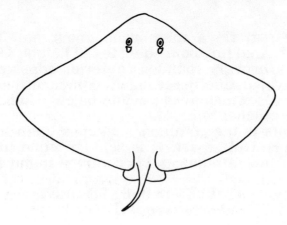

A stingray without a sting. Tail very short, the dorsal and anal present only as very low keels. The disk is wider than long, with sharply angled outer corners. Grayish, brown, greenish, to purple above, with darker and lighter spotting. Light ventrally. Up to three feet in width.

A common ray in shallow to moderate water out to thirty fathoms or more. It is rare in bays.

42. YELLOW STINGRAY
Urolophus jamaicensis (Cuvier)

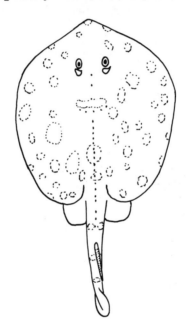

A stout-tailed stingray with a large and distinct caudal fin a short distance behind the sting. Disk oval. Background color usually sandy tan with a distinct but highly variable darker reticulation. Disk width to about fourteen inches, total length to over two feet.

A tropical species very rarely found in our area, although there are several literature records. Definitely known from southwestern Florida and southern Texas.

This genus is often placed in the separate family Urolophidae, which it would seem to deserve.

Family **MYLIOBATIDAE** — eagle rays

Large rays with the snout elevated to form a distinct forehead and also set off from the pectoral fins. Tail slender, usually spined and with a large dorsal fin anterior to spine; no caudal. No cephalic horns. Mouth ventral. Three species in our area.

43. SPOTTED EAGLE RAY
Aetobatus narinari (Euphrasen)

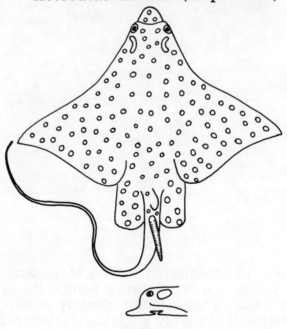

Head (lateral)

Dorsal fin inserted over pelvics. Snout depressed, sharply set off from forehead and narrower than width of head. Edges of disk very acutely angled. Dark brown with numerous round white spots about as large as eye over entire dorsum. Commonly three to five feet in width, but said to reach ten feet across the disk.

A common ray in shallow to moderately deep water. Often caught by anglers.

44. BULLNOSE RAY
Myliobatis freminvillei Lesueur

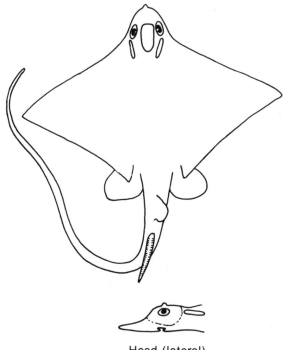

Head (lateral)

The only eagle ray with the dorsal fin entirely behind the pelvic fins. The snout is depressed but slopes upward into the forehead without a sharp angle. Males with a small tubercle over eye. Brownish to gray above, lighter below. Usually two or three feet wide.

An uncommmon ray in shallow or moderate waters of the northern Gulf.

45. COWNOSE RAY
Rhinoptera bonasus (Mitchill)

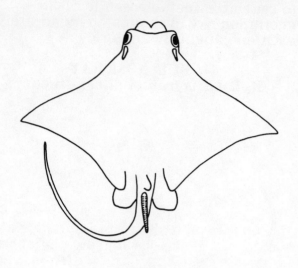

Head (lateral)

Dorsal fin over pelvics. Forehead projecting over snout, with a broad and shallow median indentation; snout notched similarly to forehead and slightly projecting. Brownish, lighter below. Two to five feet wide.

Not uncommon in shallow to deep water.

Family **MOBULIDAE** — mantas

Only one species seems to occur in the northern Gulf.

46. ATLANTIC MANTA
Manta birostris (Walbaum)

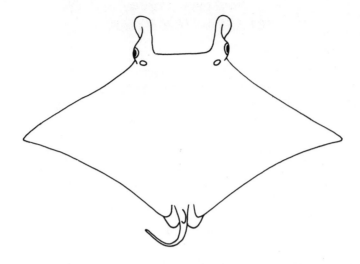

Gigantic rays with prominent cephalic fins before the eyes. Disk with sharply angled corners. Tail short, without spines, but with a large dorsal fin over the pelvics. Mouth terminal, large. Only the lower jaw has teeth. Reddish to black, sometimes with vague white patches on shoulders. Reaches a disk width in excess of fifteen feet, perhaps as great as twenty-two feet.

This fantastic pelagic fish never fails to draw comment when seen. It would appear to be relatively common in blue-water and is often seen moving at or just above the surface. They are often harpooned for "sport" — a hazardous and unnecessary "sport" to say the least.

The smaller devil ray, *Mobula hypostoma* (Bancroft), is recorded for our area but probably does not occur so far north. Its mouth is inferior, not terminal, and has teeth in both jaws.

Reference: The only comprehensive work on our skates and rays is Bigelow & Schroeder, 1953 (*Fishes of the Western North Atlantic, Volume 2*). Many of the more common species of skates, rays and sharks are also covered in the several free publications put out by the federal and various state governments.

THE BONY FISHES
CLASS OSTEICHTHYES

Included in this order are the remainder of our fishes, and of course the great majority of the species. All are easily recognizable by having only a single external gill opening usually covered by a moveable set of bones called the operculum. In some groups the operculum is no longer moveable and is covered by skin. These fishes, especially some eels and the puffers, are still obviously not sharks or rays and present no identification problems. Nineteen orders, ninety- two families, about four hundred and fifty-six species.

ORDER ACIPENSERIFORMES — sturgeons and allies

Primitive fishes with heterocercal caudal fins (the notochord continued into the upper lobe). Pelvic fins abdominal, pectorals set low on body. Mouth small, inferior, with barbels; long flattened rostrum. One family, one species.

Family **ACIPENSERIDAE** — sturgeons

Only one species in the northern Gulf of Mexico.

47. **ATLANTIC STURGEON**
Acipenser oxyrhynchus Mitchill

Dorsal and anal fins small, set far posteriorly. Head with long fleshy snout and long nasal barbels. Five rows of bony scutes on otherwise naked body, one row middorsal, one row laterally and one ventrolaterally on each side. Blackish dorsally, white ventrally; scutes colored similar to body. Reaches about six to ten feet in length, but now rare at large sizes.

This distinctive fish is found in our area only west of the Mississippi River delta area to about the Timbalier Islands of Louisiana. It is anadromous, ascending rivers to spawn, and is locally common in shallow water. Occasionally caught by commercial fishermen. Our subspecies is *A. o. desotoi.*

ORDER SEMIONOTIFORMES — ganoid fishes

Mostly fossil groups recognized by the distinctive ganoid scales of layered bone. Caudal fin heterocercal. Pelvics abdominal, pectorals low on body. One family, one species in brackish water.

Family LEPISOSTEIDAE — gars

Heavily armored fishes with arrowhead-shaped scales and long, heavily toothed snouts. Of the four mainly freshwater species in the southern United States, only one is commonly found in full salt water, although all the species may occasionally be found in bays and brackish river mouths. See any good freshwater book for fuller coverage of the species.

48. ALLIGATOR GAR
Lepisosteus spatula Lacepede

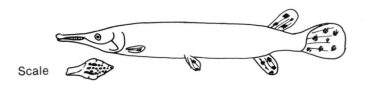

Scale

Cylindrical fishes with bony heads and relatively short, very broad snout, the snout length (tip of snout to angle of jaw) less than remainder of head length. Head without spots above. Olive green, grayish, to blackish, without spots. Large adults commonly exceed five or six feet in length, sometimes reaching nine feet.

A common species of both fresh and brackish water, sometimes common in shallow areas of the open Gulf. The decomposing bodies of this species are in some areas common on beaches, and the disarticulated jaws with their large conical teeth are often found in beach drift.

ORDER ELOPIFORMES — tarpons and relatives

Primitive fishes with the pelvic fins abdominal, the pectorals set low on the sides, the caudal fin deeply forked, the adipose fin absent, and a gular plate anteriorly between the gill membranes in some families. Two families, three species.

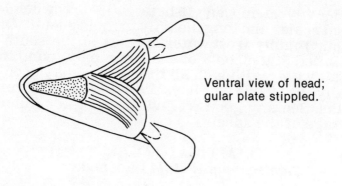

Ventral view of head; gular plate stippled.

Family ELOPIDAE — tarpons

Moderate to very large fishes with the mouth large and terminal or dorsal. A gular plate is present. Two species.

49. LADYFISH
Elops saurus Linnaeus

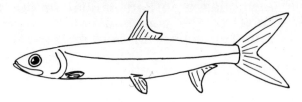

Body cigar-shaped, with 105 to 120 small silvery scales in a lateral series. The dorsal fin lacks an elongated last ray and is inserted only slightly posterior to the pelvic fins. Silvery, appearing bluish in life. Normally ten to thirty inches in length.

A common fish found in bays, along shores, and in open shallow water. There is a leptocephalus-like larva, but the spawning grounds are unknown.

50. TARPON
Megalops atlantica Valenciennes

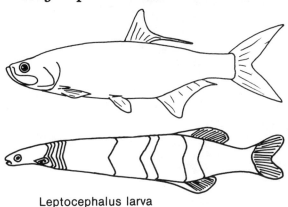

Leptocephalus larva

A coarse-bodied fish with very large scales, 41 to 48 in a lateral series. The last dorsal ray is prolonged. Insertion of the pelvic fins is anterior to the dorsal origin by at least one pelvic fin length. Silvery, appearing bluish to greenish. Three to eight feet.

A common sportsfish usually found in shallow or moderate water, sometimes in bays. The leptocephalus larva has a forked caudal unlike the rounded caudal of the common eel. The genus *Tarpon* is sometimes used instead of *Megalops*.

Family **ALBULIDAE** — bonefishes

Famous sportsfishes. Gular plate absent. Mouth small, inferior, under a short pig-like snout. One species.

51. BONEFISH
Albula vulpes (Linnaeus)

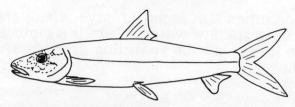

Scales moderate, about 65 to 71 in a lateral series. Pelvic fins are inserted under the posterior part of the dorsal fin. Silvery, appearing bluish with vague darker lengthwise stripes. One to two-and-a-half feet long.

A tropical species characteristic of shallow salty to brackish flats. Strays northward in our area to the central Texas coast, where rare; also southern Florida. Absent in north-central Gulf (Louisiana records are unsubstantiated).

References: For the orders Acipenseriformes to Elopiformes, see various chapters of volume three of *Fishes of the Western North Atlantic* (1963).

ORDER ANGUILLIFORMES — the eels

Body elongated, with long dorsal and anal fins. Pelvic fins always absent. Pectoral and caudal fins may be normal, reduced, or absent. Scales absent or, if present, small and embedded. Gill openings reduced to a slit or pore, opercular bones not distinct and not easily moveable externally. All other eel-like fish families either have pelvic fins or have a normal, moveable operculum. Seven families, twenty-four species.

This large and complicated group is often considered difficult, and many of the genera and species are poorly defined. The names used here are probably subject to change with further study of the osteology and life cycles of the various groups, especially in the Ophichthidae. The families are easy to recognize from the following key:

1a. Lower jaw projecting; body stout, dark; embedded scales present............Anguillidae
1b. Lower jaw not projecting; no scales.........2
2a. Jaws bony beaks with heavy fangs; body silvery, very slender ....Muraenesocidae
2b. Jaws not bony; body seldom silvery and usually not very slender........................3
3a. Anus situated just behind level with posterior edge of pectoral fin..............Dysommidae
3b. Anus posteriorly located, usually just before anal fin 4
4a. Gill opening a rounded pore; pectoral fin completely absent...................Muraenidae
4b. Gill opening a vertical or horizontal slit; pectoral fin present or absent 5
5a. Neither nostril tubular; dorsal and anal fins similar......................Moringuidae
5b. At least anterior nostril tubular, or if not, then anal fin absent 6
6a. Posterior nostril a pore located above the upper lip; all fins present..........Congridae
6b. Posterior nostril located on upper lip, often tubular; caudal and sometimes other fins often reduced or absent ....Ophichthidae

Family **ANGUILLIDAE** — freshwater eels

Large eels with a prominently projecting lower jaw. Body covered with small embedded scales. Caudal fin present. One species.

52. AMERICAN EEL
Anguilla rostrata (Lesueur)

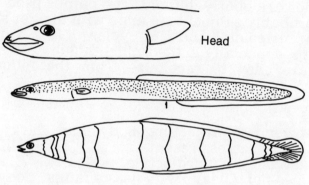

Leptocephalus larva

Dorsal fin begins between tip of pectoral and the vent, but closer to vent. Dark brown to blackish. Two to five feet long, sometimes larger.

A common fish in open salt water, brackish bays, and freshwater. Catadromus, spawning in the Sargasso Sea and the leptocephalus larvae (caudal rounded) eventually moving into inshore brackish and freshwaters for transformation. Although the American *Anguilla* has received many names because of its variability, there is a growing opinion that it is not really distinct from the virtually identical European species.

Family **MORINGUIDAE** — spaghetti eels

A small family based mostly on osteological and larval characters and very poorly known. One rare species in our area.

53. SLENDER PIKE EEL
Neoconger mucronatus Girard

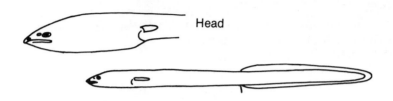

Head

Neither nostril tubular, both open pores. Posterior nostril located well above upper lip and just anterior to middle of eye. Pectoral large. Dorsal fin low, beginning about over vent; anal fin starting slightly behind dorsal; caudal distinct. Two to three rows of palatal teeth. Silvery brown. Small, usually under one foot.

A rare species very poorly known. Found only west of the Mississippi delta in fifteen to at least seventy fathoms.

Family MURAENIDAE — morays

Gill opening a circular pore. Pectoral fins absent. Anterior nostril tubular, the posterior nostril a pore near the anterior or upper edge of eye. Head often distinctly set off from body by gibbous nape. Two species.

54. SPOTTED MORAY
Gymnothorax moringa (Cuvier)

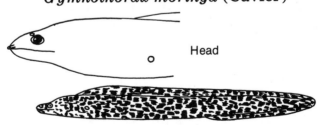

Head

Teeth entire. Two or three median anterior fangs on palate. Background color white to yellowish with numerous stripes and spots of brownish or blackish, resulting in a reticulated pattern. Fins white-bordered posteriorly. Two to three feet.

Status in the northern Gulf of Mexico unknown; possibly not uncommon on snapper banks and other hard bottoms.

55. BLACKEDGE MORAY
Gymnothorax nigromarginatus (Girard)

G. n. saxicola

G. n. nigromarginatus

Teeth distinctly serrated. No median anterior fangs on palate. Color dark dorsally, with numerous small white spots or streaks. Anal fin black, the dorsal fin with interrupted black margin. One to two feet.

Common in about ten to thirty-five fathoms, rarely shallower.

Two subspecies are recognizable:

G. n. nigromarginatus (Girard)—body with discrete small white spots relatively widely separated by dark background; head without stripes. Texas to about Pensacola, Florida.

G. n. saxicola Jordan & Davis—white spots large, dark background narrower, appearing reticulated; head with distinct stripes. West coast of Florida west to about Mobile Bay, Alabama. The two subspecies overlap and intergrade between Mobile Bay and Pensacola.

Family MURAENESOCIDAE — pike congers

Body extremely long and slender, round, covered with silver pigment which rubs off easily. Jaws long, bony, with a row of large palatal fangs. Posterior nostril a large oval pore. One species.

56. SILVER CONGER
Hoplunnis macrurus Ginsburg

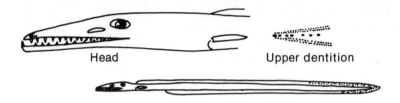

Head   Upper dentition

Tail about three times as long as trunk. Caudal fin long for an eel. Upper jaw teeth in two rows; six or seven upper median canines which are not flanked by smaller teeth. Silvery, the color apparently being guanine and easily rubbed off. Posterior part of dorsal, anal, and caudal black. Six to eighteen inches long, but extremely slender for length.

Common in twelve to forty fathoms, but easily missed by large-meshed nets.

Two other species which are very similar externally occur in deeper water and possibly stray into our depth range. They may be distinguished by tooth characters. *H. tenuis* Ginsburg: three rows of upper jaw teeth, small teeth flanking median canines, anterior inner teeth of lower jaw larger than in outer row and widely spaced; *H. diomedianus* Goode & Bean: three rows of upper jaw teeth plus small teeth flanking canines, anterior inner teeth smaller than outer and closely spaced.

Family **CONGRIDAE** — conger eels

Anterior nostril tubular, the posterior nostril a pore set well above the upper lip. Distinct lip folds usually present on upper and/or lower lip. Pectoral and caudal fins both well developed. Five species, all in moderate to deep water.

57. BANDTOOTH CONGER
Ariosoma impressa (Poey)

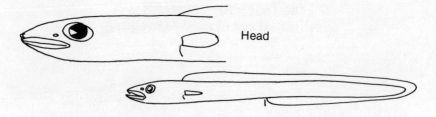

Head

Head does not look distinctly higher than body. The teeth in the upper jaws are pointed and in many rows. Gill opening extending to about middle of pectoral base. Dorsal fin originates about over base of pectoral fin. Silvery-brown, the fins dark edged posteriorly. Six to twelve inches long.

An uncommon eel in about ten to fifty-five fathoms.

58. YELLOW CONGER
Congrina flava (Goode & Bean)

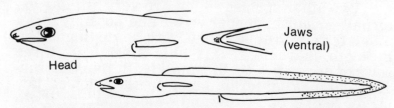

Jaws
(ventral)

Head

Snout longer than lower jaw, distinctly projecting. The premaxillary teeth form an exposed patch in front of the mouth. Body strongly tapered posteriorly. Pectoral fin long, the dorsal fin origin over pectoral base. Caudal fin short, its length less than body depth just anterior to vent. Predorsal length about 13-17% of total length. Silvery brown, the fins dark-edged posteriorly. Said to reach four feet in length, but usually only two feet long.

Moderately uncommon off our coast in about twelve to ninety fathoms depth. Specimens of this genus taken in more than thirty or forty fathoms may represent *Congrina* species not in this manual, but are usually easily recognizable as not being *C. flava*.

59. DOGFACE CONGER
Congrina macrosoma Ginsburg

Snout longer than lower jaw, projecting, the premaxillary tooth patch exposed. Body not strongly tapered posteriorly, appears distinctly stubby. Pectoral fin long; dorsal origin over pectoral base. Caudal fin long, equal to or greater than body depth just anterior to vent. Antedorsal length about 20% of total length. Straw brown in preservative. One foot long.

An apparently rare and poorly known species from off the Louisiana coast in twenty to thirty fathoms. This species is not in the AFS *Checklist*, and the common name dogface conger is proposed here as new. I have examined two specimens from off Grande Isle, Louisiana in twenty fathoms which agree in all respects with the description of Ginsburg's unique holotype from off Isle Deniere, Louisiana. The species is easily distinguished from the sympatric *Congrina flava* by the relatively stubby body, long caudal fin, and longer antedorsal distance. The appearance of the head is also subtly different from that of *C. flava*.

60. MARGINTAIL CONGER
Paraconger caudilimbatus (Poey)

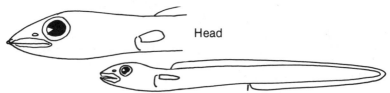

Head

Skull with inflated mucous cavities, the head appearing distinctly higher than the slender body. Teeth in the upper jaw closely spaced, blunt, and in one prominent row. Gill opening extending to upper edge of pectoral base. Dorsal fin origin over middle of pectoral fin. Silvery brown, the fins darker posteriorly. Six to fourteen inches long.

An uncommon eel from depths greater than ten fathoms.

61. THREADTAIL CONGER
Uroconger syringinus Ginsburg

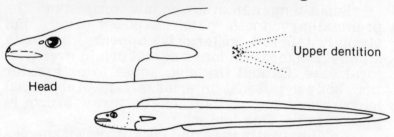

Upper dentition

Head

Snout blunt, shorter than in *Congrina*, premaxillary teeth not exposed. Upper jaw teeth in two rows. A row of about twelve strong median palatal fangs or canines. Gill opening extending to lower edge of pectoral fin. Dorsal fin origin over pectoral base. Body strongly tapered posteriorly, more so than in our other conger species except *Congrina flava*. Brownish, the sensory pores dark; fins dark posteriorly. Twelve to sixteen inches long.

An apparently rare species known in our area from off the Louisiana and Texas coasts in twenty to fifty fathoms. This species is not listed in the AFS *Checklist*, and the common name used here is new. It is easily recognized by the row of palatal fangs, the anterior origin of the dorsal, the short gill opening, the tapered tail, and the unusually conspicuous sensory pores on the head and body. The snout is also distinctly short and blunt compared to the lower jaw.

Family OPHICHTHIDAE — snake eels and worm eels

Small to very large eels with the fins highly variable in development. The pectoral and caudal fins may be large and well developed or absent.

The one distinctive character is the presence of the posterior nostril on the edge of the upper lip; the anterior nostril is tubular (one exception), the posterior tubular or not. Several of the genera and species are of doubtful distinctiveness. About thirteen species in the northern Gulf of Mexico.

62. KEY WORM EEL
Ahlia egmontis (Jordan)

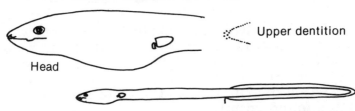

No palatal teeth. Dorsal fin low, beginning about over vent. Caudal and pectoral fins present. Pale brown. Eight to fourteen inches long.

A species associated with hard bottoms and reefs, apparently rare and not extending west beyond the Mobile Bay area. An offshore species in our area.

63. WHIP EEL
Bascanichthys scuticaris (Goode & Bean)

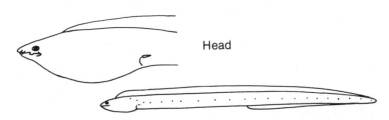

Anterior mandibular teeth not distinctly enlarged. Pectoral fins present, very small; caudal fin absent. Dorsal fin beginning on nape, well in advance of vertical gill openings; anal fin present; both fins low. Very slender, the body depth only 1.1 to 1.6% of total length and about half of predorsal distance. Yellow to brownish, sometimes with a row of white spots laterally. Dorsal and anal fins lighter than body. Two to three-and-a-half feet long.

A rarely seen burrowing eel found from the shoreline to moderate depths.

64. SOOTY EEL
Bascanichthys teres (Goode & Bean)

Identical in all respects to *Bascanichthys scuticaris* except for body depth. Depth 1.7 to 2.6% of total length and only slightly less than predorsal distance. This is probably not a distinct species.

Same distribution as the whip eel, and sometimes found with it.

65. BLOTCHED SNAKE EEL
Callechelys muraena Jordan & Evermann

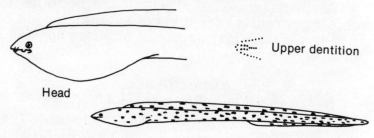

Anterior mandibular teeth not distinctly enlarged. Pectorals and caudal fin completely absent. Dorsal fin beginning on nape; anal fin present. Gill opening nearly horizontal, very low on body, completely visible from below. Yellowish, with numerous small cloudy brown spots over entire body. About two feet long.

In our area seems to prefer hard offshore bottoms. Not known west of the Mobile Bay area. Other species may also occur, but this genus is very poorly known.

66. HORSEHAIR EEL
Gordiichthys irretitus Jordan & Davis

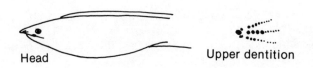

Head   Upper dentition

Anterior mandibular teeth distinctly larger than posterior ones. Palatal teeth in one row of four large teeth anteriorly and six smaller ones posteriorly. Dorsal origin at back of head. Pectoral fin presumably absent; anal fin unknown. Body extremely slender, thread-like. Color unknown. Nearly three feet long.

An extremely rare eel known from a single mutilated specimen taken from the stomach of a snapper or grouper off Pensacola, Florida. Supposedly other specimens have been taken, but these have not yet been described.

67. THREAD EEL
"Gordiichthys" springeri Ginsburg

Upper dentition

Anterior mandibular teeth distinctly larger than the posterior ones. Five large palatal teeth arranged in two rows, not followed by smaller teeth. Dorsal fin originates on top of head; anal present. Pectoral and caudal absent. Body extremely slender. Body and tail with large brown spots. Fifteen inches long.

Another rare species known from a single mutilated specimen taken from the stomach of a shark off Florida. Very poorly known and probably does not belong to *Gordiichthys* but to another genus. The gill openings are horizontal much as in *Callechelys*.

68. SAILFIN EEL
Letharchus velifer Goode & Bean

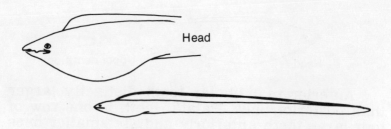

Head

Anterior mandibular teeth not distinctly enlarged. Anterior nostril not tubular. Dorsal fin high anteriorly, beginning behind angle of mouth. Pectoral, caudal, and anal fins absent. Gill openings nearly horizontal, fully visible from below. Uniform brown, the dorsal fin lighter and with a black distal margin. To about twenty inches in length.

Offshore hard bottoms of the west coast of Florida.

69. SPECKLED WORM EEL
Myrophis punctatus Lutken

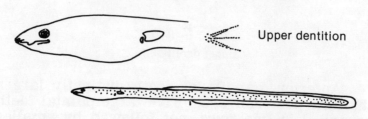

Upper dentition

One to two rows of palatal teeth. Dorsal fin low, beginning about half way between pectoral fin and vent. Pectoral and caudal fins present, well developed. Brownish, distinctively speckled with numerous small black spots. Six to sixteen inches long.

A common burrowing eel found in bays and shallow water. Rare offshore.

70. SPOTTED SPOON-NOSE EEL
Mystriophis intertinctus (Richardson)

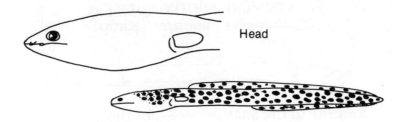

Head

A heavy-bodied eel with the dorsal fin beginning about one pectoral length behind the pectoral fin. Caudal fin absent. Gill slit vertical. Upper jaw not projecting. Palatal and anterior jaw canines present. At about three feet in length, the yellow background color is covered with numerous large brown spots arranged in about three rows between dorsal fin and light venter. The largest spots are about equal in length to the snout plus the eye; spots larger in smaller specimens. Two to four feet long.

An uncommon eel found in ten to thirty-five fathoms of water. Somewhat less common than the snapper eel, but much more common than the stippled spoon-nose eel.

71. SNAPPER EEL
Mystriophis mordax (Poey)

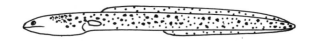

Morphologically indistinguishable from the spotted spoon-nose eel and the stippled spoon-nose eel, differing only in color. In three-foot-long specimens the spots are relatively smaller, about four to six rows on each side, the largest spots about equal to snout length. The spots are larger and in about two rows in two-foot-long specimens. To four or more feet.

This is the most common *Mystriophis* in central northern Gulf waters, commonly taken in ten to thirty-five fathoms.

72. STIPPLED SPOON-NOSE EEL
Mystriophis punctifer (Kaup)

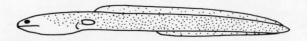

Similar to the snapper eel, but the spots even smaller. In a two-foot-long specimen the spots are arranged in about six rows on each side and are smaller than the snout length. Three-foot-long specimens have the spots in about ten rows and appearing as stipples rather than distinct spots. Four feet.

The least common *Mystriophis* in our area and sometimes taken with the other two species. It is also the most distinctively patterned species. One should not expect to be able to accurately identify all specimens of this genus found in commercial trawl catches because of the variation in color pattern with size; the differentiation is particularly hard between *M. mordax* and *M. intertinctus*.

73. SHRIMP EEL
Ophichthus gomesi (Castelnau)

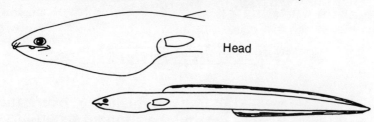

Head

A supple but heavy-bodied eel. The dorsal fin originates about over the pectoral fin. Caudal fin absent. Two to four rows of palatal teeth. Upper jaw distinctly overhanging lower. Color generally an unmarked brownish-yellow, lighter below. Fins dark posteriorly. Two to three feet long.

An abundant eel in shallow sandy and muddy bottoms and also in water up to about fifteen fathoms deep.

74. PALESPOTTED EEL
Ophichthus ocellatus (Lesueur)

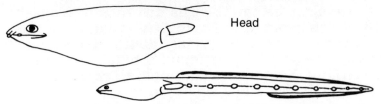

Head

A very large, very heavy-bodied eel. The dorsal fin originates anywhere from over the tip of the pectoral to over one fin length beyond the pectoral. Caudal fin absent. One row of palatal teeth. Upper jaw projecting. Brown, generally with a lateral row of large white spots; variable. Three to over six feet long.

An uncommon species sometimes taken by sportsfishermen off hard bottoms in five to eighty fathoms. More than one species may be involved, as the species is highly variable in dorsal origin, color pattern, and maximum adult size.

Family **DYSOMMIDAE** — arrowtooth eels

Stout eels with rounded snouts. The anus and anal fin are situated just behind the level of the pectoral fin tip. One species.

75. SHORTBELLY EEL
Dysomma anguillare Barnard

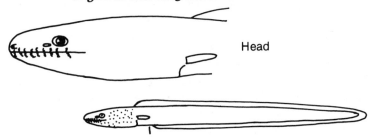

Head

Dorsal fin origin slightly in front of pectoral base. Teeth of lower jaw larger than those of upper. Three or four median palatal fangs. Skin thick, often looks wrinkled. Silvery. Eight to thirteen inches long.

In our area the records are mostly from off the Texas coast in thirty to fifty fathoms, but the species is much more widely distributed and will probably eventually be found throughout the northern Gulf. Sometimes common. *Dysomma aphododera* Ginsburg is a synonym.

References: The only general work on the eels of the northern Gulf is Ginsburg, Issac, 1951 (*Texas Journal of Science,* 3(3):431-485). Although still a useful and necessary paper, it is now outdated as regards family placements and some species names.

ORDER CLUPEIFORMES — herrings and anchovies

Generally deep-bodied silvery fishes with abdominal pelvic fins, pectoral fins set low on the body, and the caudal fin deeply forked. The dorsal fin is generally at about the middle of the body; there is no adipose fin. The scales of the ventral profile are often keeled and spinous. Two families, eighteen species.

Family CLUPEIDAE — herrings and menhaden

Mouth usually terminal or dorsal, the body usually deep; if mouth is ventral then the snout is not distinctly pointed. Maxillary relatively short, not extending beyond eye in most forms. Usually no silvery lateral band. Thirteen species, several commercially important.

76. ALABAMA SHAD
Alosa alabamae Jordan & Evermann

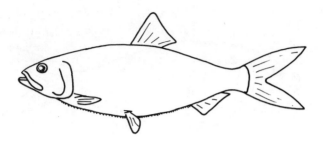

Body relatively deep. Pelvic fins under the anterior part of the dorsal fin. The gill rakers are close-set at the base, numerous, more than forty on the first arch. In large specimens the lower jaw lacks teeth. Silvery blue. Ten to twenty inches long.

A freshwater fish which also occurs in salt water, especially east of the Mississippi River. Seldom common.

77. SKIPJACK HERRING
Alosa chrysochloris (Rafinesque)

Body relatively slender. The pelvic fins originate under the posterior part of the dorsal fin. The gill rakers are few, about twenty to twenty-five, and their bases are distinctly separated. The lower jaw has teeth at the symphysis in all specimens, the teeth easily felt with the finger. Silvery blue. Twelve to eighteen inches long.

A freshwater fish widely distributed in lakes and rivers and also in bays and estuarine waters. Not edible and often a commercial nuisance.

78. FINESCALE MENHADEN
Brevoortia gunteri Hildebrand

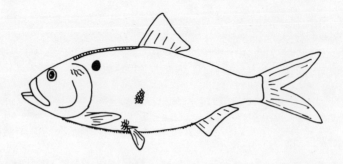

Two rows of enlarged middorsal scales running from the nape to the dorsal origin. Scales numerous, small, not in regular rows, and difficult to count. Shoulder spot not followed by smaller spots. Twenty-seven to thirty ventral scutes. Two to four horizontal rows of scales between the tip of the pectoral and the base of the pelvics. Silvery, the caudal fin with a pale margin. Six to twelve inches in length.

The two small-scaled menhadens (*B. gunteri* and *B. smithi*) both are not slimy to the touch and have the radiating striae on the operculum weak and short. The large-scaled menhaden (*B. patronus*) is very slimy and the opercular striae are long and distinct.

A moderately common fish in inshore and shallow waters generally west of the Mississippi delta. Intermediates with the yellowfin menhaden occur.

79. GULF MENHADEN
Brevoortia patronus Goode

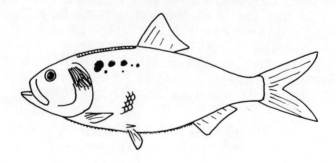

Scales large, in regular rows, and easily countable. Shoulder spot usually followed by several smaller spots. Opercular striae long and distinct. Very slimy. Silvery, more greenish above. Caudal fin with a dark margin, the other fins often yellow. Six to ten inches. The predorsal scales are enlarged as in other menhadens.

An important and abundant commercial fish in shallow Gulf waters.

80. YELLOWFIN MENHADEN
Brevoortia smithi Hildebrand

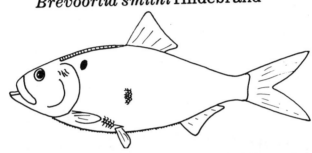

Enlarged predorsal scales. Scales small, in irregular rows and hard to count. Shoulder spot not followed by smaller spots. Thirty to thirty-two ventral scutes. Five to eight horizontal rows of scales between the tip of the pectoral fin and base of the pelvic fin. Silvery, the caudal and other fins yellow; caudal with a pale margin. Six to thirteen inches in length.

Not uncommon in shallow water mostly east of the Mississippi delta.

81. GIZZARD SHAD
Dorosoma cepedianum (Lesueur)

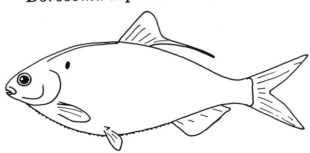

Narrow naked ridge between nape and dorsal origin. Last dorsal ray elongated. Dorsal fin origin over pelvic base. Mouth inferior, the snout blunt. Scales in lateral series more than fifty. Silvery, often with a dark shoulder spot. Six to twelve inches.

A common freshwater fish which is also often found in shallow bay areas.

82. THREADFIN SHAD
Dorosoma petenense (Gunther)

Naked ridge from dorsal fin to nape. Last dorsal ray elongated. Dorsal fin origin over pelvic base. Scales in lateral series forty-one to forty-eight. Mouth terminal, the snout sharp. Silvery, often with dark shoulder spot. Four to seven inches.

A freshwater fish which commonly enters brackish to somewhat salty estuarine areas.

83. ROUND HERRING
Etrumeus teres (DeKay)

Body rounded, not compressed. No ventral scutes. Dorsal rays seventeen to twenty. In adults the pelvic fins are behind the dorsal, but in young they are anterior to the dorsal, moving back with growth. Olive silvery. Eight inches in adults.

A rare fish in the northern Gulf of Mexico, known mostly from juvenile specimens taken in five to twenty fathoms.

84. FALSE PILCHARD
Harengula clupeola Valenciennes

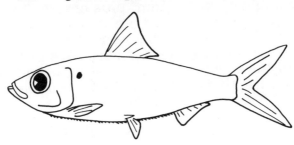

Mouth terminal. Last dorsal ray not elongated. Body deep, compressed, silvery, with relatively large and prominent scales. Pelvic fins about under middle of dorsal fin. Dorsal and ventral profiles both convex, similar. Distance from occiput to dorsal origin 66% or more of body depth. A dark humeral spot is nearly always present. Dark bluish above, shiny silver on sides. Six to eight inches.

A tropical species rarely recorded from our area but perhaps confused with the very similar scaled sardine.

85. REDEAR SARDINE
Harengula humeralis Cuvier

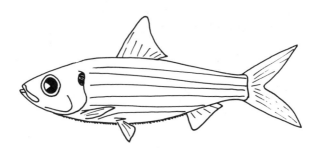

Mouth terminal. No elongated dorsal ray. Body deep and compressed, the scales slightly deciduous. Pelvic fins originate near the front of the dorsal fin. Dorsal and ventral profiles convex and similar. Humeral spot consistently absent. Silvery, bluish above. A distinctive orange spot at upper angle of operculum, plus orange highlights on head and vague orange stripes along scale rows on sides. Grows to nine inches.

This tropical species is very rare in our area, most of the records probably being based on misidentified scaled sardines. Most common on west coast of Florida near shore.

86. SCALED SARDINE
Harengula pensacolae Goode & Bean

A deep bodied, very flat fish with shining silvery scales on the sides. The mouth is terminal. The dorsal fin lacks elongated rays and the pelvics are about under the middle of the dorsal. The dorsal profile is distinctly straighter compared to the strongly convex ventral profile. In addition, the eyes are distinctly larger than in the other *Harengula* species in our area. The humeral spot is normally present but may be weak or absent. Silvery, bluish above. Usually three to six inches long.

A very common little fish in shallow waters of high salinity.

87. ATLANTIC THREAD HERRING
Opisthonema oglinum (Lesueur)

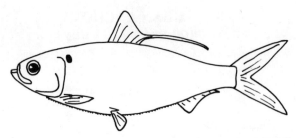

Last dorsal ray greatly elongated. Middorsal area between dorsal origin and nape scaled. Mouth large, terminal. Pelvic fins about under middle of dorsal fin. Shoulder spot present. Silvery, bluish above. Reaches eight to ten inches, but seldom this long.

Common in higher salinity waters, usually near shore.

88. SPANISH SARDINE
Sardinella anchovia Valenciennes

Body slender, slightly rounded or at least not as compressed as most of our herrings. Dorsal profile straight. Last two rays of anal fin distinctly longer than preceding rays. Dark blue-black above, silvery below. Four to six inches.

Rare in the northern Gulf and usually found in moderate depths with high salinities.

Family **ENGRAULIDAE** — anchovies

Mouth inferior, overhung by a large, usually protruding snout. Maxillary reaching well beyond eye, sometimes to edge of operculum. Silvery lateral band present. Five species.

89. CUBAN ANCHOVY
Anchoa cubana (Poey)

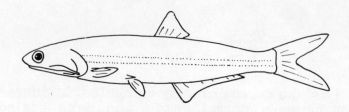

Maxillary posteriorly pointed. Anal fin origin under middle or posterior fourth of dorsal fin. Snout overhanging mouth, prominent. Relatively slender bodied. Silver lateral band narrower than width of eye. Gill rakers forty-four to fifty. Translucent tan, lighter below, with silver band. About four inches.

Rare in our area, the few records covering almost our entire area, however. Usually in high salinity water.

90. STRIPED ANCHOVY
Anchoa hepsetus (Linnaeus)

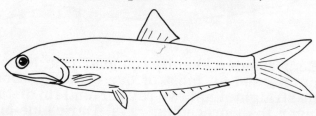

Maxillary pointed posteriorly. Origin of anal fin about under middle or posterior fourth of dorsal fin. Snout prominent, overhanging mouth. Body relatively deeper than in the Cuban anchovy and seems more firm than most anchovies. Gill rakers thirty-five to forty-one. Silvery lateral band narrower than eye. Four to six inches, our largest anchovy.

An abundant species in shallow to moderate waters of high salinity; rarely inshore.

91. BAY ANCHOVY
Anchoa mitchilli (Valenciennes)

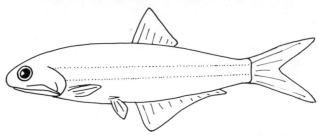

Maxillary pointed posteriorly. Anal fin originates only slightly behind the dorsal fin origin. The snout is relatively short and does not greatly overhang the mouth. Body deeper than in our other species and very fragile, the tissue easily destroyed in nets. Silvery lateral band of variable width. Two to four inches long.

The abundant anchovy in shallow water and bays of low salinity. Rarely found in deep water of high salinity.

92. LONGNOSE ANCHOVY
Anchoa nasuta Hildebrand & Carvalho

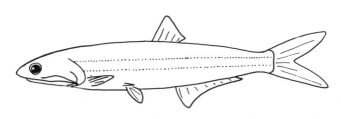

Anal fin origin under or behind the last dorsal ray. Snout greatly overhanging mouth, appearing longer than in the striped anchovy. Silvery lateral band usually as wide as or wider than the eye. Body slender. Two to three inches.

A rare but widely distributed species in the northern Gulf, usually found with *Anchoa hepsetus* in offshore waters of high salinity. Gulf specimens were formerly misidentified as *Anchoa lyolepis.*

101

93. FLAT ANCHOVY
Anchoviella perfasciata (Poey)

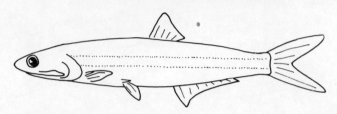

Posterior end of maxillary truncate, somewhat shorter than in *Anchoa*. Anal fin origin under or slightly behind last dorsal ray. Snout long, overhanging mouth. Silvery band about as wide as eye. Two to four inches.

Rare in our area, generally in offshore high salinity waters.

References: The most comprehensive work on the Clupeidae and Engraulidae is Hildebrand, S.F., 1963 (*Fishes of the Western North Atlantic, Volume 3*). This volume also contains a great deal of information on the natural history of these fishes.

ORDER MYCTOPHIFORMES — lanternfishes, lizardfishes, and allies

This order contains a great variety of mostly deep sea families. For our purposes the order is recognizable by the presence of an adipose fin and the absence of mouth barbels. Only one shallow water family, with eight species.

Family SYNODONTIDAE — lizardfishes

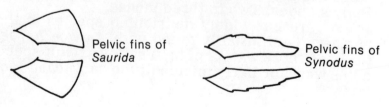

Pelvic fins of *Saurida*

Pelvic fins of *Synodus*

Cigar-shaped fishes with heavy scales, large mouths, prominent adipose fins, and large abdominal pelvic fins. Eight species.

94. LARGESCALE LIZARDFISH
Saurida brasiliensis Norman

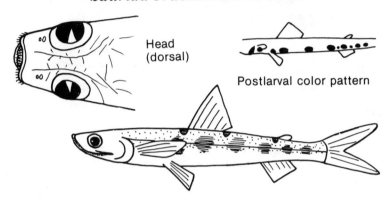

Head
(dorsal)

Postlarval color pattern

Pelvic fins truncate, the inner and outer rays about equal in length. Lower jaw distinctly longer than upper and visible in dorsal view. Scales in lateral series forty to fifty. Silvery, with brown dorsal saddles and lateral blotches. Two to four inches.

Relatively common in waters of ten to one hundred fathoms, especially beyond the twenty-five fathom line.

95. SMALLSCALE LIZARDFISH
Saurida caribbaea Breder

Pelvic fin truncate. Lower jaw longer than upper, visible from above. Scales in lateral series fifty-four to sixty. Silvery, with vague brownish areas and blotches. Three to five inches.

Rare in the northern Gulf of Mexico. Record-ed only from east of the Mississippi delta in three (rare) to over two hundred fathoms.

96. SHORTJAW LIZARDFISH
Saurida normani Longley

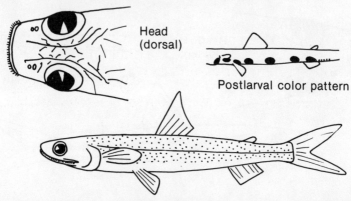

Head
(dorsal)

Postlarval color pattern

Pelvic fin truncate. Upper jaw longer than the lower, the lower not visible in dorsal view when the mouth is closed. Scales fifty-one to fifty-six. Silvery, with little darker pattern. Large, to thir-teen inches.

A rare species, seldom found in less than fifty fathoms in our area.

97. INSHORE LIZARDFISH
Synodus foetens (Linnaeus)

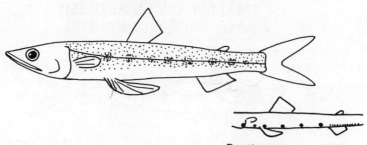

Postlarval color pattern

Pelvic fin with inner rays much longer than outer, pointed. Lower jaw without distinct fleshy knob at symphysis. Dorsal fin concave posteriorly, its anterior rays, when laid back, longer than most succeeding rays. The pectoral fin does not reach the base of the pelvics. Lateral scales fifty-five to sixty-four. Anal rays eleven or twelve. Color brown, usually with a series of indistinct mid-lateral diamond-shaped brown marking, fading with growth. Tip of snout without a black spot. Ten to sixteen inches.

This is the common lizardfish of all shallow northern Gulf waters and the only species likely to be found inshore. It also ranges into moderate depths, at least twenty-five fathoms, where it is somewhat replaced by the offshore lizardfish and the various *Saurida*.

98. SAND DIVER
Synodus intermedius (Agassiz)

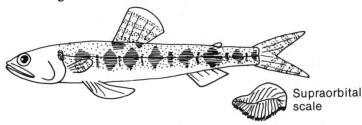

Supraorbital scale

Pelvic fin with inner rays longest. Lower jaw without a fleshy knob. Dorsal fin straight posteriorly, its anterior rays not longer than the other rays when laid back, although equal in length to a few. Scales forty-three to fifty in lateral series. Large scale anterodorsal to eye with posterior margin strongly serrated. Grayish-brown with eight distinct crossbands. A prominent black spot at the upper edge of operculum, mostly under the operculum. Eight to sixteen inches long.

Uncommon in our area, with most records coming from east of the Mississippi delta. It is most common between twenty and sixty fathoms, rarely in shallower waters.

99. OFFSHORE LIZARDFISH
Synodus poeyi Jordan

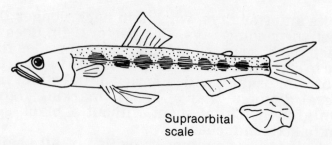

Supraorbital scale

Pelvic fin with the inner rays longest. Lower jaw ending in a prominent fleshy knob at symphysis. Dorsal fin concave, its anterior rays equaling or exceeding the posterior rays. Lateral scales forty-three to forty-eight. Large scale between nostril and upper anterior part of eye with its posterior margin smooth. Grayish to brown, with indistinct lateral blotches. No dark spot under operculum. Six to eight inches long.

The most common offshore lizardfish, replacing *Synodus foetens* at about fifteen fathoms. This species and the sand diver also differ from the inshore lizardfish in having shorter snouts and larger eyes.

100. RED LIZARDFISH
Synodus synodus (Linnaeus)

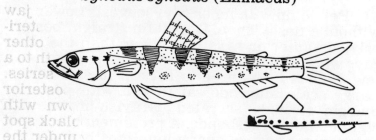

Postlarval color pattern

Pelvic fin with inner rays longest. Generally similar to the common *Synodus foetens*. Differs in having a longer pectoral which greatly exceeds the base of the pelvics. Anal rays eight to ten. Color similar to S. *foetens*, but the tip of the snout has a conspicuous small black spot. Reddish in life. About ten inches in length.

Although this species is common in the tropics, it appears to be very rare in the northern Gulf, there being few verified records. These are mostly from offshore hard bottoms.

101. SNAKEFISH
Trachinocephalus myops (Forster)

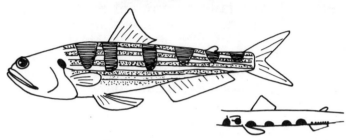

Postlarval color pattern

Pelvic fin with inner rays longer than outer. Head short and stout, the whole body form being stouter than in *Synodus* or *Saurida*. Anal rays fourteen to sixteen. Pelvic fin separated from anal fin by less than its own length (more than its own length in other lizardfishes). Snout shorter than eye. No knob on lower jaw. Grayish to brown, with indistinct brown dorsal saddles and lateral blotches. Dark spot on upper edge of operculum. Four yellow lateral stripes in life. Six to fifteen inches in length.

Uncommon in offshore waters of twenty to fifty fathoms, and very rare in shallower water.

References: Anderson, Gehringer, and Berry, 1966 (*Fishes of the Western North Atlantic, Volume 5*). Also, by the same authors, 1966, *U.S. Fish. and Wildlife Serv., Circular* 245:1-12.

ORDER SILURIFORMES — catfishes

In our single family, the dorsal fin is located just behind the head, there is a prominent adipose fin, the caudal fin is deeply forked, and there are barbels present on the jaws. Body without scales. One family, two species.

Family **ARIIDAE** — sea catfishes

Nostrils without barbels; one or two pairs of barbels on lower jaw; prominent maxillary barbels. Males of some species mouthbrooders. Two species.

102. SEA CATFISH
Arius felis (Linnaeus)

Maxillary barbel and filament from dorsal spine not greatly prolonged and flattened. Two pairs of barbels on lower jaw. Grayish, lighter below. One to one-and-a-half feet long.

Very common in all bays and shallow water, also extending out to at least fifteen fathoms. Formerly placed in the genus *Galeichthys*.

103. GAFFTOPSAIL CATFISH
Bagre marinus (Mitchill)

Maxillary barbel, dorsal spine filament, and pectoral filament greatly prolonged and flattened. Only one pair of barbels on lower jaw. Gray, lighter below, the filaments black. One to two feet in length.

A common fish in all bays and shallow waters along our coast. Often a great nuisance to both line and net fishermen, along with the sea catfish, the pointed, dorsal and pectoral spines making the fish dangerous to handle.

ORDER BATRACHOIDIFORMES — toadfishes

Robust, large-headed fishes with large terminal or dorsally inclined mouths and heavy teeth. Body without scales. Pelvic fins inserted near isthmus, with less than five soft rays. One family, three species.

Family **BATRACHOIDIDAE** — toadfishes and midshipmen

First dorsal fin low, with two or three heavy spines almost covered with heavy skin. Soft dorsal and anal long, caudal peduncle short. Caudal fin rounded. Three species.

104. GULF TOADFISH
Opsanus beta (Goode & Bean)

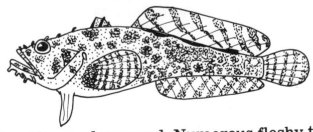

Head large, depressed. Numerous fleshy tabs and filaments around mouth and on head. Three dorsal spines. Dorsal rays twenty-four or twenty-five, pectoral rays usually eighteen or nineteen. Brown, heavily mottled with darker in a lichenose pattern. Mouth white. Often a dark line under soft dorsal. Pectorals and caudal rather regularly banded with dark. Eight to twelve inches.

A common fish in protected habitats such as oyster reefs. Occurs from shallow bay areas to offshore hard bottoms in at least twenty fathoms.

105. LEOPARD TOADFISH
Opsanus pardus (Goode & Bean)

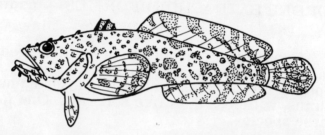

Similar in form to the Gulf toadfish. Dorsal rays average twenty-six; pectoral rays twenty or more. Color light tan with rather discrete and irregular darker brown spots; the pattern is not as lichenose as in the Gulf toadfish. Pectoral and caudal fins with dark broken bars and spots, usually irregular. This looks like a light fish with many dark spots, while the Gulf toadfish looks like a dark fish with many small lighter areas. Mouth white within. Reaches at least a foot in length.

This is the common toadfish of offshore hard bottoms in the northern Gulf, usually in fifteen or more fathoms.

106. ATLANTIC MIDSHIPMAN
Porichthys porosissimus (Valenciennes)

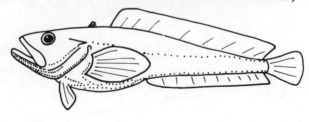

A lightly built toadfish with few or no fleshy tabs on the head. Two dorsal spines. Grayish-olive above, golden below, shiny. Lateral line and all other lines of pores golden. The pores contain luminescent material, this being our only shallow water luminescent species. Five to ten inches.

A common fish in shallow to moderate water and rarely in bays. Seems to prefer mud bottoms.

Reference: Walters, V. and C.R. Robins, 1961 (*American Museum Novitates, #2047*).

ORDER GOBIESOCIFORMES — clingfishes

Small depressed fishes which lack a spinous dorsal fin. Pelvic fins modified into a sucking disk bearing papillose areas. Body scaleless. One family, two species.

Family GOBIESOCIDAE — clingfishes

Head broadly rounded. Eyes small. Caudal long, rounded. Two species.

107. STIPPLED CLINGFISH
Gobiesox punctulatus (Poey)

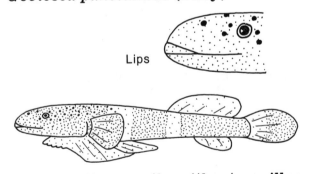

Lips

Edges of upper lip smooth, without papillae. Anal fin short, about half length of dorsal fin base. Dark brown, with wide lighter bands on body at level of pectoral and at origin of dorsal fin. Top of head with small but distinct dark spots. About two-and-a-half inches long.

A tropical species found in our area only in southern Florida and extreme southern Texas. Inshore bays and protected shallow water.

108. SKILLETFISH
Gobiesox strumosus Cope

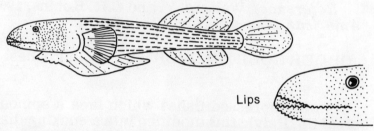

Lips

Upper lip and chin with edges strongly papillose. Anal fin about as long as dorsal fin. Color variable, usually light tan with vague darker broken horizontal stripes. Head without small dark spots. Two to four inches long, said to reach six inches.

A very common fish in protected shallow water, including bays.

ORDER LOPHIIFORMES — frogfishes and batfishes

Bizarrely-shaped fishes with the pelvic fin modified into a moveable support for the body; a distinct "elbow" at the base of the pectoral. Gill opening a round or oval pore near the base of the pectoral. Caudal fin rounded. Body without true scales. First dorsal spine modified into a lure. Two families, ten species.

Family ANTENNARIIDAE — frogfishes

Mouth large, dorsally inclined. Body oval in

cross-section and not much longer than high. An external dorsal fin of separated spines. Four species.

109. OCELLATED FROGFISH
Antennarius ocellatus (Bloch & Schneider)

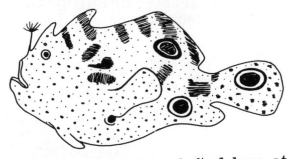

First dorsal spine with a tufted lure at tip. Three ocellated spots, one on caudal fin, one at base of soft dorsal, and one above base of anal fin near midside. Brownish, belly lighter. Many small dark spots on lower part of body and on caudal and anal fins. Large, to fifteen inches in length.

An uncommon species in the northern Gulf, generally found offshore.

110. SINGLESPOT FROGFISH
Antennarius radiosus Garman

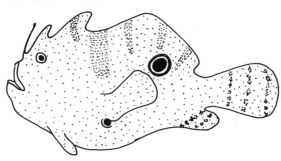

First dorsal spine with a bulbous lure at tip. Dark, with a single ocellated spot below base of soft dorsal fin. Body otherwise mottled, as are fins. Small, seldom exceeding six inches.

This is the common resident frogfish of the northern Gulf of Mexico. Although it is found in inshore waters, it is most common offshore out to at least twenty-five fathoms. Often abundant in shrimp trawls offshore.

111. SPLITLURE FROGFISH
Antennarius scaber (Cuvier)

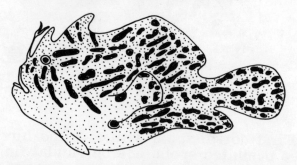

Lure of first dorsal spine split into two soft, curling processes. Two common color patterns: *one*) virtually all black; *two*) dark spots or short streaks scattered over brownish body and fins except light ventrally. No large ocellated spots. Four-and-a-half inches.

A rare species in our area, with few reliable records. Sometimes placed in the genus *Phrynelox*. "*Phrynelox nuttingi*" is the name given to the uniformly dark pattern, which might represent mature females.

112. SARGASSUMFISH
Histrio histrio (Linnaeus)

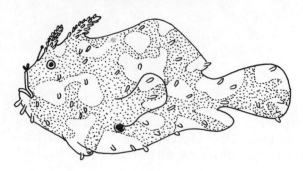

First dorsal spine very short compared to long second dorsal spine. Body covered with fleshy tabs and processes. Two of these tabs (dermal cirri) located on middorsal line of snout before base of first dorsal spine. Variable in color, usually yellowish or orange blotched and/or spotted with a darker reddish-brown; cirri usually yellowish. A very attractive species. Average maximum size about six inches.

A very distinctive and common fish seemingly associated only with the mats of *Sargassum* algae which commonly wash in from the open Gulf. Biological laboratories are commonly besieged with specimens of this fish brought in by interested beachcombers. Many synonyms, including *Histrio gibba*.

Reference: Schultz, Leonard, 1957 (*Proc. U.S. Nat. Mus.*, 107(3383):47-105).

Family **OGCOCEPHALIDAE** — batfishes

Strongly depressed fishes with a distinctly triangular or rounded anterior disk and an elongate trunk. Mouth small, ventral. First dorsal spine a fleshy lure (esca) hidden in a chamber under a protruding rostrum; no external dorsal spines.

Esca of: a, *Ogcocephalus*; b, *Zalieutes*; c, *Halieutichthys*.

The taxonomy of this family is greatly confused, with several undescribed species incorrectly assigned to previously described species. The treatment of the genus *Ogcocephalus* is based largely on information and photos supplied by Dr. Margaret Bradbury, the authority on the group. The species *O.* sp. A and *O.* sp. B will be described soon by Dr. Bradbury.

113. PANCAKE BATFISH
Halieutichthys aculeatus (Mitchill)

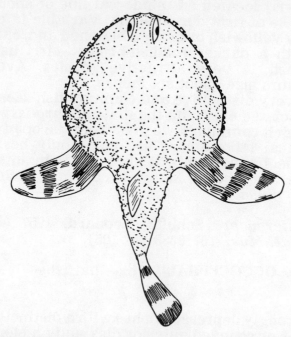

Head broadly rounded anteriorly, the rostrum not developed. Esca simple, without lobes. Numerous small spines dorsally. Trunk short. Pectorals large, broad. Brown above, white below, with a darker reticulum dorsally. Caudal fin banded, pectoral with variable bands. Two to four inches long.

A common, sometimes abundant, fish taken in trawls in water deeper than twelve fathoms.

114. ROUGHBACK BATFISH
Ogcocephalus parvus Longley & Hildebrand

Head (lateral)

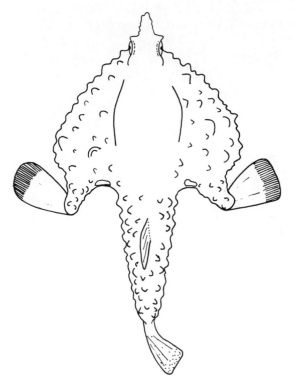

Head disk roundly triangular, with a short, slightly upturned rostrum. Esca with three lobes (also applies to other *Ogcocephalus*). Pectorals plain except for wide black distal band. Disk and trunk plainly colored, without large black spots. Three or four inches long.

Uncommon. Sixteen to sixty-eight fathoms.

115. POLKA-DOT BATFISH
Ogcocephalus radiatus (Mitchill)

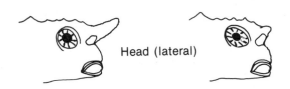

Head (lateral)

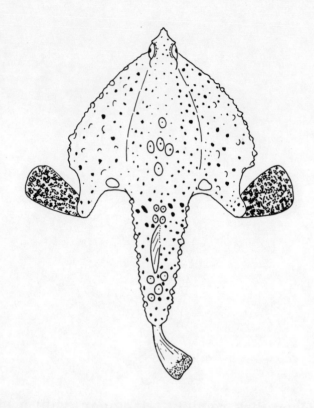

Head disk roundly triangular. Snout variable
with age: long and thick in smaller specimens,
becoming reduced with growth to a small upturned button. Pectorals heavily reticulated with
dark. Body and disk with numerous round black
spots in most specimens. Reaches ten to fifteen
inches.

This appears to be the common species of batfish in shallow waters of the northern Gulf. Specimens from the eastern Gulf are somewhat different than those from the western Gulf. The stout,
upturned rostrum and reticulated (or spotted)
pectorals are usually distinctive. Shallow water,
including bays, to thirty-seven fathoms.

116. PALESPOT BATFISH
Ogcocephalus sp. A, Bradbury

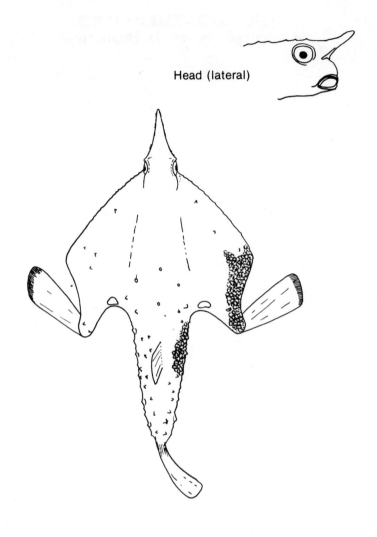

Head (lateral)

Head disk broadly triangular and relatively smooth. Rostrum always long, evenly tapered, upturned. Pectoral fins light with narrow dark distal margin. Disk and body gray with numerous small light spots. Five to six inches.

Uncommon, offshore in sixteen to one hundred and twenty-five fathoms.

The uniformly long, smooth rostrum and the numerous pale spots are distinctive.

117. THICK-TAIL BATFISH
Ogcocephalus sp. B, Bradbury

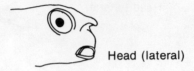

Head (lateral)

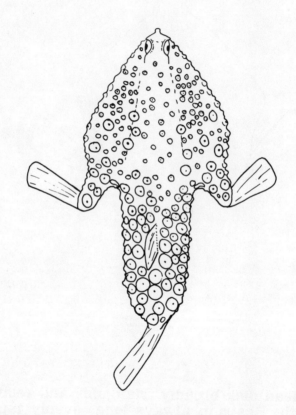

Head disk narrowly triangular; the trunk is very wide and robust compared to our other species. Numerous large tubercles of nearly equal size. Rostrum very short, downturned. Pectorals plain. Body brown with vaguely darker spots. Four or five inches long.

Not uncommon, two to one hundred fathoms.

118. TRICORN BATFISH
Zalieutes mcgintyi (Fowler)

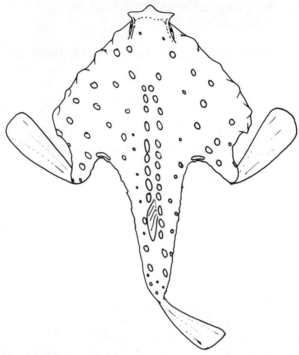

Head disk very depressed, broadly triangular. Two laterally directed preorbital spines plus a similar sized rostrum present a distinctly tricorned appearance. Disk and trunk weakly armored. Pectorals plain. Esca with weakly developed lateral lobes; gill rakers large thin plates bearing minute teeth. Three to four inches.

Uncommon. Twenty-one to two hundred and eighty fathoms.

Reference: Bradbury, Margaret, 1967 (*Copeia*, 1967(2):399-422).

ORDER GADIFORMES — cods and cusk-eels

Mouth large, terminal or slightly inferior.

Pelvic fins inserted anterior to pectorals, usually reduced to two or three rays inserted on the isthmus. Separate first dorsal fin may be present or absent. Soft dorsal and anal fins long. Four families, fifteen species.

Family **BREGMACEROTIDAE** — codlets

Only one species in our area.

119. ANTENNA CODLET
Bregmaceros atlanticus Goode & Bean

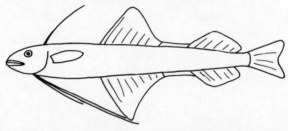

An elongate, slender fish with a long single dorsal spine located on the nape over the posterior margin of the eye. Second dorsal and anal similar, both consisting of a high lobe, then a low section, then another high lobe. Pelvic fins very long, three-rayed. Caudal fin forked in adults. Two to three inches. Silvery with dusky areas.

Uncommon in twenty to one hundred or more fathoms; pelagic.

Reference: Clancey, J.F., 1956 (*Bull. Mar. Sci.*, 6(3):233-260).

Family **GADIDAE** — cods and hakes

Dorsal fin in two parts, the anterior one higher and shorter than the second. Lateral line distinct. Barbel at tip of lower jaw. Pelvics usually filamentous. Caudal usually distinct. The luminous hake, sometimes placed in the separate family Steindachneridae, differs in lacking the barbel, having normal pelvics, lacking the caudal fin, and having an anal fin consisting largely of low separate rays. Four species.

120. LUMINOUS HAKE
Steindachneria argentea Goode & Bean

Head large, body strongly tapered to pointed tail. Pelvics large, under pectorals. Second dorsal very long. Anal fin of a large rounded anterior lobe and a long row of low, membraneless rays. No caudal fin. At least ten inches long.

Rare in our depth area, generally in more than thirty fathoms but recorded in as little as eleven.

121. GULF HAKE
Urophycis cirratus (Goode & Bean)

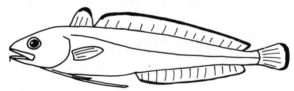

First dorsal fin broadly rounded. Anal fin about two-thirds length of second dorsal. Caudal truncately rounded. Mandibular barbel very short. Pelvic fins of two conspicuous rays, one several times longer than other. Uniformly pale brownish, the fins edged with darker. Lateral line lacks white spots. Ten inches.

This is an offshore species which almost certainly does not occur in our depth range. The report of this as a common species in a few fathoms off Texas almost certainly refers to the southern hake.

122. SOUTHERN HAKE
Urophycis floridanus (Bean & Dresel)

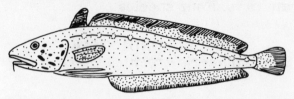

First dorsal relatively high. Anal almost as long as second dorsal. Caudal roundly truncated. Pelvics long filaments, the two branches of about equal length. Mandibular barbel about three-fourths as long as diameter of eye. Scales very small, hard to count, about 120. Light tan, with large black spots and streaks. Mandibular barbel with dark band at middle. Lateral line of dark brown sections interspaced by large round white spots. All fins dusky, darker at edges. First dorsal completely dark. Six to twelve inches long.

A common fish from shore to at least twenty fathoms. Seems to move inshore in winter or cold weather, otherwise mostly offshore.

123. SPOTTED HAKE
Urophycis regius (Walbaum)

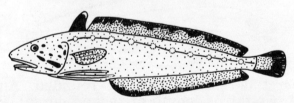

Morphologically similar to the southern hake. Supposed to have fewer rays in first dorsal and larger scales than the southern hake, but both these counts are very difficult to make and not really necessary for separation. In the spotted hake the mandibular barbel is very short, less than half the eye diameter. In addition, the distal portion of the first dorsal fin in the spotted hake is distinctly white. Otherwise the color patterns of the two species are similar.

This seems to be a rare species in our area, if it occurs at all. Most records of the spotted hake from shallow northern Gulf waters seem to really refer to the southern hake.

FAMILY **OPHIDIIDAE** — cusk-eels and brotulas

A single dorsal fin, often continuous with the similar anal. Body elongated, usually tapering to a point. Caudal fin separate or continuous with dorsal and anal. Pelvics inserted anteriorly under head, more-or-less filamentous. Scales very small. Nine species.

The taxonomy of this family is very unsettled. Many taxonomists recognize two families, the Brotulidae and the Ophidiidae, for the brotulas and cusk-eels respectively. Our two brotulas are not easily confused, and the same thing can be said for the shallow water species of *Lepophidium*. However, the genera and species of the remaining cusk-eels are all uncertain. Only two genera, *Ophidion* and *Otophidium*, are used here, although two others are probably recognizable. Separation is primarily on internal characters and not very clear-cut. There are also several undescribed species in our area, some of which perhaps occur in relatively shallow water. There is also the problem of *Rissola marginata*, an Atlantic seaboard species commonly reported from the northern Gulf and closely related to the supposedly distinctively patterned *Ophidion welshi*. The Gulf specimens of *R. marginata* I have seen have all definitely represented juvenile, unpatterned stages of *O. welshi*. For this reason I have not included *R. marginata* in this manual, as I cannot separate the two taxa.

124. BEARDED BROTULA
Brotula barbata (Bloch & Schneider)

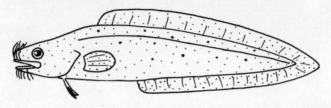

Dorsal and anal fins continuous with caudal; caudal pointed. Pelvics filamentous, inserted on level between eye and pectoral base. Lower jaw and snout with numerous short filaments. Scales very small, overlapping. Reddish brown, sometimes with scattered dark spots of small size. Fins darker. Eight to eighteen inches.

A common large species in water deeper than ten fathoms.

125. GOLD BROTULA
Gunterichthys longipenis Dawson

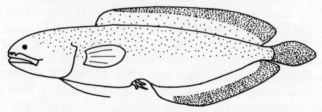

Head large, without scales. Dorsal and anal fins separate from long, rounded caudal. Pelvic fin of one obvious ray, inserted on the isthmus. Body scales small, barely overlapping. Male with external copulatory organs. Golden brown with the fins dark posteriorly. Two to three inches.

A poorly known species which seems to burrow in soft bottoms of estuarine waters. Usually in shallow water, in areas which are seldom collected extensively. Recorded from the vicinity of Mobile Bay to the marshes north of Grand Isle, Louisiana, but range probably more extensive.

Several specimens were taken in small trawls being used to capture commercial shrimp in the extensive shallow, low salinity marshes north of Grand Isle, Louisiana, in April and May. These were associated with *Erotelis smaragdis*, *Microgobius gulosus* and *thalassinus*, and *Gobionellus boleosoma* and *shufeldti*. The species is probably quite common if the proper habitat is collected.

126. BLACKEDGE CUSK-EEL
Lepophidium graellsi (Poey)

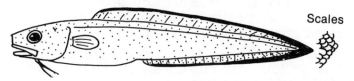

Scales

Dorsal and anal connected to caudal; body tapering to point. A prominent rostral spine. Body scales normal, small, overlapping. Gill bar black. Gill rakers 4 + 7, the upper four about one-and-a-half times higher than wide; lower seven in a steadily decreasing series, the last about one-and-a-half times higher than wide. Color uniform straw brown, the fins dark-edged. Six to twelve inches long.

This is the most common cusk-eel in waters twelve to at least twenty-five fathoms deep. Beyond this point it is to some extent replaced by other species of the genus which usually differ in color pattern and gill raker morphology.

Lepophidium brevibarbe was formerly used for this species and is still the preferred name used by some taxonomists.

127. MOTTLED CUSK-EEL
Lepophidium jeannae Fowler

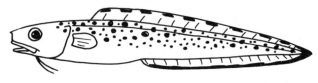

Prominent rostral spine and overlapping scales. Gill bar light, with rakers 2 + 6, the upper two rakers rudimentary and the lower first four of nearly equal size (slightly decreasing in height), the last two lower rakers rudimentary. Color pattern freckled, with numerous dusky spots on the upper two-thirds of the body and head, the spots usually smaller than pupil. Edge of dorsal fin with alternating dark and light sections; anal fin with dark edge. Eight inches.

An uncommon species in our depth range.

Three other species occur in deeper waters in the northern Gulf of Mexico and probably do not normally enter our depth range. They are briefly diagnosed here:

Fawn cusk-eel, *L. cervinum* (Goode & Bean): brownish yellow with numerous subcircular spots of white along upper half of body; fins narrowly dark-edged. Gill bar black, rakers 2 + 7, upper two rudimentary, lower seven in progressively shorter series, the last two rudimentary.

Offshore cusk-eel, *L. profundorum* (Gill): Uniformly brownish, the fins narrowly dark-edged. Gill bar light, rakers 3 + 7, upper three about as high as wide, lower seven with four about same size and three in which the height equals the width. Externally similar to the blackedge cusk-eel and perhaps confused with it. One specimen from twenty fathoms off Grand Isle, Louisiana seemed to belong to this species; it was taken with many *L. graellsi*.

Marbled cusk-eel, *L. marmoratum* (Goode & Bean): Gray, marbled with olive on upper half of head and body; fins dark-edged. Gill bar light, rakers 4 + 8, upper four about one-and-a-half times higher than wide, the lower eight in a steadily decreasing series, the last similar to upper rakers.

128. LONGNOSE CUSK-EEL
Ophidion beani Jordan & Gilbert

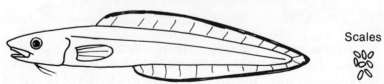

Scales

An elongate cusk-eel with small, embedded scales not overlapping. Dorsal and ventral profiles parallel anteriorly. The snout is prominent and distinctly overhangs the lower jaw. The pelvic rays are short and only reach to the beginning of the scaled area on the isthmus: Uniformly brown without pattern; fins dark-edged. About one foot.

Little known in our area, generally offshore and on hard bottoms.

129. BLOTCHED CUSK-EEL
Ophidion grayi (Fowler)

A blotched cusk-eel with body scales not overlapping. Pectoral fin rounded, middle rays longest. Dorsal fin inserted behind operculum. No distinct dark humeral spot. Body with numerous large brown spots over upper two-thirds and on occiput. Dorsal fin with most of black pigment in the membrane and marginal. Anal fin mostly light. Eight inches.

Range poorly known, mostly from offshore hard bottoms in ten to thirty fathoms, but also from mud bottoms in less then five fathoms.

130. BANK CUSK-EEL
Ophidion holbrooki (Putnam)

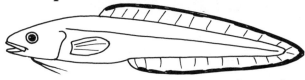

Scales in groups, embedded, not overlapping. Deep bodied anteriorly, in adults the body distinctly deeper at the dorsal fin origin than at the anus. Snout not greatly overhanging lower jaw. Pelvic fins long, extending well into scaled area of isthmus. Uniformly brown, the fins with black edges. One foot long.

Not uncommon in five to twenty fathoms.

131. CRESTED CUSK-EEL
Ophidion welshi (Nichols & Breder)

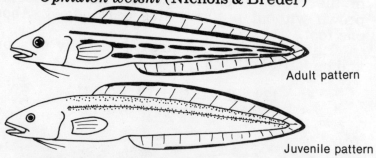

Adult pattern

Juvenile pattern

A large cusk-eel with the scales in groups and not overlapping. Nape of large males swollen. Yellowish, with three narrow brown stripes on each side, one at base of dorsal fin, one on lateral line, one on lower sides; stripes commonly broken and irregular. Young specimens uniformly golden and silver with only vague indications of stripes; stripes at dorsal base sometimes observable. Fins dark-edged. Six to eighteen inches.

A common fish from shore line to at least twenty fathoms, but usually in less than ten fathoms. Prefers soft bottoms. Juveniles common in bays with low salinity water. Gulf records of *Rissola marginata* are probably based at least in part on juveniles of this species.

132. POLKA-DOT CUSK-EEL
Otophidium omostigmum (Jordan & Gilbert)

A small yellow cusk-eel with scattered brown spots. Scales small but somewhat overlapping anteriorly; no rostral spine. Pectoral fin pointed, the upper rays longer. Dorsal fin inserted over edge of operculum. A distinct and very dark humeral spot. Brown spots few and scattered on body, absent from occiput. Black pattern of dorsal fin submarginal; anal fin largely black. Four to six inches.

A rare and poorly known species which appears to be widely distributed off both coasts of Florida and off Mexico.

References: Dawson, C.E., 1966 (*Proc. Biol. Soc. Washington*, 79:205-214; description of *Gunterichthys*); Robins, C.R., 1957 (*Bull. Mar. Sci.*, 7(3):266-275; *grayi* and *omostigmum*); Robins, C.R., 1959 (*Bull. Mar. Sci.*, 8(4):360-368; *Lepophidium*); Robins, C.R., letters of Feb. 1971 and Feb. 1973.

Family **CARAPIDAE** — pearlfishes

Only a single species in our area.

133. Pearlfish
Carapus bermudensis (Jones)

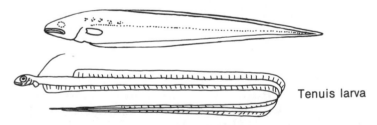

Tenuis larva

Transparent, eel-like fish with the dorsal and anal fins similar and continued around the caudal. Pectoral fins large, but pelvic fins absent. Anus located just behind the head. Eyes small, covered with skin. Transparent to translucent silvery, few dark areas of pigment. Vertebral column visible through the musculature. About four inches. Shallow water.

This tropical species is more typical of the

Florida Keys area, but has been recorded west almost to Mobile Bay. The tenuis larvae, which are extremely elongate and have a long free spine at the back of the head, are more widespread in the northern Gulf and are taken in plankton tows.

Of course this is the famous fish usually associated with sea cucumbers, freely entering and leaving their hosts through either the mouth or the anus. Only large, surface-dwelling species are inhabited, not the smaller burrowing types. Also associated with conchs and bivalves on occasion.

Formerly called *Fierasfer affinis* by many authors.

ORDER ATHERINIFORMES — flyingfishes, killifishes, silversides, and relatives

Pelvic fins abdominal, pectorals located rather high on sides. Lateral line absent or near ventrolateral surface of body. Spinous dorsal absent or very short and widely separated from the soft dorsal. Body often squarish in cross-section, the dorsum nearly flat. Five families, thirty-three species.

Family EXOCOETIDAE — flyingfishes and halfbeaks

No spinous dorsal fin, the soft dorsal located posteriorly. Caudal fin with lower lobe usually longer than upper. Lower jaw elongated and/or pectoral fin greatly elongated. Lateral line on ventrolateral surface. Thirteen species.

The halfbeaks are sometimes considered a distinct family, the Hemiramphidae, but show a complete transition to the typical flyingfish form.

134. CLEARWING FLYINGFISH
Cypselurus comatus (Mitchill)

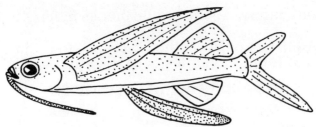

Adult: Pectoral fin extending beyond mid-point of dorsal fin; pelvic fins reaching at least to anal fin midpoint; anal fin base shorter than dorsal fin base; second pectoral ray divided; body triangular in cross-section (these characters apply to all *Cypselurus* adults). Dorsal fin low, clear; pectoral fin without pigment pattern. *Juvenile:* Color pattern as in adults. Barbel single, more than 40% of standard length. Caudal fin light. Reaches eight inches. Pelagic.

Adults sometimes within three hundred miles of land; juveniles sometimes inshore.

In juveniles of this genus specimens under 15 mm long may have the second pectoral ray simple, so be careful identifying very small flying-fishes. Such small fish also have the fins shorter and the color pattern poorly developed.

Only juveniles of this genus are illustrated, as few adults are likely to be taken within our range.

135. MARGINED FLYINGFISH
Cypselurus cyanopterus (Valenciennes)

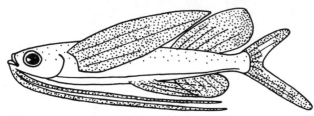

Adult: Dorsal fin high, pigmented; caudal evenly and duskily pigmented; pectoral fin solid blue. *Juvenile:* Barbels paired, very long, up to more than 100% of body length. Dorsal fin high; both caudal lobes with dusky areas; pectoral fin without bands. About twelve inches in length. Pelagic.

Adults usually within three or four hundred miles of land. Juveniles occasionally inshore.

136. BANDWING FLYINGFISH
Cypselurus exsiliens (Linnaeus)

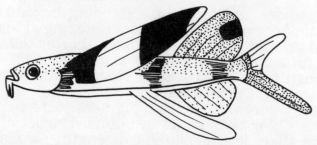

Adult: Dorsal fin high, with black spots; pectoral fin barred with dark; upper caudal lobe clear, lower dark. *Juvenile:* A pair of short, flattened flap-like barbels. Upper caudal lobe clear; dorsal fin high, dark, with darker spot(s); pectoral fin banded with dark. Eight or nine inches.

Pelagic, adults sometimes within a few miles of shore.

137. SPOTFIN FLYINGFISH
Cypselurus furcatus (Mitchill)

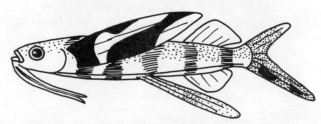

Adult: Dorsal fin low and unpigmented. Caudal fin lightly pigmented. Pectoral fin black, distinctively pigmented with wide light crossband. *Juvenile:* A pair of moderately long barbels, usually more than 16% of standard length. Dorsal fin low and unpigmented; dark body bars vague; pectoral distinctly pigmented, the light band widest distally and not divided by a dark spot. Ten to twelve inches.

Pelagic, but even adults sometimes inshore.

138. ATLANTIC FLYINGFISH
Cypselurus heterurus (Rafinesque)

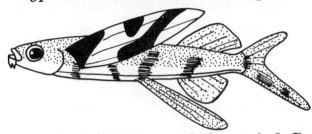

Adult: Dorsal fin low and pigmented. Caudal fin uniformly dusky. Pectoral fin gray, with light crossband widest medially, usually divided distally by a dark spot. *Juvenile:* A pair of short, triangular barbels. Dorsal fin low and unpigmented; pectoral fin with light band widest near middle; body bands dark and distinct. To almost fourteen inches in length.

Adults occur within four hundred miles of land but seldom inshore. Juveniles often inshore.

This species is very close to the spotfin flyingfish and the pectoral patterns of both vary a great deal with age. Juveniles are best separated by the longer barbels of *C. furcatus* (over 16% standard length) than those of *C. heterurus* (less than 16% standard length). Adults of *C. furcatus* have the posterior margin of the light pectoral band narrow; the first pectoral ray is less than 38% of the standard length. In *C. heterurus* the posterior edge of the light band is wide and the first pectoral ray is more than 38% of standard length.

139. FLYING HALFBEAK
Euleptorhamphus velox Poey

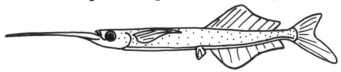

Lower jaw much longer than the upper, which is normal. Body very elongate and greatly compressed. Pectoral fin longer than head without lower jaw. Dorsal and anal fins very long, high. Pelvic fin short, posteriorly inserted. Silvery blue. One to two feet long.

Pelagic, uncommon in offshore waters.

140. OCEANIC TWO-WING FLYINGFISH
Exocoetus obtusirostris Gunther

Barbels absent in juveniles. Pelvic fin short, not reaching anal base. Dorsal fin low, its origin slightly behind anal fin origin. Pectoral fin clear, with a triangular or semicircular black blotch on basal anterior third, separated by wide light area from curved long posterior dark area. Seven inches long.

Offshore blue waters. Uncommon.

141. BALAO
Hemiramphus balao Lesueur

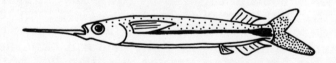

Upper jaw without scales, much shorter than lower jaw. Caudal fin deeply forked, the lower lobe much longer than the upper. Pectoral fin long, its length more than the distance from the pectoral base to the anterior nostril. Silvery, brownish above with a vague dark lateral stripe. Upper lobe of caudal red at tip then bluish violet. Anal fin inserted distinctly posterior to dorsal origin. Fourteen inches.

Tropical species which rarely straggles into the southern edges of our area. Perhaps confused with the very similar ballyhoo.

142. BALLYHOO
Hemiramphus brasiliensis (Linnaeus)

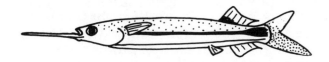

Upper jaw much shorter than elongate lower jaw, lacking scales. Caudal fin deeply forked, upper lobe shorter than lower. Anal fin origin well behind the dorsal fin origin. Pectoral fin short, its length less than the distance from its base to the anterior nostrils. Brownish to greenish above, silvery below, with vague dark lateral stripe. Upper caudal lobe entirely orangish. Ten to fifteen inches long.

A surface dweller in shallow waters throughout our area. Generally uncommon.

143. FOURWING FLYINGFISH
Hirundichthys affinis (Gunther)

Pelvic and pectoral fins both long and extending at least to middle of dorsal and anal fins. Dorsal fin low, about same length as anal fin. Pectoral fin mostly dark with transparent rectangular area extending about three-fourths way across posterior median part of fin. Twelve inches.

Offshore blue water. Uncommon.

144. HALFBEAK
Hyporhamphus unifasciatus (Ranzani)

Lower jaw much longer than short upper; upper jaw with scales. Caudal fin shallowly forked, the lower lobe not much longer than the upper. Anal fin long, its origin almost under dorsal fin origin. Greenish above, silvery below, with dark lateral stripe. Eight to twelve inches long.

Common inshore and in shallow water of high salinity.

145. SAILFIN FLYINGFISH
Parexocoetus brachypterus (Richardson)

Pelvic fin moderately long, reaching about to anal fin origin. Anal about as long as dorsal fin, the dorsal fin being high and rounded. Juveniles with a pair of barbels. Silvery, darker above. Distal half of dorsal fin black, other fins transparent or lightly dusky. Five inches.

Offshore blue water.

146. BLUNTNOSE FLYINGFISH
Prognichthys gibbifrons (Valenciennes)

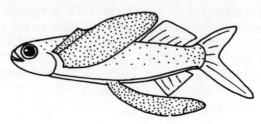

Pelvic fin long, extending beyond middle of anal fin. Anal fin base shorter than dorsal base, both fins low. Second pectoral ray simple, not forked (*caution:* almost any flyingfish less than 15 mm long may have a simple second ray). Pectoral fin uniformly brownish; pelvic fins blackish. Dorsal and caudal fins pale. Eight inches.

Offshore waters, but also both juveniles and adults occasionally inshore.

References: Lewis, J.B., 1961 (*Bull. Mar. Sci.,* 11(2):258-266); Miller, R.R., 1945 (*Proc. U.S. Nat. Mus.,* 96(3195):185-193); Staiger, J.C., 1965 (*Bull. Mar. Sci.,* 15(3):672-725).

Family BELONIDAE — needlefishes

Elongated fishes with a single dorsal fin similar to the anal fin in shape and position. Lateral line on ventrolateral surface. Both jaws elongated into bony beaks with large teeth. Pectoral fin about equal to postorbital part of head. Six species.

147. FLAT NEEDLEFISH
Ablennes hians (Valenciennes)

X-section of body

Gill rakers absent. Head and body strongly compressed laterally. Dorsal rays twenty-one to twenty-six; anal rays twenty-five to twenty-eight. Anal origin anterior to dorsal origin. Greenish above, silvery below. Dark vertical bars on sides. Dorsal fin dark at posterior tip. Two to three feet in length.

An offshore species, seldom collected in the northern Gulf.

148. KEELTAIL NEEDLEFISH
Platybelone argalus (Lesueur)

Caudal peduncle (dorsal)

X-section of body

Gill rakers present. Caudal peduncle strongly compressed, with lateral keels. Dorsal rays four or five fewer than anal rays; anal fin longer than dorsal base. A very slender fish. Silvery, greenish above. Fifteen inches.

A rare tropical straggler in the northern Gulf. An offshore species.

149. ATLANTIC NEEDLEFISH
Strongylura marina (Walbaum)

Maxillary and suborbital

Body round in cross-section. No gill rakers. Anal fin with sixteen to twenty rays. Ventral margin of maxillary not covered by suborbital when mouth is closed. Predorsal scales 213-304. Preorbital area weakly pigmented, the pigment generally not extending below middle of eye. Lateral line not marked with dusky. Greenish, with a dusky lateral band which is not widened between the dorsal and anal fins. Three feet.

This is the common needlefish of the entire northern Gulf of Mexico, the other two species of *Strongylura* being much rarer and the other genera offshore tropical stragglers.

150. REDFIN NEEDLEFISH
Strongylura notata (Poey)

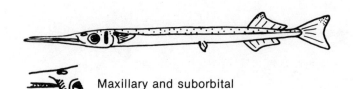

Maxillary and suborbital

Body round in cross-section. Gill rakers absent. Anal rays thirteen to sixteen. Maxillary completely covered by suborbital when mouth is closed. Predorsal scales 84-117. Greenish above, silvery below, with a narrow dusky lateral stripe. Prominent vertical dark bar on gill covers. Tip of upper caudal lobe and dorsal fin red. Two feet long.

Rare in the northern Gulf, but can be found mixed with most large collections of the Atlantic needlefish. Often inshore.

151. TIMUCU
Strongylura timucu (Walbaum)

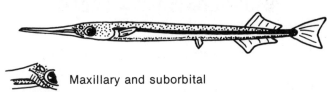

Maxillary and suborbital

Generally similar to the Atlantic needlefish, the maxillaries exposed when the mouth is closed. Predorsal scales 120-185. More dark pigment on head, the pigment extending to lower edge of suborbital. Dark lateral stripe widened between dorsal and anal fins. Lateral line dark.

A tropical species found in our area mostly east of Mobile Bay. Easily confused with the abundant Atlantic needlefish, with which it sometimes occurs.

152. AGUJON
Tylosurus acus (Lacepede)

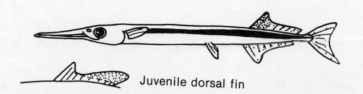
Juvenile dorsal fin

Body squarish in cross-section. No gill rakers. Bill shorter and stouter appearing than in other species. Caudal fin more deeply forked than in other needlefishes, the lower lobe distinctly longer than the upper. Anal rays twenty to twenty-one; posterior lobe of dorsal fin very large in juveniles. Greenish above, silvery below, the lateral band indistinct. Up to five feet in length.

A tropical species, rare in our area.

References: Berry, F.H. and L.R. Rivas, 1962 (*Copeia,* 1962(1):152-160); Collette, B.B., 1968 (*Copeia*, 1968(1):189-192).

Family **CYPRINODONTIDAE** — killifishes

Mouth small, terminal or dorsal. Lateral line absent. Caudal rounded or truncate. Dorsal and anal fins similar. Male anal fin similar to that of female. Nine species. Several other freshwater species may occur in brackish water and are not covered here.

153. **DIAMOND KILLIFISH**
Adinia xenica (Jordan & Gilbert)

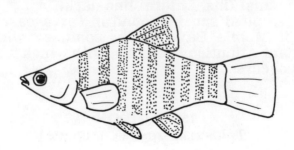

Upper edge of opercle joined to body above pectoral base. Body deepest at middle, both anterior dorsal and anterior ventral profiles converging to snout, presenting a diamond-shaped body outline. Dorsal fin origin well before anal. Anal rays eleven to twelve. Lateral scales about twenty-five. Greenish silvery with numerous dark crossbars. Fins heavily mottled with dark. Two inches.

Locally common in brackish water, but not seen as commonly as the species of *Fundulus* and *Cyprinodon*.

154. SHEEPSHEAD MINNOW
Cyprinodon variegatus Lacepede

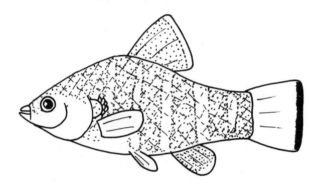

Body deep, stout, dorsal profile sloping toward snout. Dorsal fin set before anal fin. Caudal truncate. Humeral scale (behind upper edge of operculum) enlarged. Operculum free above. Anal rays ten; lateral scales twenty-six. Yellowish to bronzy with darker and irregular stripes. Dorsum iridescent blue in breeding males. Dorsal and caudal fins clear, sometimes with black margins. Two to three inches.

A common fish in brackish water all along the northern Gulf.

155. GOLDSPOTTED KILLIFISH
Floridichthys carpio (Gunther)

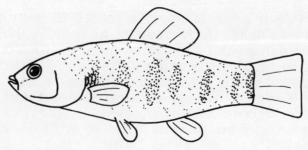

Body stout, deep, the dorsal profile not strongly sloping to snout. Dorsal fin set distinctly before anal. Caudal truncate. Humeral scale not enlarged. Operculum free above. Anal rays nine; lateral scales twenty-four. Silvery or olive with orange or golden spots or blotches along midsides. Fins clear. Two to three inches.

A brackish water fish common along the western coast of the Florida peninsula. Not found west of the Pensacola area.

156. MARSH KILLIFISH
Fundulus confluentus Goode & Bean

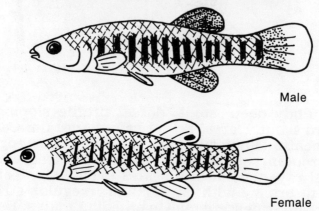

Male

Female

Body cylindrical, flatter dorsally, as in all *Fundulus*. Dorsal origin over or slightly behind anal origin. Dorsal rays eleven; lateral scales about forty. Longitudinal streaks on each scale row and about fourteen dark vertical bars. Female with additional small spots on body. Fins of male dark, with a few small light spots; dorsal of female light, with a large dark spot posteriorly. Two to three inches long.

Inshore brackish water of the eastern northern Gulf, west to about Mobile Bay. Probably intergrading there with the bayou killifish.

157. GULF KILLIFISH
Fundulus grandis Baird & Girard

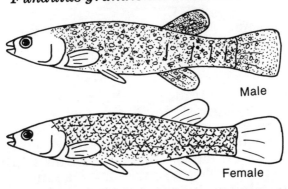

Male

Female

Body cylindrical but robust. Dorsal fin inserted anterior to anal fin. Snout short and blunt, not longer than eye diameter. Anal rays about eleven; lateral scales about thirty-one to thirty-four. Fins mostly dark, at least in male. Body bronzy, with numerous pearly spots, not strongly banded; female mostly plain brownish. Four to eight inches long.

An abundant fish in brackish water and shallow higher salinity water as well.

158. SALTMARSH TOPMINNOW
Fundulus jenkinsi (Evermann)

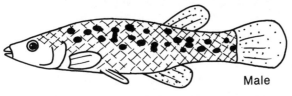

Male

Cylindrical. Dorsal rays eight to nine, anal rays about twelve; dorsal fin origin distinctly behind anal origin. Brownish, with two rows of large

spots above axis of body, the spots sometimes fused. Body and fins with a profuse dusting of fine brown points. Two inches.
Locally common in brackish water.

159. BAYOU KILLIFISH
Fundulus pulvereus (Evermann)

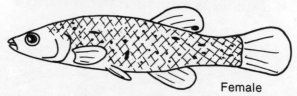

Female

Generally similar to the marsh killifish, of which it is almost certainly just a subspecies. Dorsal rays usually ten, fin inserted behind anal. Female without vertical bars, but with larger dark spots on sides, these sometimes fused into short streaks. Two to three inches long.
Locally common in brackish water from Texas to about Mobile Bay.

160. LONGNOSE KILLIFISH
Fundulus similis (Baird & Girard)

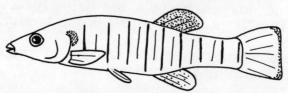

Body appears elongate because of sloping snout profile. Dorsal fin origin anterior to anal fin origin. Snout long, pointed, longer than eye diameter. Dorsal rays about twelve or thirteen. Lateral scales thirty to thirty-two. Fins light, except with black ocellus in young and generally dusky in breeding males. A dark spot at upper edge of operculum. Silvery brown to greenish, the females and non-breeding males with narrow vertical bars, breeding males with body darker, the bars diffuse. Caudal truncate. Six inches or more in maximum length.

An abundant killifish in brackish and high salinity salt water. Usually found with *Fundulus grandis*.

161. RAINWATER KILLIFISH
Lucania parva (Baird)

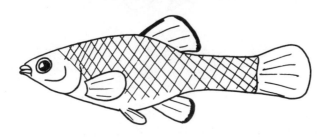

Deep-bodied, with a long caudal peduncle. Dorsal about over anal. Dorsal rays about ten to twelve, anal rays nine to ten. Twenty-five to twenty-six lateral scales. Grayish brown, the scales outlined in darker, the sides having the appearance of a distinct dark meshwork. Fins sometimes with dark margins or creamy white with orange. Two inches.

Common in inshore brackish to fresh waters. Looks like a female *Gambusia*, but easily distinguished by fin position and mesh appearance of sides.

References: Brown, J.L., 1957 (*Journ. Wash. Acad. Sci.*, 47(3):69-77); Carr, A. and C.J. Goin, 1959 (*Guide to the Reptiles, Amphibians, and Freshwater Fishes of Florida*; Univ. Fla. Press, Gainesville, Fla.); Miller, R.R., 1955 (*Occ. Papers Mus. Zool., U. Mich.*, #568).

Family POECILIIDAE — livebearing killifishes

Generally similar to the Cyprinodontidae, but the anal fin of the male is modified into an intromittent organ. Anal fin often distinctly anterior to dorsal fin. Three species.

162. MOSQUITOFISH
Gambusia affinis (Baird & Girard)

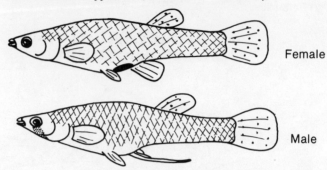

Female

Male

Small slender grayish fishes with the dorsal fin short and entirely behind the anal fin base. Sides faintly reticulated with brown on gray. Usually a broad black band under eye and, in females, a black area near anus. Fins usually with small spots. One to two inches.

A common freshwater fish which occasionally ventures into brackish water. Generally not abundant in brackish water.

163. LEAST KILLIFISH
Heterandria formosa Agassiz

Female

Tiny fish with the origin of the dorsal fin distinctly behind the anal origin. Pale brown with dark lateral band ending in a spot at caudal base, other lateral spots present. Black spot at base of dorsal and anal fins. Fins clear except for orange to reddish areas and the black spots. One-half to one inch in length. Our smallest fish.

Locally common in coastal brackish and freshwater ditches mostly east of the Mississippi River, but extending west at least to Calcasieu Parish, Louisiana.

164. SAILFIN MOLLY
Poecilia latipinna (Lesueur)

Male

Dorsal fin long, its origin in front of anal; fin sexually dimorphic, much higher and more colorful in males than females. Caudal peduncle stout. Brownish-silver with about six rows of brown or black spots on sides. Dorsal and caudal fins with rows of black spots. Four inches.

Common in brackish coastal water and also in protected higher salinity waters.

Formerly in the genus *Mollienesia*.

Family ATHERINIDAE — silversides

Small fish with silvery lateral band and a forked caudal fin. A small spinous dorsal fin is present and well separated from the soft dorsal. Anal fin longer than soft dorsal. Two species.

165. ROUGH SILVERSIDE
Membras martinica (Valenciennes)

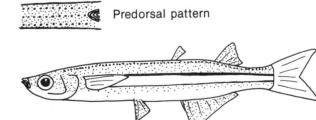

Predorsal pattern

Silver stripe wider than eye. Area between nape and dorsal origin with three rows of small black spots, the scales ctenoid. Caudal and pectoral fins pale. Body greenish brown above, translucent below. Three inches.

Common in bays and shallow salt water.

166. TIDEWATER SILVERSIDE
Menidia beryllina (Cope)

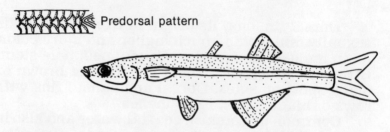

Predorsal pattern

Silver stripe narrower than or equal to eye. Area between nape and dorsal origin with numerous black semicircles caused by pigment on the cycloid scale edges. Caudal and pectorals yellow. Three inches.

Common in bays and shallow salt water.

ORDER BERYCIFORMES — armored fishes

Head with serrated bony plates. Scales usually large. Pelvic fins with more than five rays. One family, three species.

Family HOLOCENTRIDAE — squirrelfishes

Silvery and red fishes with strong dorsal and anal spines, the dorsal fin deeply notched. Caudal fin forked. Strong spines at preopercular angle and on operculum and above maxillary. Pelvic fins thoracic. Three species.

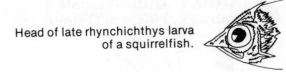

Head of late rhynchichthys larva
of a squirrelfish.

167. SQUIRRELFISH
Holocentrus ascensionis (Osbeck)

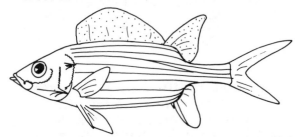

Caudal fin deeply forked, the upper lobe distinctly longer than the lower. Soft dorsal fin pointed. Silvery with red lateral stripes. Fins all dusky, including spinous dorsal. One to two feet long.

Rare in deep water over hard bottoms.

168. DEEPWATER SQUIRRELFISH
Holocentrus bullisi Woods

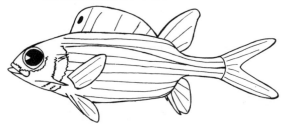

Caudal moderately forked, the lobes equal and rounded. Soft dorsal fin rounded. Reddish with alternating silver stripes. Axilla of pectoral and edges of caudal lobes not distinctly dusky. Small black spot between first two dorsal spines. Seven inches.

Rare, hard bottoms in twenty-five to sixty fathoms.

This species is commonly placed in the genus *Adioryx*.

169. DUSKY SQUIRRELFISH
Holocentrus vexillarius (Poey)

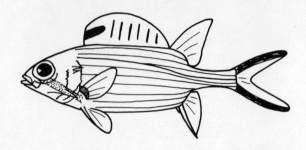

Caudal moderately forked, lobes equal and rounded. Soft dorsal fin rounded. Dusky reddish and silver stripes alternating on sides. Dusky or black spot in pectoral axilla. Edges of caudal lobes dark. Membranes between dorsal spines one and three with dark streaks. Six inches long.

A rare species in the northern Gulf, generally found only in deep water near offshore snapper banks. Commonly placed in the genus *Adioryx*.

ORDER ZEIFORMES — dories

Body compressed, oval or orbicular. Spinous dorsal fin continuous with soft dorsal, of few spines. Pelvics thoracic. One family, one species.

Family CAPROIDAE — boarfishes

One deep water species in our area.

170. DEEPBODY BOARFISH
Antigonia capros Lowe

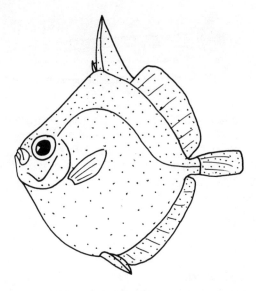

Body oval, with small upturned mouth. Eight dorsal spines, the second very high and heavy. Pelvic spine heavy. Soft dorsal and anal low, the anal very long. Silvery-pink. Ten to twelve inches long.

Rarely found in water less than forty fathoms deep.

ORDER LAMPRIDIFORMES — oarfishes and ribbonfishes

Body very elongate, compressed. Mouth small, upturned. Dorsal long, beginning over eye. Pelvic fins reduced or absent. One family, one species.

Family REGALECIDAE — oarfishes

A single species.

171. OARFISH
Regalecus glesne (Ascanius)

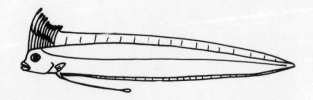

Anterior dorsal rays greatly elongated. Anal
fin a series of spiny tubercles. Pelvic fin a long
single ray ending in a small bulb. Lateral line low
on body. The small caudal fin is almost always absent in stranded specimens. Reddish and silver.
Reaches at least eleven feet in length.

A poorly known fish, either deep sea or pelagic but exact habitat unknown. The specimens
seen are almost always dead or dying and cast up
on shore. Few records for the northern Gulf of
Mexico, all apparently from the west coast of Florida during the spring or summer.

ORDER GASTEROSTEIFORMES — tube snouts

Generally long-tailed fishes with heavy dermal armor and long snouts ending in a small terminal or dorsal mouth. Pectoral large; pelvic abdominal or absent. Three families, fifteen species.

Family AULOSTOMIDAE — trumpetfishes

One tropical straggler in the northern Gulf.

172. TRUMPETFISH
Aulostomus maculatus Valenciennes

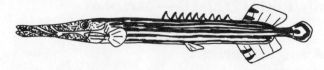

An elongate fish with a seahorse-like mouth,
but with teeth. Nine separate low dorsal spines be-

fore dorsal fin. Caudal fin **large, peduncle short.**
No tail filament. Brown or red, with silvery
streaks and bands and black spots. One to three
feet long.

A coral reef species which rarely straggles into the northern Gulf.

Family **FISTULARIIDAE** — cornetfishes

A single species in our area.

173. BLUESPOTTED CORNETFISH
Fistularia tabacaria Linnaeus

Snout long, seahorse-like. No dorsal spines.
Body straight, ending in a long tail filament extending from between the lobes of the caudal fin.
Three to six feet in length. Olive with darker mottling and small blue spots.

A tropical species which is not uncommonly
found in our area. There may be resident populations on the offshore snapper banks and coral
heads.

Family **SYNGNATHIDAE** — pipefishes
and seahorses

Body and tail covered with encasing circles of
bony plating. Pelvic fins absent; anal fin small or
absent. Caudal section of body long, slender. Dorsal fin large, located about over anus. Thirteen
species.

The pipefishes, which comprise ten of our
thirteen species, are notoriously hard to separate.
However, careful counts of body and tail rings
and dorsal rays, used in conjunction with snout
length and general color pattern, will usually al-

low specimens to be placed in the proper species. Caudal rings are often difficult to count. Sometimes it is helpful to know if the females, which lack a brood pouch, are flat-bellied or V-bellied. This simply refers to whether there is a crest on the midventral line of the trunk (V-bellied) or not (flat-bellied); there are several intermediate conditions, however.

174. PIPEHORSE
Amphelikturus dendriticus (Barbour)

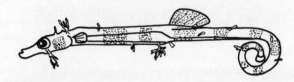

Intermediate between pipefishes and seahorses. Head with short, wide snout and slightly angled to body. Tail prehensile but with a small caudal fin. Several clusters of branched cirri. Brown with darker mottling or entirely dark brown. Three inches.

This supposedly rare species was recently reported to be not uncommon in plankton samples in the northern Gulf of Mexico.

175. LINED SEAHORSE
Hippocampus erectus Perry

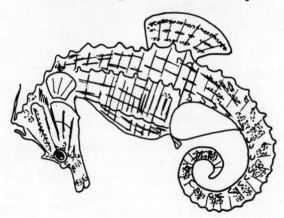

Juvenile

The common large seahorse. Tail prehensile, without caudal fin; head angled to body. Dorsal rays seventeen to twenty-one. Caudal segments thirty-three to thirty-eight. There are about three body tubercles at the base of the dorsal fin. Brownish, variably marked with stripes, both vertical and horizontal. Three to six inches in length.

Common in the northern Gulf, especially in shallow weedy water, but also out to at least twenty-five fathoms. Any seahorse over two inches long is this species.

It is unfortunate that the more familiar name *H. hudsonius* was replaced by the obscure and rather dubious name given by a second-rate zoologist in an obscure publication.

176. DWARF SEAHORSE
Hippocampus zosterae Jordan & Gilbert

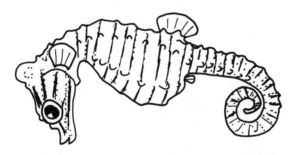

Tail prehensile, without caudal fin; head at angle to body. Dorsal rays only ten to fourteen, the fin over two body tubercles. Caudal segments twenty-eight to thirty-four. Brownish, sometimes mottled. One-half to one-and-a-half inches.

A common dwarf species almost restricted to shallow beds of various sea grasses. The name

Hippocampus regulus is considered insufficiently distinct to recognize as a full species.

177. FRINGED PIPEFISH
Micrognathus crinigerus (Bean & Dresel)

Snout short, concave dorsally. Anal fin absent. Dorsal fin entirely behind anus. Trunk very short, tail very long. Caudal fin large. Dorsal rays sixteen to eighteen. Trunk rings fourteen to sixteen, tail rings thirty-seven to thirty-nine; brood pouch over seventeen to eighteen rings. Brown with regular rows of large white spots and light streaks from eye. Three black spots on trunk. Fins light. Four to five inches.

Uncommon in shallow water, few Gulf populations known.

178. OPOSSUM PIPEFISH
Oostethus lineatus (Kaup)

Body very slender, the snout very long. Trunk and tail ridges modified into conspicuous spines. Anal fin present. Dorsal rays forty to forty-seven, the fin larger than in our other pipefishes. Trunk rings twenty-one; tail rings twenty to twenty-six; brood pouch under trunk. Brownish, with dark streak through eye; caudal fin black; dorsal fin with brown streaks between rays. Three to five inches.

This seems to be a rare species in our area, but the records indicate that it is rather continuously distributed; shallow water.

179. SHORTFIN PIPEFISH
Syngnathus elucens Poey

Snout moderate, about 1.9 to 2.2 in head. Anal fin present (as in all our species of *Syngnathus*). Dorsal fin origin about over anal. Dorsal rays twenty-two to twenty-four. Trunk rings seventeen; tail rings thirty-one to thirty-four. Brown, with regularly arranged rows of light spots on trunk and spots or spots fused into vertical bands on tail. Fins light dusky. Six inches.

A tropical species recently taken in offshore waters of the northern Gulf. Rare.

180. DUSKY PIPEFISH
Syngnathus floridae (Jordan & Gilbert)

A long-snouted species, the snout 1.6-1.7 in head. Trunk rings seventeen to eighteen; tail rings thirty to thirty-five. Dorsal of thirty to thirty-three rays. Brood pouch on fifteen to eighteen rings. Grayish-brown with lighter and darker mottling and spots. Caudal fin black. Dorsal fin with dark streaks between rays. Ten inches.

A common large pipefish found in both inshore and offshore waters.

181. NORTHERN PIPEFISH
Syngnathus fuscus Storer

Snout short, 2.0-2.4 in head. Dorsal rays thirty-six to thirty-nine. Trunk rings eighteen to nineteen; tail rings thirty-three to thirty-six. Brood pouch on twelve to fifteen tail rings. Female flat-bellied. Light brown mottled with darker brown. Caudal fin dark. Dorsal fin with brown blotches. Eight inches.

A very rare pipefish in the northern Gulf, representing a distinct subspecies, *S.f. affinis*, of the common Atlantic seaboard species. Very few specimens are known, mostly from offshore waters of Texas and Louisiana.

182. DWARF PIPEFISH
Syngnathus hildebrandi Herald

Snout very short, only 2.5 to 2.9 in head length. Head and body with a few cirri. Dorsal fin about over anal fin. Trunk rings seventeen; tail rings thirty-three to thirty-four. Dorsal rays nineteen to twenty-one. Caudal dark; dorsal clear. Uniformly brownish. Three to four inches.

Uncommon. West coast of Florida in seven to eleven fathoms over rocky bottoms. Possibly more widely distributed.

183. CHAIN PIPEFISH
Syngnathus louisianae Gunther

Snout long, 1.6 to 1.9 in head length. Trunk rings nineteen to twenty-one; tail rings thirty-six or thirty-seven. Dorsal rays thirty-three to thirty-six. Brood pouch on seventeen rings. Female flat-bellied. Light brown with darker brown even rectangles on dorsal surface and on tail. Caudal dark; dorsal clear. Reaches fifteen inches.

An uncommon species usually taken in deeper water.

184. SARGASSUM PIPEFISH
Syngnathus pelagicus Linnaeus

Snout moderate, 1.75-2 in head. Trunk rings sixteen to eighteen; tail rings thirty to thirty-four. Dorsal rays twenty-eight to thirty-one. Brood pouch on twelve to fifteen rings. Female V-bellied. Light brown, the lower part of trunk almost black, with wide white vertical spots dividing this dark area into even dark and light areas. Caudal light; dorsal fin with brown bands and blotches. Seven inches.

Recently recorded from the northern Gulf in offshore plankton tows. Uncommon.

185. GULF PIPEFISH
Syngnathus scovelli (Evermann & Kendall)

Snout short, 2 to 2.5 in head. Trunk rings sixteen or seventeen; tail rings thirty to thirty-four. Dorsal rays twenty-seven to thirty-five. Brood pouch on eleven to thirteen rings. Female V-bellied. Pale tan, with a broad dark stripe from snout along midside to caudal fin; dorsum light; a few black V-shaped marks laterally at base of tail. Fins light. To about six inches.

The common inshore pipefish in shallow or brackish water. Also recorded from freshwater.

186. BULL PIPEFISH
Syngnathus springeri Herald

Snout moderate, 1.96 to 2.13 in head. Trunk rings twenty-three to twenty-four; tail rings thirty-six or thirty-seven. Dorsal rays thirty-three to thirty-six. Brood pouch on sixteen to seventeen rings. Females flat-bellied. Pattern like that of the chain pipefish, pale brown with darker evenly spaced rectangles. Caudal dark; dorsal light. Fourteen or more inches long.

A strictly offshore species known in depths of ten to seventy fathoms. In our area known only from the west coast of Florida.

SYNGNATHUS MERISTICS

Species	Trunk rings	Tail rings	Dorsal rays	Snout/ head	Brood P.
springeri	23-24	36-37	33-36	1.96-2.13	16-17
louisianae	19-21	36-37	33-36	1.6-1.9	17
fuscus	18-19	33-36	36-39	2.0-2.4	12-15
floridae	17-18	30-35	30-33	1.6-1.7	15-18
pelagicus	16-18	30-34	28-31	1.75-2	12-15
elucens	17	31-34	22-24	1.9-2.2	—
scovelli	16-17	30-34	27-35	2-2.5	11-13
hildebrandi	17	33-34	19-21	2.5-2.9	—

References: Ginsburg, I., 1937 (*Proc. U.S. Nat. Mus.*, 83(2997):497-594; *Hippocampus*); Herald, E.S., 1942 (*Stanford Ichty. Bull.*, 2(4):125-134; key to pipefishes, but outdated and not very usable); Herald, E.S., 1965 (*Proc. Calif. Acad. Sci.*, 32(12):363-375; updated list pipefishes, new species).

ORDER PERCIFORMES — the typical fishes

Operculum generally large. Spinous dorsal fin usually present, with definite spines, well developed. Pelvic fins, if present, with five, sometimes fewer, rays, thoracic or more anterior. About half of our marine fishes belong to this order, including most of our common game and commercial species.

The perciform families present a great diversity in size and shape, from the smallest gobies to the largest tunnies and billfishes, but most are recognizable by the prominent spinous dorsal fin and thoracic pelvic fins containing five or fewer rays. The best way to recognize the families in this group is to become familiar with the body forms shown on the following pages.

Contains forty-nine families and two hundred and fifty-eight species.

Family CENTROPOMIDAE — snooks

A single species in our range.

187. SNOOK
Centropomus undecimalis (Bloch)

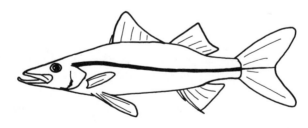

Two dorsal fins, the first with eight strong spines, separate from the soft dorsal. Head long, pointed, the lower jaw strongly projecting. Preopercle coarsely serrated; operculum without spines. Lateral line continued onto caudal fin. Second anal spine very long and strong. Silvery, the lateral line black. Two to four-and-a-half feet in length.

A popular tropical sports species, ranging north to southern Florida on the east and to the central Texas coast on the west. Not definitely recorded from Louisiana, Mississippi, or Alabama.

Family **PERCICHTHYIDAE** — temperate basses

A serranid-like family based on osteology and not easily separable on external characters. Spinous dorsal slightly separate from soft dorsal. One species.

188. STRIPED BASS
Morone saxatilis (Walbaum)

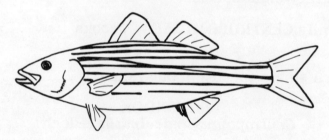

Dorsal fins two, separate. Anal fin III, 12. Silvery, with dark lateral streaks comprised of fused spots. One to four feet long.

An uncommon species on the northern Gulf coast, originally ranging west only to the Mississippi delta area. Anadromous, ascending rivers to spawn. This famous sportsfish is virtually extinct in our area, but has been widely introduced both east and west of the Mississippi. It is not yet known if these introductions will yield permanent populations.

Also commonly known as *Roccus saxatilis*, few taxonomists greatly preferring one generic name to the other.

Family **SERRANIDAE** — sea basses and groupers

"Typical basses" with three anal spines and the dorsal fins usually continuous. The upper part of the maxillary is not hidden under the suborbital when the mouth is closed, as it is in the snappers. Twenty-nine species.

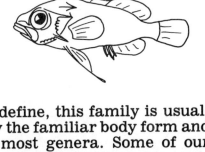

14 mm larva of an *Epinephelus.*

Although hard to define, this family is usually easy to recognize by the familiar body form and unspecialized fins in most genera. Some of our species are very common, but many are rare strays from warmer climates, putting in an appearance as juveniles during the summer. Most of these, and most serranids, for that matter, occur on or near hard offshore bottoms such as the snapper banks and coral heads. It is likely that other species occur in our range as well. The eleven genera fall into three groups based on number of dorsal spines:

D. IX
Petrometopon — body spotted, caudal rounded
Paranthias — body nearly unicolor, caudal deeply forked
D. X, about one foot maximum length
Hypoplectrus — body deep, ovoid; ventral margin preopercle with antrorse spines
Hemanthias — mouth very oblique, with strong canines on notched upper jaw
Centropristis — body round in x-section; caudal with one to three filaments
Serraniculus — body round, very small; caudal truncate; black spots along dorsal base

Diplectrum — body round; caudal forked; pre-
    opercular angle with strong spines
Serranus — body round; caudal forked or trun-
    cate; preopercle smooth or weakly armed
D. XI, commonly over two feet long
    Epinephelus — scales rough; anal rays III, 7-9
    (one species with ten dorsal spines)
    Dermatolepis — scales smooth except under
    pectoral fin
    Mycteroperca — scales rough; anal rays III, 11-
    14

189. BANK SEA BASS
Centropristis ocyurus (Jordan & Evermann)

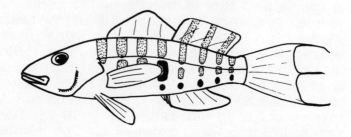

Caudal fin of adults distinctly trilobed, each
lobe often with a long filament. D. X,11; A. III,7;
Ll. 53-57. Body brown, with darker lateral bands,
the bottom part of last four or five bands distinctly rounded and very dark, looking like inky spots.
The middle portion of the band at the pectoral tip
is black. Dorsal spine tabs short, not exceeding
the spines. Twelve inches. The preopercle is
strongly serrated in all *Centropristis*.
    Uncommon, most records from moderate or
deep water over hard bottoms.

190. ROCK SEA BASS
Centropristis philadelphica (Linnaeus)

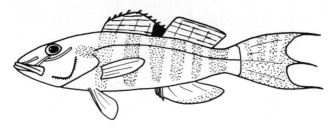

Caudal fin trilobed, the lobes filamentous. Fleshy dorsal tabs extending beyond tips of dorsal spines, yellow. D. X,11; A. III,7; Ll. 53-57. Brown, with vague darker bands, the middle band darker near the dorsal fin and continued as a black spot on the last two dorsal spines. Head with orange lines below eye and in furrow of upper jaw. Nine to twelve inches.

The common *Centropristis* in the northern Gulf, usually occurring in five to thirty fathoms.

191. BLACK SEA BASS
Centropristis striata (Linnaeus)

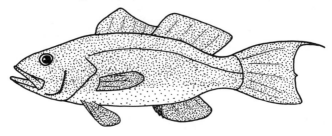

In adults, caudal fin rounded with a projecting upper lobe bearing a short filament. Dorsal spine tabs short and not exceeding spines. D. X, 11; A. III,7; Ll. 47-49. Stout bodied. Nearly uniform gray above, lighter below. Juvenile generally similar to adults. Eighteen inches.

A rare species in our area, restricted to the west coast of Florida and west to about Mobile Bay. The Gulf of Mexico population differs from the Atlantic seaboard populations and has been called a distinct species or subspecies, *C. melana* Ginsburg.

167

192. MARBLED GROUPER
Dermatolepis inermis (Valenciennes)

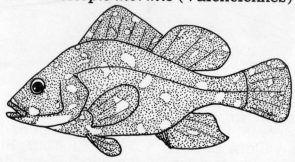

Deep-bodied species with high nape profile; soft dorsal and anal fins falcate in large individuals. D. XI,19-20; A. III,9; Ll. 85-100, irregular. Scales smooth except under pectoral, fish "slippery." Dark brown or black with large, irregular white spots over head and body, including fins; white spots from eye; variable. Two feet or more in length.

Rare in our area, a few records from the west coast of Florida.

Dermatolepis has recently been considered to be a subgenus of *Epinephelus*, an assignment not followed here, as *Epinephelus* is already too cumbersome a genus to be made even bulkier by the inclusion of readily recognizable groups.

193. DWARF SAND PERCH
Diplectrum bivittatum (Valenciennes)

Preopercle

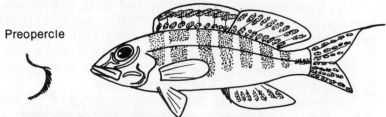

Preopercle with its lower angle strongly produced and bearing spines much longer than those above or below the angle. Caudal fin slightly forked, upper rays filamentous. D. X,12; A. III,7; Ll.

48-51. Silvery, with brown oblong spots which tend to fuse into bands or stripes. Fins clear, with red spots. Operculum orange, with large blue lines below and before eye. Four to eight inches long.

This is a very common little bass in waters of ten to forty fathoms, most common in fifteen to thirty fathoms.

194. SAND PERCH
Diplectrum formosum (Linnaeus)

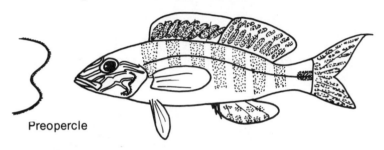

Preopercle

Posterior edge of preopercle produced into an upper and lower lobe each of which bears a group of large spines. Caudal fin lunate, the upper rays filamentous. Brownish, with stripes or bands. Blue lines on head. Fins clear, with orange spots and stripes. Two black spots on base of caudal fin. Eight to twelve inches.

Rare along the northern Gulf, most records coming from snapper banks in moderate water off central and southern Texas.

195. ROCK HIND
Epinephelus adscensionis (Osbeck)

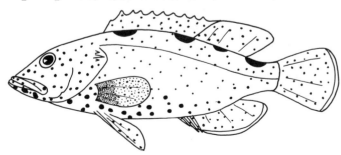

D. XI,17; A. III, 8. Caudal fin convex. Body and fins pale, whitish to olive, with numerous red to reddish-brown spots. Spots in ventral area larger than those dorsally. Three large black blotches along base of dorsal fin. Young and small adults with small caudal peduncle saddle. Eighteen inches.

One of the most common small groupers of the northern Gulf coast. Often caught by sport and commercial fishermen fishing for red snapper.

196. SPECKLED HIND
Epinephelus drummondhayi Goode & Bean

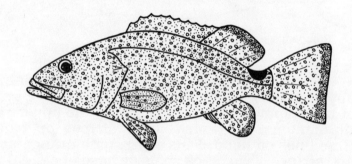

D. XI, 15-16; A. III, 9. Caudal fin straight or concave. Head, body, and fins dark brown with numerous white specks. Our only *Epinephelus* with light spots on a dark ground. Caudal saddle small, not reaching down to lateral line or forward to dorsal fin base. About two feet; thirty pounds.

A poorly known little grouper seemingly restricted to offshore hard bottoms east of the Mississippi delta area.

197. YELLOWEDGE GROUPER
Epinephelus flavolimbatus Poey

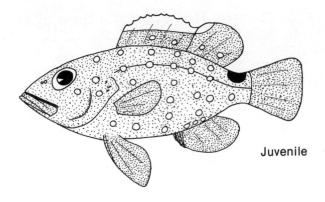

Juvenile

D. XI,13-15; A. III,9. Nostrils subequal. *Young:* Body dark brown, fins somewhat lighter. Black moustache over maxilla. Large white spots on body and sometimes on head and dorsal fin, arranged in regular lateral and longitudinal rows. Spinous dorsal and anterior part of soft dorsal broadly margined with yellow-orange. Caudal saddle black, not extending forward to dorsal fin or ventrally to lateral line. Juveniles only, six inches.

Only juvenile specimens have been taken from the northern Gulf, apparently strays from permanent populations to the east and south of our area. A nicely marked specimen was taken with a similar size (four inches) *E. niveatus* in twenty fathoms off Isle Deniere, Louisiana.

198. RED HIND
Epinephelus guttatus (Linnaeus)

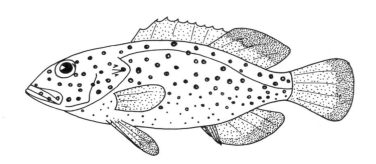

D. XI,15-16; A. III,7-8. Caudal fin convex. Yellowish to pale olive, with ocellated or plain spots of red or reddish-brown over head, body, and basal part of fins. Soft dorsal, anal, and caudal broadly edged with black. Spots small or absent ventrally. No caudal saddle. Two feet long.

Uncommon, but possibly confused with the rock hind.

199. JEWFISH
Epinephelus itajara (Lichtenstein)

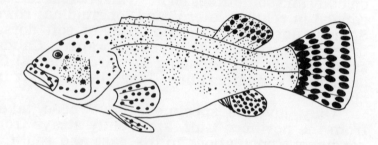

D. XI,15-16; A. III,8. Caudal convex. Head very broad, the interorbital wider than eye diameter. Dorsal spines lower than soft dorsal rays, of about equal height, and with their membranes deeply notched. *Young:* Light brown background with about five dark brown bands, the last encircling the caudal peduncle. Fins and head with black or brown spots, these becoming more widespread and numerous with age. *Adults* (over four feet): Brown, with brown spots on fins and body. Reaches over seven feet in length and seven hundred pounds.

An abundant grouper in the northern Gulf— at least as abundant as a seven hundred pound fish can be. Often called *Promicrops itaiara* in older literature.

200. RED GROUPER
Epinephelus morio (Valenciennes)

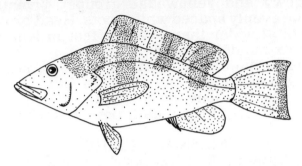

D. XI,16-17; A. III,9-10. Caudal fin emarginate or truncate. Spinous dorsal fin high, especially the second spine, its membrane unnotched. Reddish-brown, sometimes with pale blotches or indications of banding. Few scattered black spots sometimes present around eye and on head. Soft fins black-edged. No caudal saddle. Three feet and fifty pounds.

Common along the west coast of Florida, becoming rarer to the west, although there are records for most of the northern Gulf. Hard bottoms in moderate or deep water.

201. WARSAW GROUPER
Epinephelus nigritus (Holbrook)

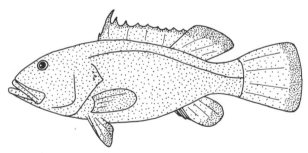

D. X,13-15; A. III,9. Our only *Epinephelus* with ten dorsal spines. Caudal fin truncate. Spinous dorsal high, second spine much longer than first, slightly longer than third. Dark gray without regular pattern, but sometimes with irregular whitish blotches laterally. Young (rare) similar to snowy and yellowedge grouper juveniles in having evenly spaced white spots. Head broad, interorbital wider than eye. Six feet in length and over six hundred pounds.

This, the black jewfish of anglers, is a common grouper along the northern Gulf. Juveniles under one foot long are very rare.

Previously known as *Garrupa nigrita*.

202. SNOWY GROUPER
Epinephelus niveatus (Valenciennes)

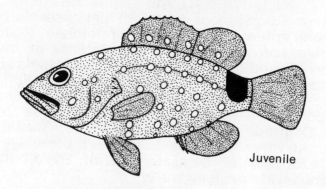

Juvenile

D. XI,13-14; A. III,9. *Juvenile:* Body dark brown, fins lighter. Black moustache over maxilla. Large white spots on body and sometimes on head and dorsal fin, arranged in regular lateral and longitudinal rows. Caudal saddle black, extending forward to dorsal fin base and ventrally to below lateral line. With growth the spots and saddle fade. No broad yellow line in dorsal fin. *Adult:* Coppery gold with eighteen narrow wavy dark bands laterally and two bands across preopercle and opercle. Posterior nostril three to five times larger than anterior nostril. Only four- to six-inch juveniles known from the northern Gulf.

An uncommon tropical straggler in waters over ten fathoms deep. Adults are at least four feet long.

203. NASSAU GROUPER
Epinephelus striatus (Bloch)

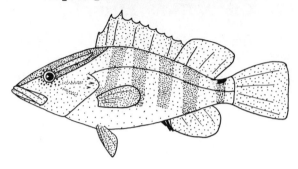

D. XI,16-18; A. III,8. Caudal fin convex. Spinous dorsal high, second and third spines of about equal height; membrane deeply notched. Light olive brown with darker lateral bands and a band through the eye and across the nape. Bands sometimes indistinct. Small black spots around eye. Black caudal saddle narrow, not reaching dorsal fin, short, not reaching lateral line. Soft fins yellowish distally. Three feet; fifty-five pounds.

Not uncommonly taken off snapper banks.

204. RED BARBIER
Hemanthias vivanus (Jordan & Swain)

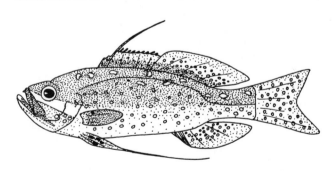

Mouth very oblique. Upper jaw indented medially, with strong canines at the corners. Third dorsal spine greatly elongated, strong and flexible. Caudal fin truncate or slightly emarginate in adults. Color basically carmine above, silvery below, with many yellow spots. A bright yellow stripe through eye. Pelvic fins yellow, with long filament. D. X,13; A. III,7-8; Ll. 48-52. At least one foot long.

Hemanthias is a deep water genus, but occasional specimens of the red barbier are taken in water of forty or fewer fathoms near snapper banks. It is occasionally taken with vermilion snapper.

205. YELLOWTAIL HAMLET
Hypoplectrus chlorurus (Valenciennes)

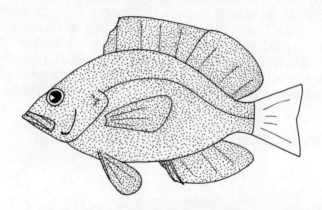

D. X,14-16; A. III,7. Body short, deeper than other basses. The horizontal edge of the preoperculum has short curved serrae directed anteriorly. Uniformly dark brown except for bright yellow caudal fin. Five inches.

A tropical serranid recorded in our area only from the southern Texas coast, where it is rare near rocky wharves.

206. BARRED HAMLET
Hypoplectrus puella (Cuvier)

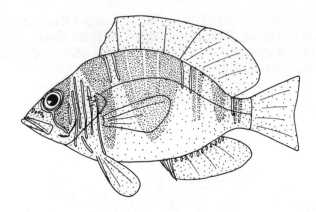

Morphologically identical with the yellowtail hamlet, differing only in color pattern. Body light brown with irregular obliquely vertical darker brown barring. Head with blue lines. Five inches.

Southern Florida, rarely straggling north along the western coast of Florida.

206X. BASSLET
Liopropoma spp.

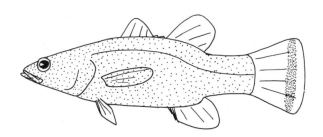

Small serranids recognized by the deeply divided dorsal fins, actually continuous but with last spines often embedded in flesh. Head conical, lower jaw projecting. Caudal fin rounded, slightly emarginate, to truncate. Color pattern variable with species, straw brown to patterned with red and black stripes. Soft dorsal and anal and caudal usually with black spots.

Although no particular species of this genus has been recorded from our area, one or more is almost certain to be found on the offshore snapper banks and coral heads. In addition, the deep water genus *Pikea* (seldom in less than fifty fathoms) is common off our coasts and is probably a synonym of *Liopropoma*.

207. BLACK GROUPER
Mycteroperca bonaci (Poey)

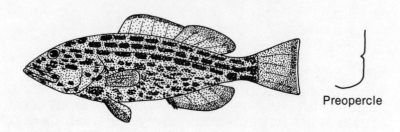

Preopercle

D. XI,16-17; A. III,11-13. Caudal fin truncate, corners only slightly or not at all extended. Preopercle with angle broadly rounded, not deeply notched. Grayish to olive, with numerous elongate dark brown blotches arranged in vague lengthwise rows. Small red or orange spots in background. Soft dorsal and anal fins broadly margined with black; caudal with narrow white margin after broad black zone. Pectoral fin brown, gradually turning orange at distal margin. Over three feet; one hundred and eight pounds.

Apparently not common on our coast, but really little known. Hard offshore bottoms.

208. GAG
Mycteroperca microlepis (Goode & Bean)

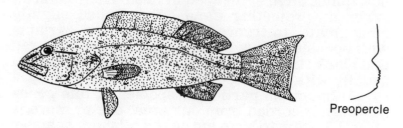

Preopercle

D. XI,16-19; A. III,11. Caudal emarginate.
Preopercle with a deep notch. Anterior and posterior nostrils subequal in size. Olive, mottled
with darker olive spots. Soft dorsal, anal, and caudal edged with blue-black, with narrow white
margins. Blue streaks from eye. Scales very
small, over 140 in lateral line. Two feet long.

The only common *Mycteroperca* in our area,
although seemingly restricted to offshore hard
bottoms mostly east of the Mississippi River.

209. SCAMP
Mycteroperca phenax Jordan & Swain

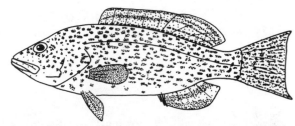

D. XI,15-18; A. III,11. Caudal emarginate, the
corners distinctly extending beyond margin. Preopercle with a deep notch set off ventrally by larger teeth. Posterior nostril larger than anterior.
Light grayish brown with numerous small brown
spots, some fused into larger blotches. Fins spotted. Two feet long.

Moderately common on hard bottoms, mostly
along the western coast of Florida but also west to
the Mississippi delta.

210. COMB GROUPER
Mycteroperca rubra (Bloch)

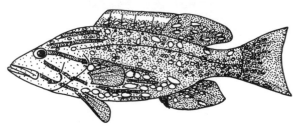

D. XI,15-17; A. III,11. Caudal nearly truncate, the corners not extended. Preopercle with a deep notch set off below by strong spines. Nostrils subequal. Olive brown with darker mottlings and dark lines on head. Body sprinkled with white spots, these especially prominent and mixed with wavy lines above anal fin. Gill rakers 45-54, much more than in any other *Mycteroperca*. About two feet long.

An apparently rare and poorly known species recorded in our area from off Texas. It has been listed in the past as *Parepinephelus acutirostris*.

This species was omitted from the AFS *Checklist*.

211. YELLOWFIN GROUPER
Mycteroperca venenosa (Linnaeus)

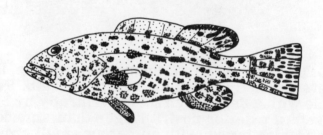

D. XI,15-16; A. III,11. Caudal fin truncate. Preopercle broadly rounded, without deep notch. Grayish to olive, with elongate brownish blotches. Much red in background in most color phases. Soft dorsal, anal, and caudal white distally with black spots and narrow black margins. Pectoral fin spotted basally, the distal third of fin abruptly orange-yellow. Reaches about three feet in length.

An uncommon grouper in the northern Gulf, straying north along the western coast of Florida from tropical seas.

212. CREOLE-FISH
Paranthias furcifer (Valenciennes)

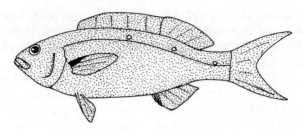

D. IX,18-19; A. III,9-10. Body moderately compressed, robust. Caudal fin deeply forked. Mouth moderately upturned. Dorsal fins not deeply notched. Generally reddish, darker above and pinkish below. Throat yellowish and fins margined with yellow to orange. Bright red triangular spot at upper base of pectoral fin. Three small white or black spots above lateral line. About one foot in length.

An uncommon fish in our area, generally in more than ten fathoms. Feeds on zooplankton above the bottom. Occurs in small schools.

213. GRAYSBY
Petrometopon cruentatum (Lacepede)

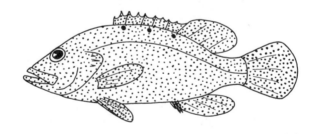

D. IX,14; A. III,8. Caudal fin convex. Light olive to brown in background color, with many small round red to brown spots. Three or four well defined black spots (white if background color is dark) below the dorsal fin base, the one under origin of soft dorsal most prominent. Interspinal membrane of dorsal fin edged with orange. Six to twelve inches.

A very rare tropical species in the northern Gulf. Recorded from off the Texas coast in forty fathoms. It should be expected on offshore hard bottoms. Because of its color pattern it might be easily confused with some of the groupers of the genus *Epinephelus*.

It has recently been proposed to combine *Petrometopon* with *Cephalopholis* and then combine *Cephalopholis* with *Epinephelus* as a subgenus. Although I cannot pass judgement on the value of the characters which separate these taxa, I can see no advantage in combining recognizable units into bulky and already complex genera like *Epinephelus*.

214. PYGMY SEA BASS
Serraniculus pumilio Ginsburg

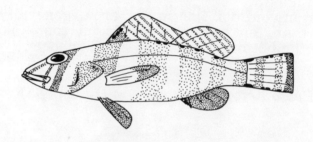

D. X,10-11; A. III,7; Ll. 44-46. Branchiostegals six (seven in all our other serranids) but difficult to count—this character is not usable for identification. A very small fish likely to be mistaken for the young of *Diplectrum* or *Centropristis*. Plump bodied. Preopercle serrate. Caudal fin truncate. Body light brownish and orange, with diffuse darker lateral bands. Orange bands from eye to isthmus. Black spots from base of posterior part of spinous dorsal to edges of caudal fin. Pelvics and anal fin black. Two to three inches long.

Apparently uncommon but widely distributed in waters six to thirty-two fathoms deep. Prefers hard bottoms, which with its small size makes it hard to collect and probably explains its apparent rarity.

215. BLACKEAR BASS
Serranus atrobranchus (Cuvier)

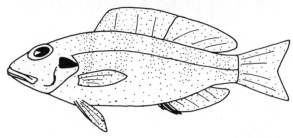

D. X,12. A. III,7. Caudal fin forked. Preopercle serrated on vertical margin. In our area, body is uniformly brownish with little indication of a body pattern. Inner surface of opercle with a well defined wedge-shaped black bar about the size of the pupil. The body is rather stout and the head blunt for this genus. Two to four inches.

Common in waters twelve to ninety fathoms deep. This is the *Paracentropristes pomospilus* of Ginsburg.

216. TATTLER
Serranus phoebe Poey

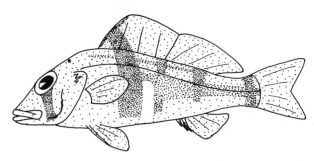

D. X,12; A. III,7. *Young:* Caudal fin truncate, uncolored. Pectoral fin plain. Body light brown with several dark bands, the most conspicuous one running from the second dorsal spine to between the pelvic and anal fins. *Adult:* Caudal shallowly forked. Body plain or with vestiges of juvenile banding. A distinct silvery band before the anus, running from the belly upward about to lateral line. Fins plain. Intermediate color patterns occur. Four to six inches.

Adult tattlers are deepwater fish, seldom being collected in less than thirty fathoms. Young specimens stray as shallow as fifteen fathoms, however. Rare, and known only from east of the Mississippi delta.

In older literature this species is called *Prionodes phoebe*.

217. BELTED SANDFISH
Serranus subligarius (Cope)

D. X,13; A. III,7. Body very deep, the head very pointed. Caudal fin truncate. Body light brown with numerous narrow darker bands. A prominent black spot on the first few soft dorsal rays. Caudal and pectoral fins banded or spotted with brown. Pelvic fins black centrally. Sides of head with many brown vermiculations in most specimens. The lustrous white belly is sharply set off from the dorsal pattern. Four inches or less.

Uncommon in our area, the adults usually found in ten or more fathoms but the young occasionally venturing closer to shore.

This is the *Dules subligarius* of older literature.

References: Miller, R., 1959 (*Tulane Stud. Zool.*, 7(2):35-68; *Centropristis*); Rivas, L.R., 1964

(*Quart. Jour. Florida Acad. Sci.*, 27(1):17-30; *Epinephelus*); Robins, C.R. and W.A. Starck, 1961 (*Proc. Acad. Nat. Sci., Phila.*, 113(11):259-314; *Serranus*); Smith, C.L., 1971 (*Bull. Amer. Mus. Nat. Hist.*, 146(2):69-241; groupers).

Family GRAMMISTIDAE — soapfishes

A single species in the northern Gulf.

218. GREATER SOAPFISH
Rypticus saponaceus (Bloch & Schneider)

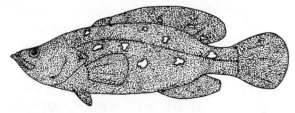

D. III,23-25. Skin thick, with small embedded scales. Dorsal and anal fins fleshy, the dorsal spines somewhat embedded. Soft dorsal and anal similar. No anal spines. Two prominent spines on preopercle, three on opercle. Head small, the lower jaw projecting. Caudal convex. Brown, lighter below. White spots about the size of the pupil on body and on dorsal fins, generally few, often clumped. Six to twelve inches in length.

Although this fish is poorly known, it does not appear to be uncommon in water fifteen to forty fathoms deep near hard bottoms. It is sometimes taken by snapper fishermen.

Family PRIACANTHIDAE — bigeyes

Body deep, compressed, usually reddish brown and silvery. Mouth large and oblique. Pelvics large, connected to body by membrane. Three anal spines. Base of soft dorsal fin shorter than that of soft anal fin. Two species.

219. BIGEYE
Priacanthus arenatus Cuvier

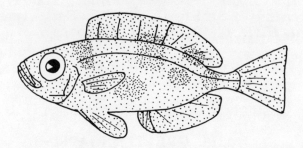

D. X,13-14; A. III,14-15. Scales about eighty to one hundred in lateral line. Body elongate. Eye large. Uniform bright red in most phases, sometimes mottled with brownish. Eight to sixteen inches in length.

Uncommon tropical species which would seem to have resident populations somewhere offshore on hard bottoms. Fifteen or more fathoms.

220. SHORT BIGEYE
Pristigenys alta (Gill)

D. X,11; A. III,9-11. Lateral line scales larger, 35 to 50. Body short and deep. Eye very large. Red, the soft fins with black margins. Six to eleven inches in length.

A deep water fish rare in our area. The genus *Pseudopriacanthus* is sometimes used.

Family APOGONIDAE — cardinalfishes

Small fishes with a very long and slender caudal peduncle. Eye and mouth large. The dorsal fins are widely separated. Two anal spines. Five species, all tropical stragglers which are very rarely seen in the northern Gulf. Most are known in our range only along the southwestern coast of Florida and are associated with hard bottoms.

221. BRIDLE CARDINALFISH
Apogon aurolineatus (Mowbray)

Pale silvery pink without conspicuous dark markings on body. Short black lines around eye and on opercle. Preopercle without long lower lobe. Body scales ctenoid. Pelvic fin not reaching anal fin base. Two-and-a-half inches.

A deep water cardinalfish found only beyond ten fathoms. Southwest coast of Florida.

222. FLAMEFISH
Apogon maculatus (Poey)

Bright red with two black spots on body; one spot, nearly circular, at posterior base of soft dorsal fin, the other broadly rectangular and covering all of posterior half of caudal peduncle. A broad black line from eye to preopercle, bordered above and below by narrow white lines continued into eye. Lower preopercular lobe not elongated. Pelvic fin not reaching anal base. Scales ctenoid. Five inches.

A widespread shallow water species associated with coral reefs. Either this species or the similar twospot cardinalfish is reported by divers to occur on the offshore oil platforms of Louisiana. Common on the Florida coast.

223. TWOSPOT CARDINALFISH
Apogon pseudomaculatus Longley

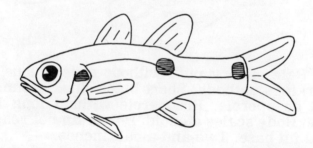

Reddish, with two black spots on body, one at posterior base of soft dorsal and other on upper edge of caudal peduncle just anterior to caudal base. Caudal peduncle spot rounded, never rectangular, and covers less than a fourth of distal half of peduncle. Dark smudge on opercle. Pelvic fins short, not reaching anal base. Scales ctenoid. Preopercular lobe not elongate. Four inches.

Same habitat as flamefish. Southwest coast of Florida.

224. BRONZE CARDINALFISH
Astrapogon alutus (Jordan & Gilbert)

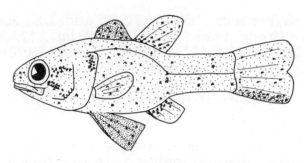

Brownish over a silvery background, with scattered darker points. Fins mostly dusky to black, the edges lighter. Body scales cycloid. Pelvic fins long, reaching to about anterior third of anal fin base. Preopercular lobe short. About three inches.

This is a shallow water inquiline in queen conchs and other large molluscs. Known from the west coast of Florida to about Pensacola.

225. FRECKLED CARDINALFISH
Phaeoptyx conklini (Silvestri)

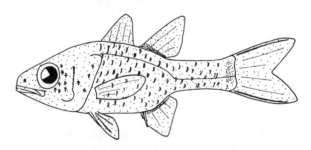

Body frail looking, translucent. Silvery with faint pinkish tinges, the body and head with large black chromatophores in regular rows. Fins dusky to dark. Scales ctenoid. Pelvics short. Lower preopercular lobe horizontally prolonged, rounded. Three to four inches.

An inquiline in tubular sponges at moderate depths on offshore reefs. Southwest coast of Florida.

References: Bohlke, J.E. and J.E. Randall, 1968 (*Proc. Acad. Nat. Sci., Phila.*, 120(4):175-206); Fraser, T.H. and C.R. Robins, 1970 (*Stud. Trop. Oceanogr.*, 4(2):302-315).

Family **BRANCHIOSTEGIDAE** — tilefishes

Elongate to moderately elongate fishes with the dorsal fins continuous, with only four to seven spines and many rays; spinous dorsal somewhat lower than soft dorsal. One anal spine, many rays. Lips thick. Scales small, over one hundred in lateral line. Caudal fin concave to lunate. Two species.

226. BLACKLINE TILEFISH
Caulolatilus cyanops Poey

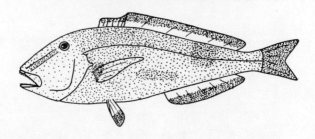

Head large, profile high, lips thick. Outer teeth canine. Caudal concave, upper lobe slightly longer than lower. D. VII,24-25; A. I,22-23; Ll. 105-120. Opercle with large flat spine. Snout naked. Reddish with yellow markings and a yellow band below eye. Dark blotch in axilla of pectoral. Dorsal fin with brown spots. One to two-and-a-half feet long.

An uncommon fish on offshore deepwater reefs and snapper banks. The proper name for this species, which may actually represent two different species, is uncertain.

227. SAND TILEFISH
Malacanthus plumieri (Bloch)

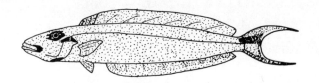

Body elongate, head conical, lips very thick. D. IV or V,53-57; A. I,50-52; Ll. 140-144. Caudal fin lunate, with long points. Bluish gray, fins yellowish, the caudal with orange lobes and dusky above the middle. One or two feet in length.

A tropical reef fish rarely found in the northern Gulf. In our area seems to like deep sandy bottoms.

Family **POMATOMIDAE** — bluefish

Only one species, worldwide in distribution.

228. BLUEFISH
Pomatomus saltatrix (Linnaeus)

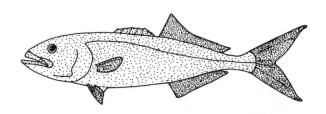

D. VIII-I,23-26; A. II-I,25-27; Ll. 95-105. Mouth large, oblique, with large teeth. Preopercle serrated. Lower jaw projecting. First dorsal fin of low and weak spines. Two spines preceding anal fin. Caudal peduncle without keels. Caudal fin forked. Greenish-blue with silvery reflections. Two to four feet long.

A common schooling game fish generally found in moderate depths.

Family RACHYCENTRIDAE — cobia

A single widespread species.

229. COBIA
Rachycentron canadum (Linnaeus)

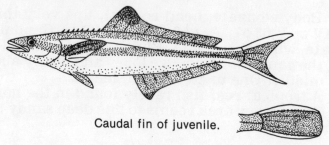

Caudal fin of juvenile.

D. VIII-I,30; A. I,23. Head depressed, the lower jaw projecting. Pectorals large, rather stiff. First dorsal fin of short, stiff, free spines. Second dorsal and anal similar, elevated anteriorly. Caudal fin strongly convex in juveniles, lunate in adults. Scales very small, embedded. Black, with a black lateral band in young bordered above by dirty white; anal and pelvic fins whitish, other fins dusky. Two to five feet long.

An abundant and popular game fish most common near oil rings and over hard bottoms.

The juvenile bears an amazing resemblance in color and shape to the sharksucker.

Family ECHENEIDAE — remoras

Elongated fishes with dorsal mouths, projecting lower jaw, and the first dorsal fin modified into a sucking disk of paired laminae. Soft dorsal and anal fins similar. Six species. Only the sharksucker is common, the other species being very rare and usually associated with large offshore fish, sharks, and turtles.

230. SHARKSUCKER
Echeneis naucrates Linnaeus

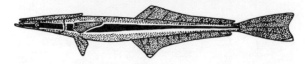

Disk laminae twenty-one to twenty-seven. Pectoral fins acute. Grayish-brown with a wide black lateral band bounded above and below by a narrow white band. Caudal, anal, and dorsal with lobes white. One to three feet.

Widespread and common. Usually attached to a variety of large fish, but also commonly found free-swimming.

231. SLENDER SUCKERFISH
Phtheirichthys lineatus (Menzies)

Disk laminae nine to eleven. Pectoral fin acute. Color pattern like the sharksucker. Body shape like a very slender sharksucker. Thirty inches.

Rare. Found on sharks.

232. WHALESUCKER
Remora australis (Bennett)

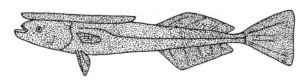

Disk laminae twenty-four to twenty-eight, the disk equal to about half the body length. D. 20-27; A. 20-26. Pectoral fin rounded, 21-24 rays. Body stout. Light gray through blues and violet to black, as are all the remaining species. Thirty inches.

Rare. Usually on whales.

233. SPEARFISH REMORA
Remora brachyptera (Lowe)

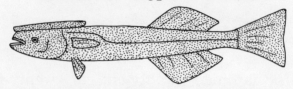

Disk laminae fourteen to seventeen, the disk not reaching beyond pectoral tip. D. 27-34; A. 25-30. Pectoral fin rounded, 23-27 rays. Body stout. Light brown to grayish, darker below. Twelve inches.
Rare. On swordfish and billfishes.

234. MARLINSUCKER
Remora osteochir (Cuvier)

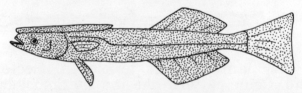

Disk laminae sixteen to twenty, the disk extending well beyond tip of pectoral fin. D. 20-27; A. 20-26. Pectoral fin rounded, the rays stiff and ossified; rays 20-24. Body stout. Brown. About a foot long.
Rare. On billfishes, swordfish, and wahoo.

235. REMORA
Remora remora (Linnaeus)

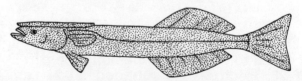

Disk laminae sixteen to twenty, the disk not extending beyond pectoral tip. D. 21-27; A. 21-25. Pectoral fin rounded, 26-30 rays. Black. Almost three feet long.

Rare in our area, but more common than other *Remora*. Found on sharks, sea turtles, ships, etc.

Family **CARANGIDAE** — jacks, scads, pompanos, and relatives

A large and variable family, generally recognized by the absence of scales or very small and embedded scales, deeply forked caudal fin, and the presence of two anal spines in front of the rest of the anal fin. Spinous dorsal fin short, usually low, sometimes embedded in skin and tissue, as also may be anal spines. Lateral line commonly armored with high, spiny scutes posteriorly; base of caudal fin with skin folds. Body ovoid to elongate, round-bodied to deeply compressed. Often shiny yellowish, bluish, or silvery. Twenty-five species.

The numerous and often common species are best recognized by general body shape and armature of lateral line.

Lateral line scutes

Jacks — body relatively deep and compressed; caudal peduncle armored. *Alectis, Caranx, Hemicaranx, Uraspis*

Scads — body slender, round in x-section; mouth terminal; caudal peduncle armored. *Decapterus, Selar, Trachurus*

Pompanos — body deep, rounded; caudal peduncle unarmed; dorsal spines low. *Trachinotus*

Amberjacks and runners — large sportsfishes, generally elongate to moderately deep bodied; often distinctive color patterns; lateral line unarmed; dorsal spines low. *Elagatis, Naucrates, Seriola*

Miscellaneous — usually of rounded, deep body form with very weakly armored or naked lateral line. *Chloroscombrus, Oligoplites, Selene, Vomer*

236. AFRICAN POMPANO
Alectis crinitus (Mitchill)

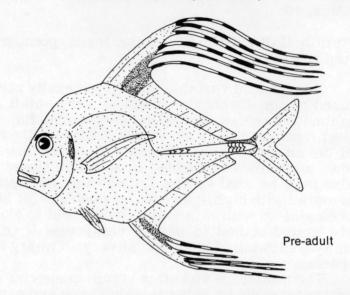

Pre-adult

Very deep bodied when young, becoming more elongate with age. Caudal peduncle with heavy scutes, the points directed caudally. D. VII-I,18-19, the first dorsal covered with tissue in medium to large fishes. Anal II-I,15-16, first two spines commonly embedded in tissue. Snout blunt. Dorsal and anal rays greatly elongated, especially in juveniles, banded with black and white. Silvery, the juvenile with black vertical bands. Adult silver, with constant black blotches on operculum and on dorsal surface of caudal peduncle. Three feet.

An uncommon fish in the northern Gulf, usually found as juveniles. Adults sometimes taken by fishermen. Sometimes called *Alectis ciliaris* or *Hynnis cubanus*.

Jacks — genus *Caranx*. Our six species of *Caranx* are distinguishable by the heavily armored caudal peduncle with scute points directed posteriorly, two dermal keels on the caudal peduncle, no elongated dorsal and anal rays, and maxillary wi-

dened posteriorly. D. VIII-I,x; A. II-I,x. Young
are banded with black and are all very similar.

237. YELLOW JACK
Caranx bartholomaei Cuvier

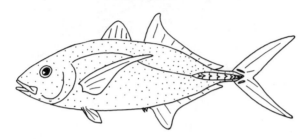

Head distinctly conical. Dorsal rays 25-28;
anal rays 21-24; scutes 20-31. Silvery with a yellowish cast. No opercular spot or dark line on caudal peduncle. One to three feet in length. Lower
gill rakers 18-21.

Common. Young with dark bars angled backward or joined into mottled pattern.

238. BLUE RUNNER
Caranx crysos (Mitchill)

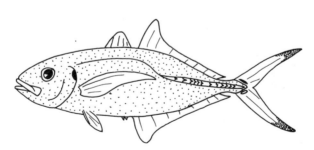

Head conical. Dorsal rays 22-25; anal 19-21;
scutes 46-56. Silvery. A distinct dark opercular
spot. One to three feet long. Lower GR 23-28.

Common. There has been a recent trend to
call this species *Caranx fuscus*. Young usually
with seven broad dark bands.

239. CREVALLE JACK
Caranx hippos (Linnaeus)

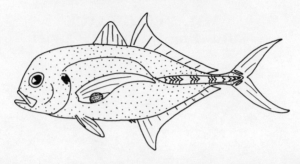

Blunt headed, the forehead strongly sloping. Dorsal rays 19-21; anal 16-17; scutes 26-35. Chest mostly naked, with only a small patch of scales anterior to pelvic fins. Silvery, with a black opercular spot, spot at pectoral axilla, and spot on lower part of pectoral. One to three-and-a-half feet.
Common. Young with five broad black bands.

240. HORSE-EYE JACK
Caranx latus Agassiz

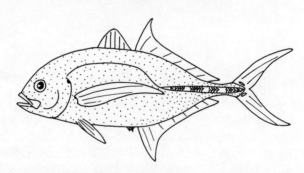

Blunt headed, the forehead moderately sloping. Dorsal rays 19-22; anal rays 16-18; scutes 32-39. Chest fully scaled. Opercle with small black spot; pectoral fin and axilla without black. One to two feet long.
Common. Young like that of *Caranx hippos*.

241. BLACK JACK
Caranx lugubris Poey

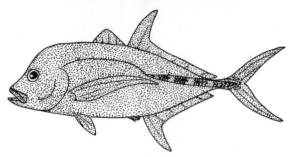

Forehead steeply sloping; head blunt. Dorsal rays 21-23; anal rays 17-20; scutes 29-33. Uniformly dark brown or sooty black; a vague black opercular spot. Three feet long. Lower gill rakers 19-21.

Very rare, usually offshore in deep water over twenty fathoms. Young not known.

242. BAR JACK
Caranx ruber (Bloch)

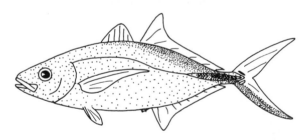

Head conical. Dorsal rays 26-30; anal rays 23-26; scutes 23-29. Silvery, with a broad black line from origin of soft dorsal along body profile through caudal peduncle to tip of lower caudal lobe; this black line is bordered below by a bright blue line which also runs forward to snout. No opercular spot. Two feet. Lower gill rakers numerous, 31-35.

A tropical species which is rarely recorded from our area, perhaps through confusion with the yellow jack. Young without distinct stripes.

243. ATLANTIC BUMPER
Chloroscombrus chrysurus (Linnaeus)

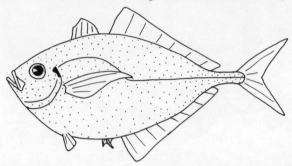

D. VIII-I,26-27; A. II-I,26-28. Anal spines strong. Lateral line unarmored. Ventral profile very strongly curved compared to nearly straight dorsal profile. Mouth very oblique. Fins low. Silvery, the fins yellow. A small opercular spot and a spot on the caudal peduncle. Four to ten inches.

A very common little jack in shallow to moderately deep high salinity water. The larger specimens come from further offshore.

244. ROUND SCAD
Decapterus punctatus (Agassiz)

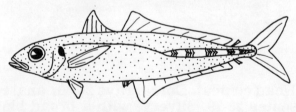

A slender, round-bodied fish. D. VIII-I,28-33-1; A. II-I,24-27-1. Last dorsal and anal ray a separate finlet. Scutes 36-44, about three-fourths as high as eye diameter, present only along straight posterior portion of lateral line. Mouth small, ending under anterior edge of eye. Silvery, blue above, with a black opercular spot. Four to twelve inches.

Moderately common in high salinity waters.

245. RAINBOW RUNNER
Elagatis bipinnulata (Quoy & Gaimard)

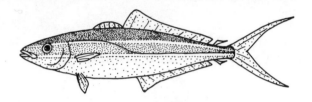

Body slender, elongate. D. VI-I,24-27-2; A. II-I,15-17-2; last two dorsal and anal rays detached finlets. Lateral line without scutes. Caudal fin deeply lunate. Olive dorsally, then a narrow blue band, a broad yellow band, a narrow blue band, and a narrow yellow band, the belly pale olive to whitish; a broad yellow band through eye. Two to four feet in length.

A popular sportsfish which is not uncommon offshore. Pelagic.

246. BLUNTNOSE JACK
Hemicaranx amblyrhynchus (Cuvier)

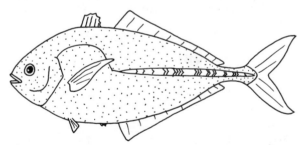

Generally similar to a small *Caranx*, but: maxillary not expanded posteriorly; outer jaw teeth not enlarged; caudal base without dermal keels. Anterior part of lateral line very high, almost semicircular, while in *Caranx* it is elliptical. Scutes weak, about fifty. D. VII-I,28; A. II-I,25. Fins low, the lobes not well developed. Pelvic fin short, not extending half way to anal base. Brownish blue above, silvery below. Generally juveniles under six or eight inches.

An uncommon and poorly known fish, said to be associated with jellyfishes and floating debris. This is probably not the oldest name for the species.

247. PILOTFISH
Naucrates ductor (Linnaeus)

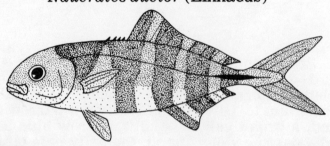

D. III or VI-I,24-29; A. I or II-I,15-18. Head broadly conical, the fins all low. Dorsal spines very low and separate, without membranes. Body silvery blue with five or six dark vertical bars extending into fin bases. Two feet long.

A widespread pelagic fish which has been vaguely reported from the entire Gulf of Mexico, but is probably only to be found far offshore.

248. LEATHERJACKET
Oligoplites saurus (Bloch & Schneider)

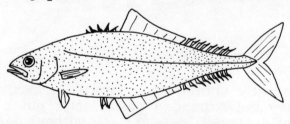

D. V-I,19-21; A. II-I,18-21. First dorsal and anal spines very strong, prominent. Posterior rays of dorsal and anal fins with deeply notched membranes. Mouth terminal, the premaxillaries not protractile. Body very compressed, the dorsal and ventral profiles similar. Silvery, the fins yellow. Six to twelve inches long.

Common in shallow to moderate water, the largest specimens coming from deepest water.

249. BIGEYE SCAD
Selar crumenophthalmus (Bloch)

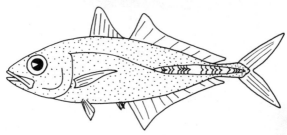

Round bodied elongate fish with terminal mouth. D. VIII-I,23-26; A. II-I,20-23. Last rays not separate finlets. Scutes restricted to straight posterior part of lateral line, about half of eye diameter in height, thirty to forty-four. Eye noticeably large. Silvery, no opercular spot. Six to fifteen inches long.

The least common scad, seemingly found only in deeper offshore waters.

250. LOOKDOWN
Selene vomer (Linnaeus)

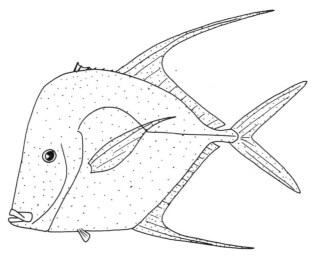

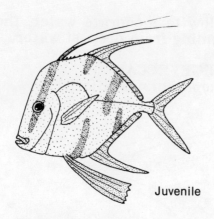

Juvenile

D. VIII-I,21-22; A. II-I,18-19. Lateral line unarmed. Snout and anterior profile very steep, almost perpendicular. Anterior anal and dorsal rays produced. Juveniles with the first dorsal spine very long and slender. Six to twelve inches long. Adult pelvic fins very short.

A common fish. Young specimens are commonly confused with young African pompanos, but lack the vertical stripes and banded fin rays of that species; in the lookdown the first dorsal spine is long, but the dorsal spines of young *Alectis* are very short.

Amberjacks — *Seriola*. Probably the most confusing genus of Carangidae, the species all very similar and varying greatly with growth. They are best identified by comparison with the illustrations after measuring the specimen. The genus is recognized by having a strong fleshy keel on the caudal peduncle, no bony scutes on the lateral line, the dorsal fin rays much more numerous than the anal rays, and the spinous dorsal fin with seven or eight low spines. The soft fins have high lobes. There is generally a dark line from the eye to the dorsal origin.

251. GREATER AMBERJACK
Seriola dumerili (Risso)

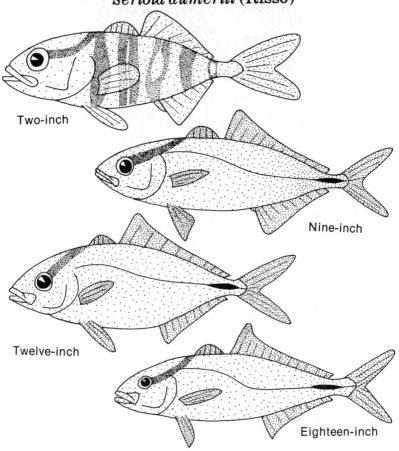

Two-inch

Nine-inch

Twelve-inch

Eighteen-inch

A consistently slender amberjack with low dorsal and anal lobes. In specimens of up to eight inches the vertical bars are split and irregular and do not extend into the dorsal and anal fins; bands usually five or six. Depths with size as % of standard length: to eight inches—33%; eight to sixteen inches—30 to 33%; sixteen to twenty four inches—27 to 30%; over two feet—23 to 27%. Gill rakers less than twenty in fishes above four inches. Reaches 170 pounds.

This is the common amberjack of fishermen; it is widely distributed.

252. LESSER AMBERJACK
Seriola fasciata (Bloch)

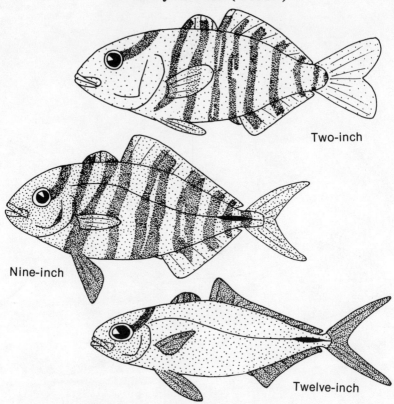

Two-inch

Nine-inch

Twelve-inch

A small, deep-bodied *Seriola*, with low dorsal and anal lobes. In this species the nuchal band angles upward sharply and fails to reach the dorsal origin. There are eight vertical bands in specimens of up to eight inches, the bands irregular, split and reaching into the webs of the dorsal and anal fins. In fish of about ten to twelve inches the bands are lacking and the eye is proportionately large. At up to eight inches, the depth is about 39% of the standard length. Up to about a foot in length.

The rarest and most poorly known amberjack in our waters. There is a possibility that the plain colored, large eyed fish over eight inches represent another species.

206

253. ALMACO JACK
Seriola rivoliana Valenciennes

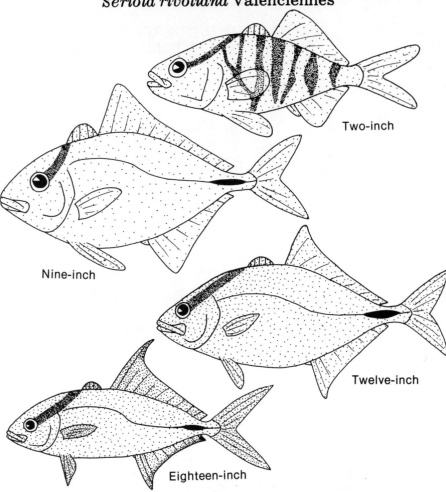

Two-inch

Nine-inch

Twelve-inch

Eighteen-inch

A large, deep-bodied amberjack with very high dorsal and anal lobes in large specimens. In specimens to about eight inches there are five or six dark vertical bands, split and irregular, which do not extend into the webs of the dorsal and anal fins. Depth with size: to eight inches—37%; eight to sixteen inches—35 to 37%; sixteen to twenty-four inches—32 to 35%; over two feet—30 to 32%. Gill rakers twenty-one or more at all sizes. To about fifty pounds.

207

A relatively common species but not as common as the greater amberjack.

254. BANDED RUDDERFISH
Seriola zonata (Mitchill)

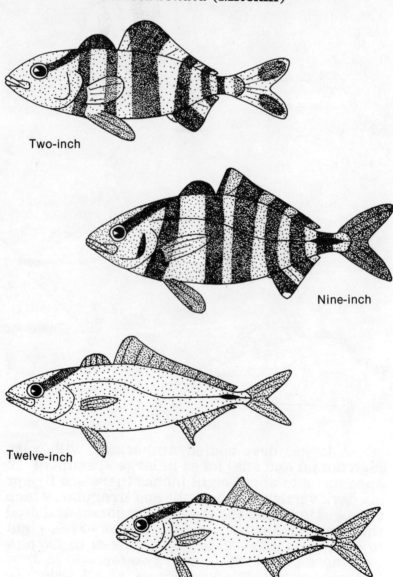

Two-inch

Nine-inch

Twelve-inch

Eighteen-inch

The most easily recognized *Seriola*, reaching about two feet and eight pounds. There are six solid, well defined vertical bars up to a length of at least ten inches. The bands extend into the dorsal and anal fins. At all sizes the soft anal fin base is about half the length of the dorsal fin base, much shorter than in the other species. Depth with size: to eight inches—33%; eight to sixteen inches—25 to 33%; sixteen to twenty-four inches—22 to 25%.

Not uncommon. The strikingly marked juvenile stages are probably more commonly seen than the unmarked adults and are also more easily recognized. The short anal fin is distinctive.

Pompanos — *Trachinotus*. Recognized by the relatively deep, silver body, the low spinous dorsal fin with six or seven spines, the short blunt snout, and the naked lateral line.

255. FLORIDA POMPANO
Trachinotus carolinus (Linnaeus)

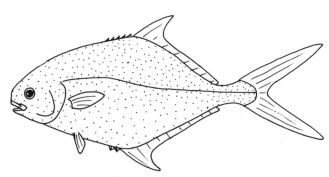

D. VI-I,23-27; A. II-I,20-22. Soft dorsal and anal fin lobes low, less than half the length of the fin, rounded. Body more elongate than round. Silvery, the fins yellowish. One to two-and-a-half feet.

A common and popular sportsfish, reknowned for its delicious flavor.

256. PERMIT
Trachinotus falcatus (Linnaeus)

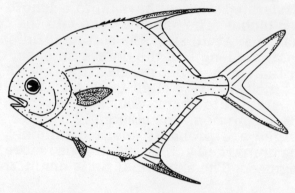

D. VI-I,18-21; A. II-I,16-18. Depth about 1.3 to 2.3 in standard length, most elongate when over two feet long. Fin lobes pointed, but not reaching beyond middle caudal rays, shortest in largest specimens. Silvery, without vertical bars. To three-and-a-half feet long, the largest pompano. A rare fish in clear offshore waters.

257. PALOMETA
Trachinotus goodei Jordan & Evermann

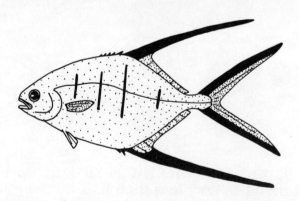

D. VII-I,19-20; A. II-I,16-18. Depth 2 (adults) to 3 (juveniles) in standard length. Lobes of fins very long, extending beyond middle caudal rays.

Silvery, yellowish below, the fins dusky. Adults with four narrow dark vertical bars. Ten to twenty inches.

Not uncommon in clear waters of the northern Gulf.

258. ROUGH SCAD
Trachurus lathami Nichols

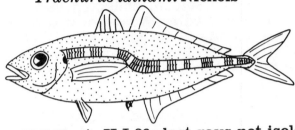

D. VIII-I,29; A. II-I,28; last rays not isolated finlets. Body relatively compressed for a scad. Entire lateral line armed with high thin scutes, which are not easily visible in moist specimens, the scutes strongest on posterior part of lateral line. Scutes about as high as eye diameter. Silvery, with a black opercular spot sometimes present. Four to nine inches in length.

Common in waters of ten to forty fathoms.

Be sure to check the anterior part of the lateral line with a needle or fingertip before deciding that the anterior scutes are absent.

259. COTTONMOUTH JACK
Uraspis secunda (Poey)

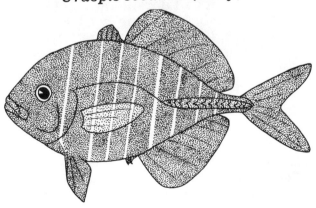

D. VII-I,29; A. I-I,22; scutes 36. Head blunt, the snout very short. Similar in body shape to *Caranx*, but the lateral line scutes with the points directed anteriorly. There are two caudal keels and enlarged outer teeth. Dull gray with darker vertical bars. The inside of the mouth is dark with large white areas. Twelve inches.

A rare and seldom collected jack generally found in deeper water. A few records from off the Mississippi delta in our area.

Uraspis heidi Fowler is a synonym, and *U. secunda* may in turn be a synonym of a Pacific species.

260. ATLANTIC MOONFISH
Vomer setapinnis (Mitchill)

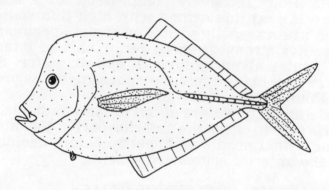

D. VIII-I,21-22; A. II-I,17-18. Dorsal spines very low. Lobes of soft dorsal and anal hardly produced, rounded. Lateral line with weak, almost invisible scutes. Forehead oblique, the snout projecting, resulting in a distinctly concave profile. Six to fifteen inches in length. Silvery, the young with a dark spot at the beginning of the straight lateral line. Adult pelvic fins very small.

A common fish in shallow to moderate water. As in the other smaller carangids, the largest specimens are taken from the deepest water.

Vomer and *Selene* are very similar genera distinguished by characters which are probably only specific in nature.

Family **CORYPHAENIDAE** — dolphins

Elongated, compressed fishes with large, forked caudal fins. The dorsal and anal fins are similar, with the spinous portion continuous with the rayed portion and not obviously distinct. The head is rounded, the forehead usually high. Lateral line irregularly jagged, the scales over 150. Two species.

261. **POMPANO DOLPHIN**
Coryphaena equisetis Linnaeus

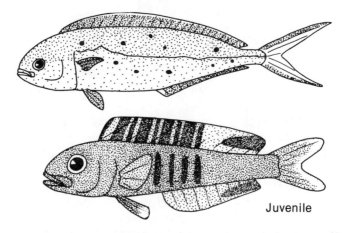

Juvenile

Dorsal elements (spines plus rays) less than fifty-five in most specimens. Lateral line scales usually less than two hundred, usually about one hundred and eighty-five. Male without gibbous nape. Twelve to thirty inches in length.

Bluish, darker above, with yellow and black spots, circles; and streaks in life, rapidly fading on death. Young generally solid dusky or with irregular dark bars on sides. The caudal and pelvic fin margins are pale.

An uncommon pelagic species seldom caught by fishermen. Few records from within our area.

The specific name is commonly spelled *equiselis*.

262. DOLPHIN
Coryphaena hippurus Linnaeus

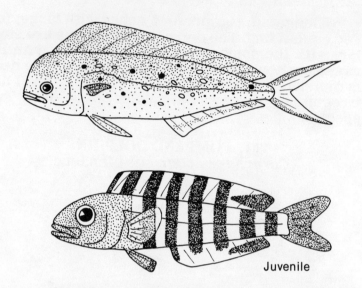

Juvenile

Dorsal elements usually more than fifty-six. Lateral line scales generally two hundred or more, usually about two hundred and sixty. Nape gibbous in adult males. Two to five feet long.

Beautifully colored in life with yellow and black on silvery blue; fades upon death to a silvery blue. The young are generally strongly barred with dark on a silvery ground. The caudal and pelvic fin margins are dark.

A very common and popular sport fish. Any dolphin over thirty inches or with a gibbous nape is this species.

Family LUTJANIDAE — the snappers

"Typical" fishes with three anal spines, a forked caudal fin, and usually a notched dorsal fin. A strong canine usually present in each upper jaw. Maxillary slipping beneath suborbital when the mouth is closed, separating the snappers from the serranids. Thirteen species.

214

The genera of this family are few and easily distinguished, but the ten species of *Lutjanus* are far from simple to identify.

D. X; dorsal and anal without scales ....
.... *Pristipomoides*

D. X; dorsal and anal scaled basally; caudal very deeply forked; yellow lateral stripe ....
.... *Ocyurus*

D. IX-XI; dorsal and anal scaled; caudal moderately forked .... *Lutjanus*

D. XII; dorsal and anal scaled ..... *Rhomboplites*

263. MUTTON SNAPPER
Lutjanus analis (Cuvier)

Vomerine patch

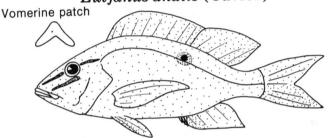

D. IX to XI,13-14; A. III,7-8. Anal fin pointed, the middle rays extending beyond the posterior rays. Canines small. Vomerine teeth in a crescent-shaped patch. Olivaceous, sometimes barred. Fins red. Blue stripes from eye onto snout. A distinct black lateral spot present at all sizes. One to two-and-a-half feet in length.

Not uncommon over hard bottoms.

264. SCHOOLMASTER
Lutjanus apodus (Walbaum)

Vomerine patch

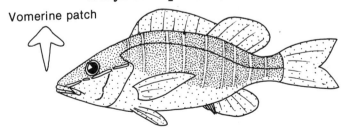

D. X,14; A. III,8. Anal fin rounded. Upper canines stronger than the lower, large. Vomerine teeth in anchor-shaped patch. Five to six rows of scales between dorsal fin base and lateral line. Depth of body 2.4 to 2.7 in standard length; pectoral fin longer than the distance from the tip of the snout to the preopercle. Olive to brown, lighter below, with narrow light vertical bars. Fins yellow. No triangular light bar below eye. Black lateral spot absent. One or two feet long.

Not uncommon over hard bottoms.

265. BLACKFIN SNAPPER
Lutjanus buccanella (Cuvier)

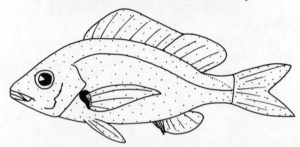

D. X,14; A. III,8. Anal fin rounded. A large, constant, black comma-shaped spot present at axilla of pectoral fin. Lateral black spot absent. Red above, silvery below. Fins yellow to red. One to two feet in length.

An uncommon to rare resident of deep offshore snapper banks and hard bottoms.

266. RED SNAPPER
Lutjanus campechanus (Poey)

Vomerine patch

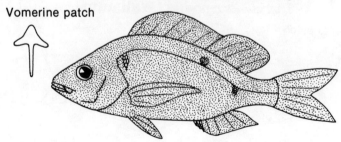

D. X,14; A. III,9. Anal fin pointed. Vomerine teeth in an anchor-shaped patch. Scales below lateral line larger anteriorly than posteriorly. Reddish, the fins also red; silvery overtones. Black lateral spot present until length of one to one-and-a-half feet. Iris red. Two to three feet long.

A common and important game and commercial fish. Common over hard bottoms, its preferred habitat commonly known as snapper banks. Extends to about eighty fathoms deep.

This is the more familiar *L. aya* and *L. blackfordi* of the literature.

267. CUBERA SNAPPER
Lutjanus cyanopterus (Cuvier)

Vomerine patch

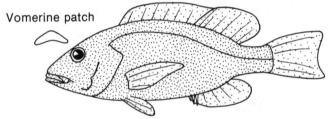

D. X,14; A. III,7-8. Anal fin rounded. Lower canines as strong as the upper, both sets large. Vomerine teeth in a crescentic patch. Lips thick. Grayish to reddish; no black lateral spot. Two to four feet long.

Apparently a very rare fish in the northern Gulf, the few records from deeper water. Perhaps confused with the gray snapper.

268. GRAY SNAPPER
Lutjanus griseus (Linnaeus)

Vomerine patch

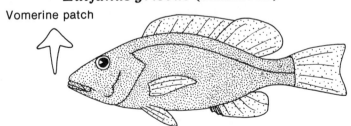

D. X,14; A. III,7-8. Anal fin rounded. Upper canines larger than the lower. Vomerine teeth in an anchor-shaped patch. Body depth 2.7-3.1 in standard length; pectoral fin short, about equal to length from tip of snout to upper preopercular margin. Olivaceous, usually with some rusty scales giving a spotted effect. No black lateral spot. One to three feet long.

A common fish both inshore and over deeper hard bottoms.

269. DOG SNAPPER
Lutjanus jocu (Bloch & Schneider)

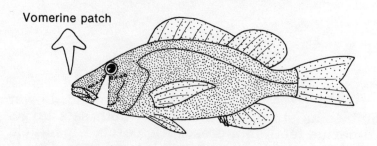

Vomerine patch

D. X,13-14; A. III,8. Anal fin rounded. Canines large, prominent, the upper larger than the lower. Vomerine teeth in an anchor-shaped patch. Body depth about 2.4-2.7 in standard length; pectoral fin longer than the snout to preopercle distance. Eight to eleven rows of scales between dorsal fin base and lateral line. Olive, the fins red and olive; blue spots or lines below eye. No lateral black spot. A prominent light triangle below the eye in life in the majority of specimens. One to two-and-a-half feet long.

Uncommon; hard bottoms.

270. MAHOGANY SNAPPER
Lutjanus mahogoni (Cuvier)

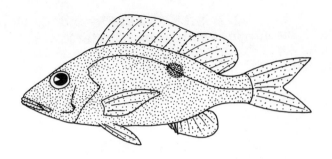

D. X,12; A. III,8. Anal fin rounded. Lower lobe
of preopercle large. A black lateral spot throughout life, extending below lateral line. Reddish-ol-
ive above, silvery below; fins red. Fifteen inches
long.

A tropical species found in our area mostly on
the west coast of Florida.

271. LANE SNAPPER
Lutjanus synagris (Linnaeus)

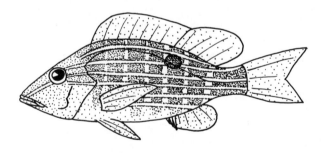

D. X,12; A. III,8. Anal fin rounded. Lower lobe
of preopercle small, not projecting. A black lateral spot throughout life, its lower margin not extending much below lateral line. Reddish pink, with
eight horizontal or oblique narrow yellow lines on
sides. Ten to fifteen inches.

A common and colorful small snapper on
shallow, usually hard, bottoms.

272. SILK SNAPPER
Lutjanus vivanus (Cuvier)

Vomerine patch

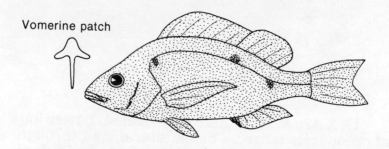

D. X,13-14; A. III,8. Anal fin pointed. Vomerine teeth in anchor-shaped patch. Scales below lateral line anteriorly about the same size as those posteriorly. Black lateral spot present until a size of one or one-and-a-half feet. Silvery red with narrow yellow lines between the scale rows. Fins red. Iris yellow. One to three feet in length.

Although this is a deepwater fish common only in water over ninety fathoms deep, it is included here because of its presence in commercial and sporting catches of red snappers and because of its general confusion with *L. campechanus.*

273. YELLOWTAIL SNAPPER
Ocyurus chrysurus (Bloch)

Vomerine patch

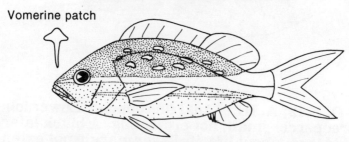

D. X,13. A. III,9. Teeth weak. Anal fin rounded. Caudal fin deeply forked, with long pointed lobes. Mouth comparatively small. Vomerine teeth in an an anchor-shaped patch. Dorsal and anal fins basally with scales, as in *Lutjanus.* Silvery, the caudal fin, caudal peduncle, and a broad midlateral stripe from eye to peduncle bright yellow. Large yellow spots above lateral line. Fins yellowish. One to two-and-a-half feet in length.

This is a common schooling species near reefs, but in the northern Gulf it appears to be rare other than on the west coast of Florida. There are scattered records, however, from offshore hard bottoms.

274. WENCHMAN
Pristipomoides aquilonaris (Goode & Bean)

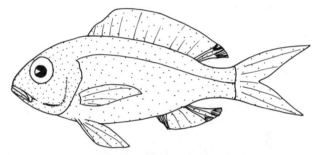

D. X,11; A. III,8. A large-headed snapper with a flattened interorbital. The dorsal and anal fins are scaleless, even basally, and the last dorsal and anal ray are distinctly longer than the preceding ray. Reddish and silvery. One to two feet long.

A deepwater species not uncommon over hard bottoms in about fifteen to ninety fathoms. *P. andersoni* is this species.

275. VERMILION SNAPPER
Rhomboplites aurorubens (Cuvier)

Vomerine patch

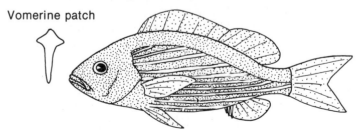

D. XII,11; A. III,8. Dorsal and anal fins with scales basally. Caudal fin forked. Anal fin rounded. Last dorsal and anal ray short. Vermilion, with narrow yellowish horizontal lines on the sides. Fins mostly red. One to two-and-a-half feet.

A common fish on deeper hard bottoms, often caught with red snapper on the snapper banks. Usually in more than fifteen fathoms.

References: Anderson, W.D., 1967 (*U.S. Fish and Wildlife Circular #252*); Rivas, L.R., 1966 (*Quart. Journ. Fla. Acad. Sci.*, 29(2):119-136).

Family **LOBOTIDAE** — tripletail

A single species in the northern Gulf.

276. TRIPLETAIL
Lobotes surinamensis (Bloch)

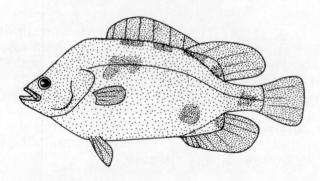

Body highly compressed, sunfish-like. Soft dorsal and anal fins rounded, equalling the caudal fin in length and shape. Mouth low on head, rather large. Preopercle with strong spines, especially in the young. One to three-and-a-half feet long. Brownish, mottled with darker. Young with black spots. Caudal fin transparent distally in the young.

A common gamefish. The young are sometimes associated with floating debris.

Family GERREIDAE — mojarras

Silvery fishes with two or three weak anal spines. Caudal fin deeply forked. Head pointed, the mouth small. Premaxillaries extremely protractile, sliding into grooves in the forehead; a naked interorbital area marks the extent of the premaxillaries. Four species.

277. SPOTFIN MOJARRA
Eucinostomus argenteus Baird & Girard

Head
(dorsal)

A. III,7; the spines weak. Lateral line scales 44 to 48. Body slender, the depth 2.6 to 3.1 in standard length. Premaxillary groove open, without scales closing or nearly closing it anteriorly; scales extend to nostrils. Silvery, with irregular bars and blotches above the lateral line, especially in young. Five to eight inches long.

A moderately common inshore fish.

278. SILVER JENNY
Eucinostomus gula (Quoy & Gaimard)

Head
(dorsal)

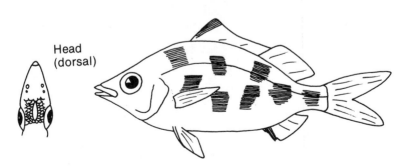

A. III,7; spines weak. Body deeper, the depth 2.2 to 2.6 in standard length. Premaxillary groove closed by scales anteriorly, leaving a naked pit behind. If groove not completely closed, it is definitely narrowed down by scales. Silvery, the young with dark bars and blotches extending below lateral line. Four to seven inches in length.

A common species, the young in bays and the adults in higher salinity waters.

279. MOTTLED MOJARRA
Eucinostomus lefroyi (Goode)

A. II,8; spines weak. Body usually slender, depth 3.1 to 3.6 in standard length. Premaxillary groove open. Silvery, with blotches and bars. Five to nine inches in length.

This is generally a tropical species, with few records from the northern Gulf. It is easily confused with the spotfin mojarra in body shape, but differs in having only two anal spines. Often placed in the genus *Ulaema*.

280. YELLOWFIN MOJARRA
Gerres cinereus (Walbaum)

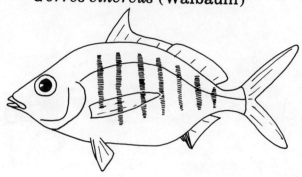

A. III,7; spines weak. Lateral line scales 39 to 44. Body deep, the depth 2.3 to 2.7 in the standard length. Premaxillary groove broad, open, the scales not extending below eye. Pelvic fin relatively long; lobe of spinous dorsal fin high and pointed, the dorsal fins only shallowly notched. Silvery, with seven narrow vertical bars. Pelvic fins yellow. Six to fifteen inches long.

A tropical species usually associated with reefs and sandy bottoms. Not common in the northern Gulf of Mexico.

Family **POMADASYIDAE** — grunts

A variable family which is hard to define. Body usually thick or only moderately compressed. Lateral line not extending onto the caudal fin. Three anal spines. Head usually pointed. Twelve or thirteen dorsal spines; anal III,7-13. Teeth absent on vomer and those in jaws not modified into molars posteriorly or incisors anteriorly. Nine species, only two common in the northern Gulf.

281. BLACK MARGATE
Anisotremus surinamensis (Bloch)

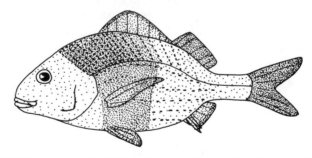

D. XII,16-18; A. III,9. Second anal spine enlarged, strong. Body deep, the mouth small, not red within; lips thick. Dorsal fin deeply notched. Scales above lateral line large, oblique. Head rounded. Gray, either uniform or with a broad

225

black blotch below the lateral line anteriorly. Fins dark. Young with a black caudal spot separate from the dark lateral stripe; a dark line from nape to under soft dorsal fin. One to two feet long.

A tropical species rarely found along the northern Gulf; generally on offshore reefs or hard bottoms.

282. BARRED GRUNT
Conodon nobilis (Linnaeus)

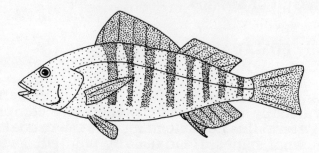

D. XII,13; A. III,7. Second anal spine strong, long. Body elongate. Mouth small, terminal, not red within. Preopercle with large serrae at the angle and antrorse serrae on lower edge. Dorsal spines high. Silvery, with about eight narrow dark bars. Fins dark. Six to twelve inches long.

A tropical species which is sometimes locally common along the southern Texas coast near wharves, jetties, and hard bottoms. Rare further east, but recorded off the Mississippi delta in over ten fathoms.

283. TOMTATE
Haemulon aurolineatum Cuvier

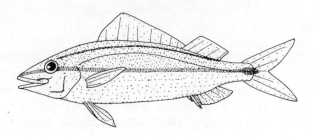

D. XIII, 14-15; A. III,9. Mouth very large, red within. Body compressed, the nape elevated. Scales above lateral line oblique, those below lateral line parallel to body axis. Median fins densely scaled (all *Haemulon*). Silvery, with two prominent bronzy horizontal lines, one from the eye and the other below the dorsal fin. A large black caudal blotch before fin. Five to ten inches long. Color pattern sometimes indistinct.

An uncommon species in our area, usually in moderate water near hard bottoms. The only *Haemulon* species likely to be collected.

This is the *Bathystoma rimator* of older literature.

284. FRENCH GRUNT
Haemulon flavolineatum (Desmarest)

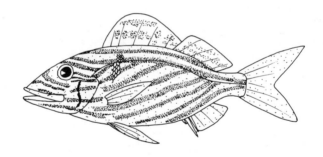

D. XII, 14-15; A. III,8. Mouth very large, red within. Body deep. Scales below lateral line in oblique rows, larger than those above the lateral line. Silvery with broad yellowish stripes, those above lateral line horizontal, those below oblique. Vertical edge of preopercle dark. One foot.

A tropical species rarely recorded from the west coast of Florida.

285. WHITE GRUNT
Haemulon plumieri (Lacepede)

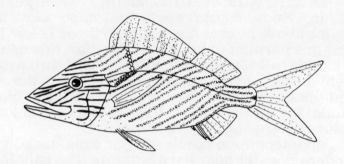

D. XII,15-17; A. III,9. Mouth large, jaws red within. Scales above lateral line larger than those below lateral line. Silvery, the head with blue and yellow stripes; body usually without distinct striping or with narrow yellow stripes. Eight to fifteen inches long.

Tropical, in our area mostly from southwestern Florida, but a few scattered records from the rest of the Gulf.

286. BLUESTRIPED GRUNT
Haemulon sciurus (Shaw)

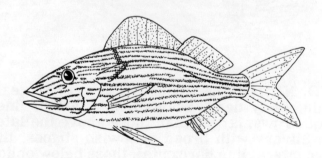

D. XII,16-17; A. III,9. Mouth large, jaws red; body deep. Scales above and below lateral line of same size. Bronzy yellow with many narrow blue stripes from the head to the caudal peduncle. One to one-and-a-half feet in length.

A tropical species rare in the northern Gulf.

287. STRIPED GRUNT
Haemulon striatum (Linnaeus)

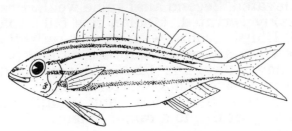

D. XIII,13-14; A. III,8. Mouth rather small, terminal. Body comparatively rounded, not compressed. Scales below lateral line oblique. Yellow, with four narrow black stripes from head to caudal peduncle. Five to nine inches long.

Rare in deep water; a tropical stray.

Juvenile Haemulon:

H. aurolineatum: 13 dorsal spines; scales below lateral line oblique; large caudal spot

H. flavolineatum: 12 dorsal spines; scales below lateral line oblique, larger than those above; caudal spot small, separate from lateral stripe

H. plumieri: 12 dorsal spines; scales above lateral line larger than those below; no black lateral stripe; caudal spot large, mostly on fin

H. sciurus: 12 dorsal spines; scales above and below lateral line same size; black lateral stripe; caudal spot on fin

H. striatum: 13 dorsal spines; scales below lateral line oblique; no caudal spot

288. PIGFISH
Orthopristis chrysoptera (Linnaeus)

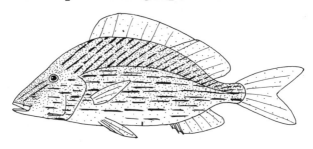

D. XIII,15-17; A. III,12-13. Dorsal fin shallowly notched; anal fin long. Mouth small, snout long, nape elevated. Second anal spine weak. Preopercle weakly serrated. Median fins only sparsely scaled. Bluish bronze with purple reflections in oblique rows above the lateral line and parallel rows below lateral line. Fins dusky except dorsal clear. One to one-and-a-half feet long.

A common fish in bays and usually shallow water. A sport fish to a minor extent.

289. BURRO GRUNT
Pomadasys crocro (Cuvier)

D. XIII,11-12; A. III,7. Second anal spine enlarged, strong. Mouth large, ventral. Preopercle finely serrate, serrae not enlarged or antrorse. Silvery, without a pattern. One to one-and-a-half feet long.

A tropical species very rare in our area.

Reference: Courtenay, W.R., 1961 (*Bull. Mar. Sci.*, 11(1):66-149; *Haemulon*).

Family **SPARIDAE** — porgies

Teeth modified into low, rounded molars posteriorly; anterior teeth often incisors. Often small, forwardly directed (antrorse) spine before the dorsal fin, partially buried in the skin. Dorsal spines eleven or twelve; anal spines three. Head usually rounded in profile. No teeth on vomer. Ten species.

290. SHEEPSHEAD
Archosargus probatocephalus (Walbaum)

D. XI or XII,11-13; A. III,10-11; Ll. 44 to 49. Anterior teeth modified into broad incisors with entire or shallowly notched margins. Body deep, the anterior profile steep. Silvery, with five or six broad black vertical bands. One to two-and-a-half feet long. An antrorse spine before the dorsal.

A common large fish, usually found out to only a few fathoms.

Genus Calamus: Anterior teeth conical, not incisors. An antrorse spine before the dorsal fin. Third dorsal spine short. D. XII,12; A. III,10.

Posterior nostril a long narrow diagonal slit before eye.

291. GRASS PORGY
Calamus arctifrons Goode & Bean

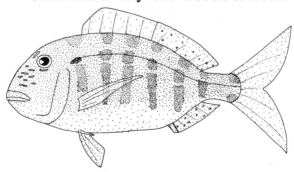

Ll. 43 to 49; no enlarged canine teeth in upper jaw at any size. Pectoral fins relatively short. A black spot at origin of lateral line. Silvery, sometimes with brown bands. Snout brownish with yellow specks. Throat orange. Anterior profile low, rounded. To about eight inches in length.

A relatively common species in grass beds along the shallow (to twelve fathoms) eastern Gulf from Louisiana to Florida.

292. JOLTHEAD PORGY
Calamus bajonado (Bloch & Schneider)

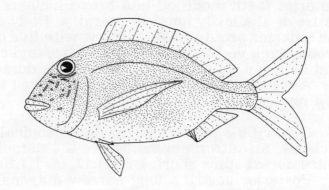

Ll. 50 to 57; enlarged canines in upper jaws of specimens over six inches long. Posterior nostril without a prominent tubercle. Forehead profile low. Body nearly plain silvery. Snout with a few blue specks, no blue horizontal lines. Twelve to twenty inches long.

A tropical species found along the western coast of Florida to Pensacola. Shallow water to twenty-five fathoms.

293. WHITEBONE PORGY
Calamus leucosteus Jordan & Gilbert

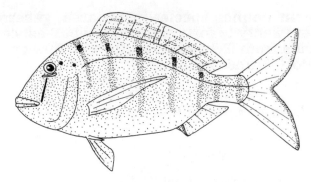

Ll. 43 to 49; upper jaw without enlarged canines at any size. Pectoral fins relatively long. Lateral line without a black spot at its origin. Silvery, with a few dark spots above lateral line, rarely forming bars. Snout without numerous blue or orange spots or stripes. Ten to fourteen inches in length.

Uncommon along the entire Gulf coast in five to fifty fathoms.

294. KNOBBED PORGY
Calamus nodosus Randall & Caldwell

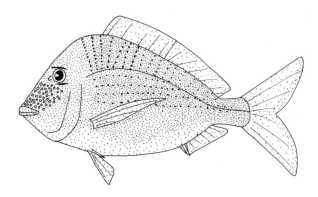

Ll. 52 to 57; upper jaw without enlarged canines. A large and prominent tubercle above the posterior nostril. Forehead steep. Silvery, with rows of small darker spots on body above midline. Snout with many bronzy or yellow spots. Ten to fifteen inches long.

An uncommon species in our area, generally in water twenty to forty fathoms deep. West coast of Florida from Pensacola south, and Texas coast from Port Aransas south.

295. LITTLEHEAD PORGY
Calamus proridens Jordan & Gilbert

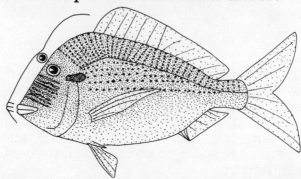

Ll. 50 to 57; upper jaws with enlarged canines in specimens over six inches long. Tubercle of posterior nostril not prominent. Forehead steep, especially so in larger specimens. Silvery, the sides with lines of dark brown spots. A dark horizontal blotch on upper edge of operculum. Snout with prominent blue lines. Ten to fourteen inches in length.

An uncommon species in our area, restricted to the northeastern Gulf in about six to thirty fathoms.

296. SPOTTAIL PINFISH
Diplodus holbrooki (Bean)

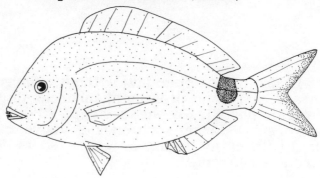

D. XII,14; A. III,13; Ll. 55-57. No antrorse spine before dorsal fin. Anterior teeth broad, unnotched incisors. Body compressed, elliptical. Forehead moderately high. Silvery, with a broad black saddle on caudal peduncle. Six to fourteen inches long.

A rarely collected tropical and Atlantic seaboard species. Most records from Florida. Two species may be involved.

297. PINFISH
Lagodon rhomboides (Linnaeus)

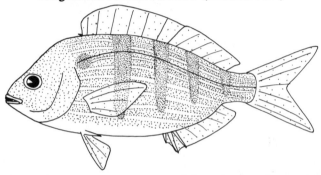

D. XII,11; A. III,11; Ll. 62-66. An antrorse spine before the dorsal. Anterior teeth deeply notched incisors. Body oblong, the nape profile low. Greenish silvery with blue and yellow horizontal stripes and vague dark crossbars. A dark spot on the shoulder. Six to twelve inches in length.

A common fish in bays and inshore areas. Common out to about twenty fathoms.

298. RED PORGY
Pagrus sedecim Ginsburg

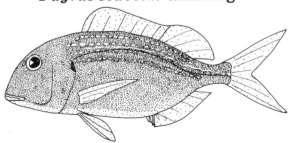

D. XII,9-11; A. III,8; Ll. 56-59. Anterior teeth canine.No antrorse spine before dorsal fin. Posterior nostril oblong, not as narrow as in *Calamus*. Reddish silvery with regular rows of small blue spots on and above the lateral line. Ten to twenty inches long.

Not uncommon off deep snapper banks on the west coast of Florida from Pensacola south. Perhaps more widely distributed.

299. LONGSPINE PORGY
Stenotomus caprinus Bean

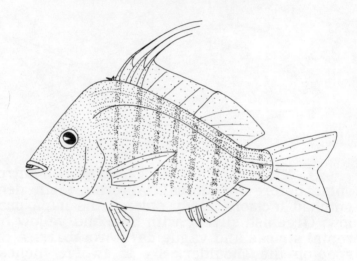

D. XII,12; A. III,12. Front teeth narrow incisors. Third dorsal spine longer than head, flexible. Body oval, the anterior profile steep. An antrorse spine before dorsal fin. Reddish silver with narrow silvery horizontal bands and vague dark vertical bars. Four to six inches.

A very common fish in waters of ten to sixty-five fathoms, rarely to three fathoms and out to one hundred.

Reference: Randall, J.E. and D.K. Caldwell, 1966 (*Bull. L.A. Co. Mus. Nat. Hist. #2; Calamus*).

Family SCIAENIDAE — drums, croakers, seatrout

A family highly variable in body form and shape of dorsal fin, but the anal fin with only one or two weak spines. Lateral line extending onto the caudal fin. One or more barbels often present on the lower jaw. Caudal fin never deeply forked, usually truncate or rounded. Sixteen species, many of great commercial and sporting interest.

300. SILVER PERCH
Bairdiella chrysura (Lacepede)

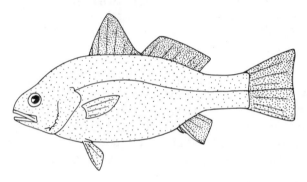

D. XI or XII,19-21; A. II,9-10. Preopercle with strong spines at the angle. Second anal spine very long and strong for a sciaenid, almost as long as anal rays. Body moderately deep, the mouth large; snout separated from nape profile by a distinct depression. Caudal fin truncate; dorsal spines high. No barbels. Uniformly silvery, fins dusky. Six to twelve inches in length.

A common inshore fish often found in bays. A minor panfish.

Seatrouts—*Cynoscion:* Slender bodied, fragile fishes with small scales and the dorsal fins separate. Two enlarged curved canines in the upper jaw near the tip. Caudal fin slightly concave. D. X-I,24-29. This genus and others like it are sometimes placed in the family Otolithidae.

301. SAND SEATROUT
Cynoscion arenarius Ginsburg

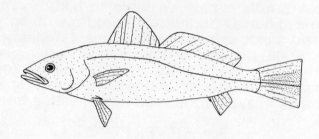

D. X-I,24-27; A. II,10-11. Soft dorsal and anal fin densely scaled. Snout long, equal to or longer than the least depth of the caudal peduncle. Silvery, the body unmarked. Caudal fin with dusky area concentrated at center of fin, yellow above and below. Anal fin often yellow. One to two feet.

A common seatrout in our waters. Although it is often said that this species is most common in shallow water and the similar *C. nothus* is most common in deeper water, I noticed no such difference in the Grand Isle, Louisiana area.

302. SPOTTED SEATROUT
Cynoscion nebulosus (Cuvier)

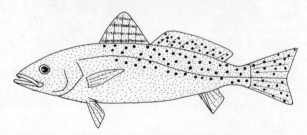

D. X-I,24-26; A. II,10-11. Soft dorsal and anal fins without scales. Silvery, greenish above, with many small round black spots above and on dorsal and caudal fins. One to two-and-a-half feet long.

A common and very popular sport and commercial fish.

303. SILVER SEATROUT
Cynoscion nothus (Holbrook)

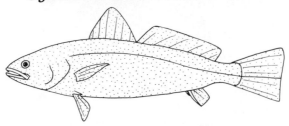

D. X-I,28-29; A. II,8-9. Soft dorsal and anal fins densely scaled. Snout short, its length less than the least depth of the caudal peduncle. Silvery, the body unmarked. Caudal fin with the dark pigment evenly dispersed along the edges of the rays; whole fin with yellow tinges, not just sides. Anal fin usually clear, seldom yellow. One to two feet long.

Common in our waters, both inshore and in deeper waters.

304. JACKKNIFE-FISH
Equetus lanceolatus (Linnaeus)

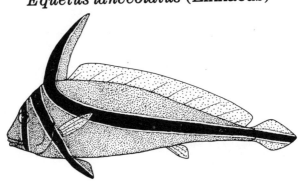

D. XIII or XIV-49-55. Dorsal fins separate. First dorsal fin very high, pointed in adults. Caudal fin pointed. No barbels. Gray with three white-bordered black bands, one through eye, one through operculum, one from first dorsal to caudal fin. Fins light. Six to nine inches long.

A tropical reef fish found in our area mostly off the west coast of Florida.

305. CUBBYU
Equetus umbrosus Jordan & Eigenmann

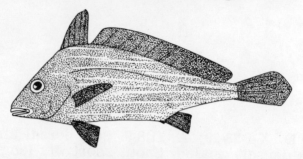

D. X or XI-37-40. First dorsal fin high and rounded. No barbels. Generally a dusky bluish-silver with about seven narrow often broken silver horizontal lines. Fins dark. Four to nine inches.

Apparently restricted to deep offshore snapper banks and reefs in the eastern Gulf, especially off the west coast of Florida.

This fish is very close to the tropical *E. acuminatus* and is probably just a very dark subspecies of that species.

306. BANDED DRUM
Larimus fasciatus Holbrook

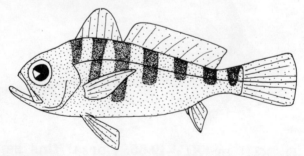

D. X-I,24-27; A. II,6-8. Body stout, snout very short, eye very large. No barbels. Mouth large, very oblique; teeth small. Preopercle not serrated. Second anal spine short and stout. Caudal fin convex (adult) to acute (young). Silvery, with seven to nine vertical black bars. Fins mostly yellow. Six to twelve inches long.

A common drum in waters ten to thirty fathoms deep.

307. SPOT
Leiostomus xanthurus Lacepede

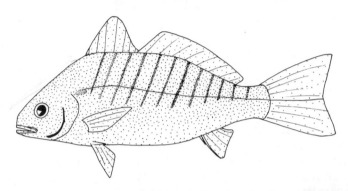

D. X-I,30-34; A. II,12-13. No barbels. Anterior profile high, the snout short and blunt; mouth inferior. Eye comparatively large. Preopercle without serrae, smooth to touch. Second anal spine short and weak. Caudal fin lunate, the lobes pointed. Silvery, darker above, with oblique yellowish bars dorsally. A black spot above pectoral base. Fins yellowish. Eight to fourteen inches in length.

A common fish from estuaries to at least twenty fathoms. Young specimens abundant in shallow water.

Kingfishes—*Menticirrhus:* Body rounded, the profile low. Snout long, overhanging inferior mouth. A single large barbel at symphysis of lower jaw. Dorsal fins separate, the first pointed, X-I, 24-27. Only one weak anal spine; A. I,7-9. Caudal asymmetrical, the lower lobe longer than the upper; shallowly notched.

308. SOUTHERN KINGFISH
Menticirrhus americanus (Linnaeus)

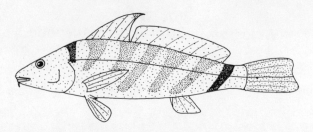

Spinous dorsal fin with the third dorsal spine short, not extending much beyond origin of soft dorsal. Chest scales not reduced, same size as those of sides. Gill cavity dusky. Body dusky silver, with seven or eight vague oblique bars dorsally, the middle bars often very indistinct. No bars fused at nape to form a V. Fins dusky, dorsal margin often narrowly black. One to one-and-a-half feet in length.

Common in bays and moderately deep water.

309. MINKFISH
Menticirrhus focaliger Ginsburg

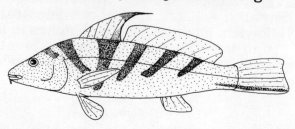

Third dorsal spine very long, greatly exceeding the origin of the soft dorsal fin. Chest scales not reduced compared to scales of sides. Gill cavity dusky. Body dusky, with well defined oblique bars, the second and third fused to form a dark V from nape to side. One to one-and-a-half feet long.

A moderately uncommon species of shallow hard bottoms. Most records come from the eastern Gulf, but there are scattered records throughout our area.

242

310. GULF KINGFISH
Menticirrhus littoralis (Holbrook)

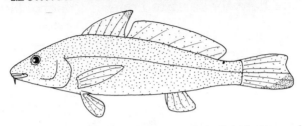

First dorsal with short spines which do not exceed the soft dorsal origin. Chest scales much smaller than scales of sides. Gill cavity pale. Silvery with no dark oblique bars. Fins plain except for black tip of dorsal and dusky lower lobe of caudal fin. Ten to fifteen inches long.

A locally common species which seems to prefer sandy surf areas.

311. ATLANTIC CROAKER
Micropogon undulatus (Linnaeus)

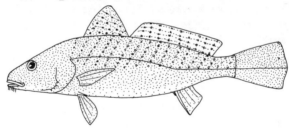

D. X-I,28-29; A. II,8. Lower jaw with short barbels. Body rather elongate, the snout long and somewhat overhanging inferior mouth. Eye small. Preopercle strongly serrate, spiny to touch. Caudal fin double concave in adults, lanceolate in young. Silvery green with many narrow wavy bars composed of small spots; bars often appear bronzy. Fins spotted. Ten to sixteen inches in length; offshore specimens largest.

A very common fish in estuarine waters out to at least twenty or thirty fathoms.

This fish is often confused with the similar and equally common spot. Besides differences in profile, eye size, and caudal shape at all sizes, the smooth preopercle of the spot contrasts greatly with the heavily serrated one of the croaker.

312. BLACK DRUM
Pogonias cromis (Linnaeus)

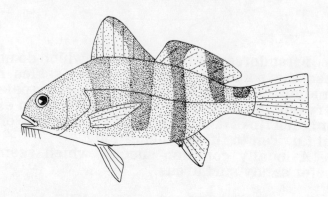

D. X-I,20-22; A. II,6-7. Second anal spine greatly enlarged. Lower jaws with numerous long barbels. Deep bodied, the mouth inferior. Preopercle entire. Caudal fin truncate. Silvery, with four or five dark vertical bars in the young; often with strong bronzy highlights. One to three-and-a-half feet in length.

A common fish in shallow bays and moderately deep water.

313. RED DRUM
Sciaenops ocellata (Linnaeus)

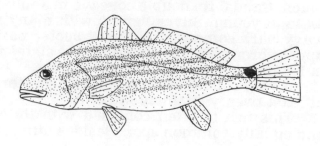

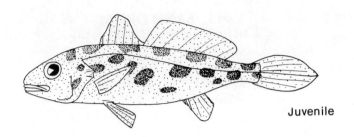

Juvenile

D. X-I,23-25; A. II,8. Chin without barbels.
Body slender, the large mouth inferior. Adult caudal fin truncate, that of juvenile lanceolate. Adult
generally bronzy with vague horizontal stripes
and a large ocellus (occasionally several) on the
upper part of the caudal peduncle. Young usually
with numerous large dark blotches. One to four
feet in length.

A common sportsfish; the young are sometimes common in bays.

314. STAR DRUM
Stellifer lanceolatus (Holbrook)

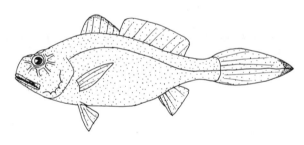

D. XII-I,21; A. II,8. Chin without barbels.
Body deep, eye and snout moderate. Mouth oblique, large, with large teeth. Numerous large
mucous chambers in the skull, giving the area
around the eye a radiated appearance. Preopercle with strong serrations. Caudal fin lanceolate.
Brownish, the tip of first dorsal black. Other fins
plain. Four to seven inches long.

A common little drum from bays to at least
thirty fathoms, but most abundant in more than
ten fathoms.

315. SAND DRUM
Umbrina coroides Cuvier

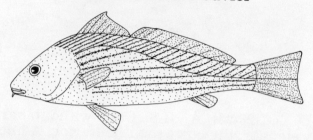

D. X-I,28. A. II,8. Body rounded. Mouth inferior, overhung by snout. Tip of lower jaw with a single large barbel. Dorsal fin low. Caudal fin slightly concave. Silvery, with vague oblique narrow dark stripes on the body, the stripes sometimes almost horizontal. Six to twelve inches long.

A tropical species found only on the extreme southern edges of our range in Florida and Texas. Prefers hard bottoms.

Family **MULLIDAE** — goatfishes

Dorsal fins widely separated, VII(or VIII)-I, 8, the first spine minute. Anal fin II,6. Caudal fin deeply forked. Body with large scales. Two long barbels on tip of lower jaw. Four species.

316. YELLOW GOATFISH
Mulloidichthys martinicus (Cuvier)

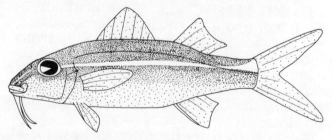

No teeth on roof of mouth. Teeth in two irregular rows at front, a single row posteriorly. Lateral line scales 34 to 39. Silvery, brownish above, with yellow fins and a yellow midlateral stripe. About one foot long.

A tropical species rarely recorded from our area.

317. RED GOATFISH
Mullus auratus Jordan & Gilbert

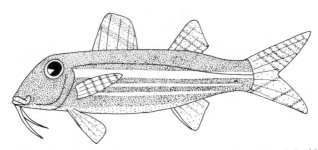

Roof of mouth with peglike teeth. No teeth in upper jaw. Lateral line scales 29 to 35. Reddish on silver, with two narrow yellow bars on side. Fins mostly yellowish or pink. Bars on caudal fin faint, seven or eight. Opercular spine absent. Four to eight inches in length.

An uncommon species in water deeper than ten fathoms.

318. SPOTTED GOATFISH
Pseudupeneus maculatus (Bloch)

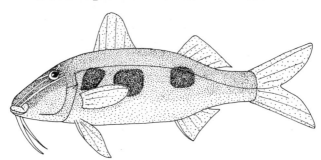

No teeth on roof of mouth. Upper jaw with canines. Opercular spine present. Lateral line scales 27 to 31. Reddish, with three large squarish blackish blotches on sides. Caudal not banded. Six to ten inches in length.

Uncommon, usually in fifteen or more fathoms.

319. DWARF GOATFISH
Upeneus parvus Poey

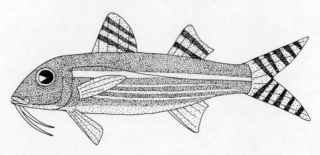

Roof of mouth with peglike teeth. Upper jaw with canines. No opercular spine. Lateral line scales 36 to 38. Red, with a broad yellow midlateral stripe and several narrower yellow stripes below this. Dorsal fin with black stripes. Caudal lobes with three to five prominent black bands. Three to six inches.

Our only truly common goatfish, but generally found only from twenty to sixty fathoms deep. Young up to almost four inches may remain silvery and pelagic. Adults are bottom dwellers.

Family **KYPHOSIDAE** — sea chubs

Only one species reported from the northern Gulf.

320. BERMUDA CHUB
Kyphosus sectatrix (Linnaeus)

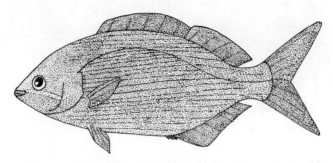

Oval, deep-bodied fish with a small terminal mouth with incisor teeth. Caudal fin deeply forked. Dorsal and anal fins low, with heavy basal sheaths of scales and skin. D. XI,12, not deeply notched, the spines low. A. III,11. Ll. 51 to 58. Dark gray with dull yellow stripes on body. One to one-and-a-half feet in length.

A tropical species but sometimes found as adults in our area. Most common near oil rigs and hard bottoms in clear water. Divers report that large schools of this species occur off Louisiana.

Family **EPHIPPIDAE** — spadefishes

One common species in our area.

321. ATLANTIC SPADEFISH
Chaetodipterus faber (Broussonet)

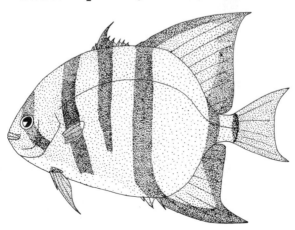

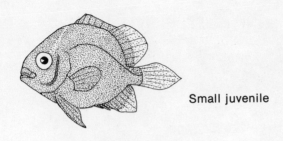

Small juvenile

Body round, the caudal peduncle short. Teeth brushlike; mouth small and terminal. Dorsal IX,21-23, the third spine very elongate in small specimens. Lobes of soft dorsal and anal high in adults. A. III,18-19. Silvery, usually with four to six broad black bands on body, these sometimes broken. Young all black, a phase sometimes seen in large adult specimens as well. One to three feet long.

Common in bays to moderate depths.

Family **CHAETODONTIDAE** — butterflyfishes

Body round or rectangular. Mouth small, terminal, with brushlike teeth. Dorsal and anal spines strong. No strong preopercular spine. Color usually silvery with yellow and black pattern. Five species.

Tholichthys larva of *Chaetodon.*

Except for the bank butterflyfish, all the species described here are considered to be tropical stragglers rare everywhere in our area. Most records in the northern Gulf are of juvenile or small specimens usually found during summer on hard bottoms.

322. BANK BUTTERFLYFISH
Chaetodon aya Jordan

D. XII,18; A. III,17. Snout longer than in other species. Dorsal and anal spines very high and strong. Silvery, with three broad black bars, the first from tip of snout to between eyes; second from end of mouth through eye to first two dorsal spines; third from fifth to eight dorsal spines downward and backward to base of soft anal fin and then angled down and forward into soft anal. Soft dorsal and face yellow. Three to five inches.

An uncommon deepwater butterflyfish known from hard offshore bottoms only east of the Mississippi delta in five (rare) to twenty-five fathoms.

323. FOUREYE BUTTERFLYFISH
Chaetodon capistratus Linnaeus

Juvenile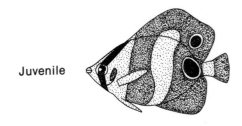

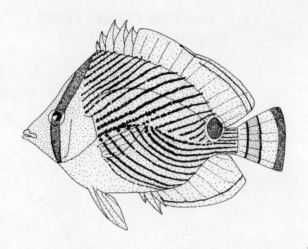

D. XIII,19-20; A. III,16-17. Body round, dorsal fin high. Gray, with narrow black oblique bars in two groups laterally: dorsal group running from head to dorsal profile, ventral group from lateral line to anal base. Black bar through eye. Large white-edged black spot at posterior base of dorsal fin. Caudal black-edged with narrow black lines, as are soft dorsal and anal. Pelvic yellow. Three to six inches.

Young with two ocellated spots, one large one at anterior base of caudal peduncle, other a small one in soft dorsal fin base. Body with two broad dusky bands on sides, running into fins.

324. SPOTFIN BUTTERFLYFISH
Chaetodon ocellatus Bloch

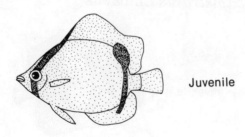

Juvenile

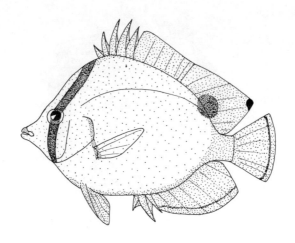

D. XII,19-21; A. III,16-18. Whitish, fins yellow. Black bar through eye. Black spot on body and lower edge of soft dorsal. Small black spot at posterior corner of soft dorsal. Narrow yellow line from upper operculum to pectoral fin base. Body round, the dorsal fin high. Four to eight inches.

Young silvery with a broad black stripe through eye to first dorsal spine and another black bar anterior to caudal peduncle, fading into anal fin below and ending in large round black spot in dorsal base.

325. REEF BUTTERFLYFISH
Chaetodon sedentarius Poey

Juvenile
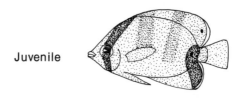

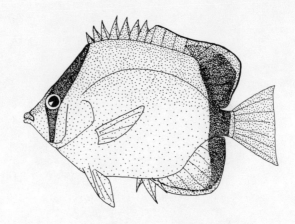

D. XIII or XIV,21-23; A. III,18-19. Body squarish, with relatively low dorsal fin. Silvery heavily washed with yellow dorsally. Black band through eye to first dorsal spine. Broad black band from soft dorsal fin through caudal peduncle onto soft anal, intensity and width varying with size. Caudal fin yellow. Three to six inches long.

Young generally similar, but posterior black band runs from caudal peduncle into anal; soft dorsal nearly unmarked except for small black spot within fin near upper posterior edge.

There may be established populations of this species in the northern Gulf on the offshore coral heads.

326. BANDED BUTTERFLYFISH
Chaetodon striatus Linnaeus

Juvenile

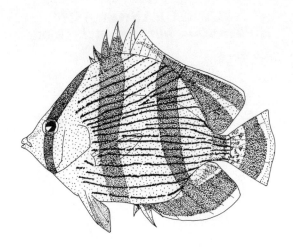

D. XII,21-22; A. III,16-18. Silvery white with pattern of narrow oblique to horizontal black bands on sides. Black bar through eye. Three broad black bars on body, the third extending from soft dorsal base onto caudal peduncle. Broad black submarginal band on caudal fin and soft dorsal and anal. Pelvic fin black. Four to six inches long.

Juveniles like adults but with large ocellated black spot in base of soft dorsal fin.

Family **POMACANTHIDAE** — angelfishes

Round-bodied fishes with small scales. Mouth small, terminal, with bristle-like teeth. Strong spine from lower angle of preopercle. Dorsal and anal fins usually prolonged into filaments. Four species.

The angelfishes are recognized as a distinct family on the basis of evidence recently presented by W. Burgess, 1974 (*Pacific Science*,28(1):57-71).

327. BLUE ANGELFISH
Holacanthus bermudensis Goode

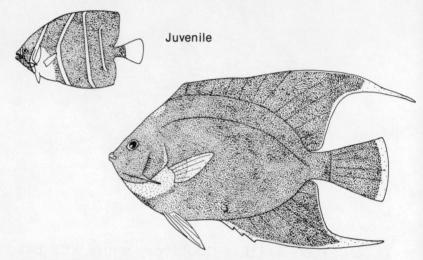

Juvenile

D. XIV,19-21; A. III,20-21. Nape and pectoral base without large ocellated black spots. Body brownish, with pale scale edgings. Caudal brownish with a yellow posterior margin. Fins edged with blue and yellow. *Young:* Three bars on the body, the second straight. One to one-and-a-half feet long.

Apparently a rare straggler on the northern Gulf coast, although divers report large numbers near offshore oil rigs in clear waters.

This species is more commonly known as *Holacanthus* (or *Angelichthys*) *isabelita* in the literature.

328. QUEEN ANGELFISH
Holacanthus ciliaris (Linnaeus)

Juvenile

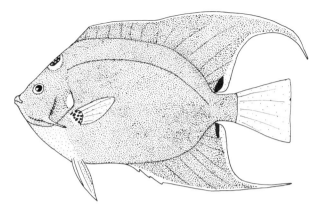

D. XIV,19-21; A. III,20-21. Nape and pectoral base with large blue-edged black spots containing small blue spots. Body blue with yellow scale edgings. Caudal fin entirely yellow. Fin margins blue and yellow. *Young:* Bluish with three blue body bars, the middle (second) one curved. One to one-and-a-half feet in length.

A rare straggler in the northern Gulf; most records are of small adults.

The fish called *Angelichthys townsendi* represents a hybrid between the blue and queen angels.

329. GRAY ANGELFISH
Pomacanthus arcuatus (Linnaeus)

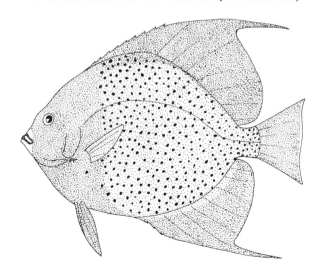

1. *Ginglymostoma cirratum*. A. Norman photo.

33. *Narcine brasiliensis*. P. Colin photo.

13. *Carcharhinus longimanus*. W.A. Starck photo.

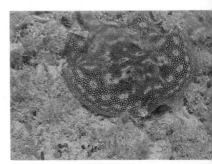

42. *Urolophus jamaicensis*. W.A. Starck photo.

24a. *Sphyrna lewini* (dorsal). S. Shen photo.

43a. *Aetobatus narinari*. G.R. Allen photo.

24b. *Sphyrna lewini* (lateral). S. Shen photo.

43b. *Aetobatus narinari* (head). G.R. Allen photo.

. *Acipenser oxyrhynchus.* H.R. Axelrod photo.

52c. *Anguilla rostrata.* From Evermann & Marsh, *Fishes of Porto Rico.*

: *Lepisosteus spatula.* H.R. Axelrod photo.

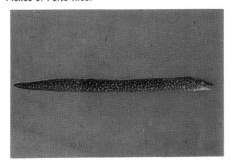

54. *Gymnothorax moringa.* W.A. Starck photo.

a. *Anguilla rostrata.* A. Norman photo.

55. *Gymnothorax n. nigromarginatus.*
W.A. Starck photo.

b. *Anguilla rostrata* (head). A. Norman photo.

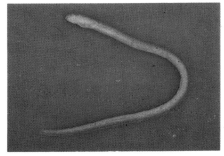

62. *Ahlia egmontis.* W.A. Starck photo.

259

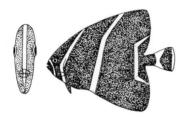

Juvenile, with front view
of head.

D. IX,31-33; A. III,23-25. Body light gray with small black spots on each scale of the body. Head and fins blackish brown. Caudal fin truncate, the corners slightly produced; margin light. Pectoral base without yellow. *Young:* Black with broad yellow bands. Caudal fin yellow with a median, nearly rectangular or semicircular, black spot nearly touching outer fin rays. Yellow line from dorsal base to snout continues through both lips to chin. One to two feet long.

A few records of this tropical straggler are known from our area, but it is rare.

330. FRENCH ANGELFISH
Pomacanthus paru (Bloch)

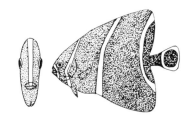

Juvenile, with front view of head.

D. X,29-31; A. III,22-24. Almost uniform velvety black, many of the body scales with narrow golden edgings. Large yellow spot at pectoral base. Caudal fin rounded. *Young:* Body black with broad yellow bars. Caudal fin yellow with nearly circular black spot which does not touch fin margins. Yellow line on snout stops at upper lip. Six to twelve inches long.

Rare along our coast, very few records.

Family **POMACENTRIDAE** — damselfishes

Small, shiny-scaled fishes with only a single nostril on each side of the head. Dorsal with twelve or thirteen spines; two anal spines. Lateral line ending under posterior base of dorsal fin, with about twenty scales. Five species, all rare to uncommon stragglers or inhabitants of deep offshore reefs.

331. SERGEANT MAJOR
Abudefduf saxatilis (Linnaeus)

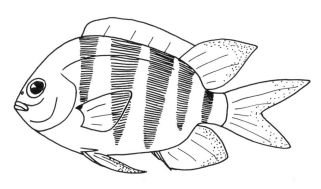

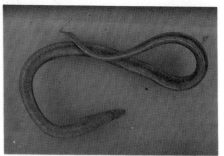

69. *Myrophis punctatus.* W.A. Starck photo.

98. *Synodus intermedius.* W.A. Starck photo.

70. *Mystriophis intertinctus.* W.A. Starck photo.

99. *Synodus poeyi.* W.A. Starck photo.

96. *Saurida normani.* W.A. Starck photo.

100. *Synodus synodus.* W.A. Starck photo.

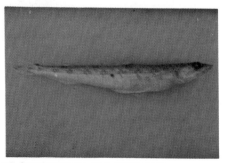

97. *Synodus foetens.* W.A. Starck photo.

101. *Trachinocephalus myops.* W.A. Starck photo.

6. *Porichthys porosissimus* (juv.).
A. Starck photo.

112. *Histrio histrio.* S. Shen photo.

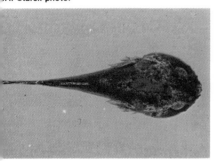

8. *Gobiesox strumosus.* W.A. Starck photo.

113. *Halieutichthys aculeatus.* W.A. Starck photo.

9. *Antennarius ocellatus.* W.A. Starck photo.

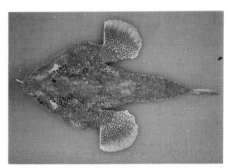

115. *Ogcocephalus radiatus.* W.A. Starck photo.

. *Antennarius scaber.* A. Norman photo.

116. *Ogcocephalus* sp. A. W.A. Starck photo.

263

Preopercle smooth. D. XIII,12-13; A. II,12-13. Ll. 21. Bluish white, washed with yellow or tan dorsally. Five black body bars, straight edged and narrower or about as wide as interspaces. Small black spot at upper base of pectoral. Four to seven inches.

A rare but regular stray to our area. Said to sometimes be locally common on the Texas coast.

The very similar night sergeant, *Abudefduf taurus*, may occur in our area on the west coast of Florida. It is very similar to the sergeant major but has only ten anal rays and the dark body bars *re wider than the narrow light interspaces.

332. YELLOWTAIL REEFFISH
Chromis enchrysura Jordan & Gilbert

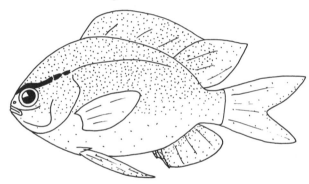

Deep-bodied fish with conical teeth and a smooth preopercle. The caudal rays are continued onto the caudal peduncle as a few short, pointed spines on each edge. Body olive-bluish, lighter below, with the soft dorsal and caudal fin yellow. A bright blue line over the eye. About four inches long.

An uncommon inhabitant of deepwater reefs and hard bottoms of the Florida west coast from Pensacola south.

333. PURPLE REEFFISH
Chromis scotti Emery

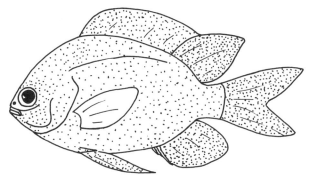

Deep-bodied and with conical teeth. The caudal rays present as short spines on edges of caudal peduncle. Preopercle smooth. Body deep purplish blue, the fins darker. About four inches.

Uncommon fish on offshore reefs of west coast of Florida north to Pensacola.

334. BEAUGREGORY
Eupomacentrus leucostictus Muller & Troschel

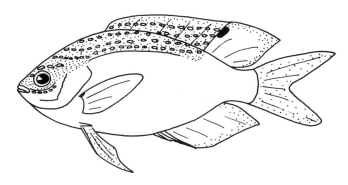

Anterior teeth incisors. Preopercle serrated. Caudal rays not continued onto edges of peduncle. About two greatly enlarged scales between edge of preopercle and edge of opercle. *Adult:* Dusky with a pale tail. Never a spot on caudal peduncle. *Young:* Yellow with a bluish wash on head and dorsum. A blue line on the head and blue spots on head, dorsum, caudal peduncle, and dorsal fin. A small oval dorsal spot toward anterior edge of soft dorsal. Two to four inches.

124. *Brotula barbata.* W.A. Starck photo.

133b. Pearlfish and host sea cucumber. W.A. Starck photo.

127. *Lepophidium jeannae* (juv.). W.A. Starck photo.

141. *Hemiramphus balao.* W.A. Starck photo.

130. *Ophidion holbrooki.* W.A. Starck photo.

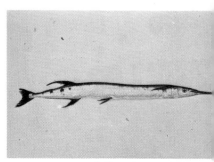

147a. *Ablennes hians.* S. Shen photo.

133a. *Carapus bermudensis.* W.A. Starck photo.

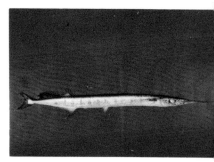

147b. *Ablennes hians* (juv.). S. Shen photo.

266

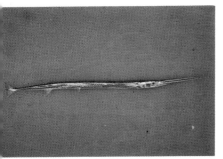

148. *Platybelone argalus*. W.A. Starck photo.

154. *Cyprinodon variegatus* (female).
A. Norman photo.

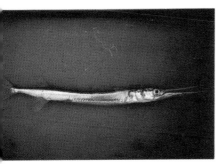

150. *Strongylura notata*. W.A. Starck photo.

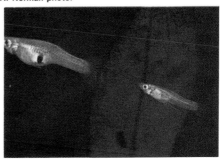

162. *Gambusia affinis*. K. Knaack photo.

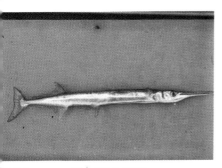

152. *Tylosurus* sp. W.A. Starck photo.

163. *Heterandria formosa*. R. Zukal photo.

153. *Adinia xenica*. A. Norman photo.

164. *Poecilia latipinna* (male). K. Paysan photo.

267

A rare straggler in the northern Gulf, usually seen as juveniles.

335. COCOA DAMSELFISH
Eupomacentrus variabilis (Castelnau)

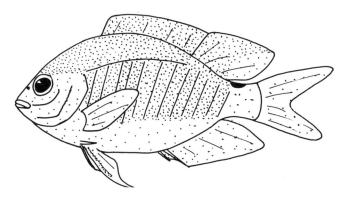

Anterior teeth incisors; preopercle serrated; caudal rays not continued onto peduncle. About three or four moderately large scales between edge of preopercle and edge of opercular membrane. *Adults:* Generally dusky, lighter below, often with a small black spot on upper edge of caudal peduncle. *Young:* Bluish olive above, yellow below, with numerous blue spots and lines on head and dorsally. Black spot on upper edge of caudal peduncle. Sometimes a black spot between soft and spinous dorsal fins, very low, almost on body. Two to four inches in length.

Rare in the northern Gulf.

Several other species of *Eupomacentrus* (sometimes placed in the genus *Pomacentrus*) are possible in our area, especially as juveniles. Because this is a complicated group and there seem to be no reliable records of other species from our area, they are not covered here.

Family **LABRIDAE** — wrasses

Colorful fishes with large scales, about twenty-five to thirty-five in the usually interrupted lateral line. Dorsal fin continuous, with strong spines; anal III,10-21. Teeth usually a few anteriorly slanted canines plus some anterior incisors. Six species, all rare in our area.

336. GREENBAND WRASSE
Halichoeres bathyphilus (Beebe & Tee-Van)

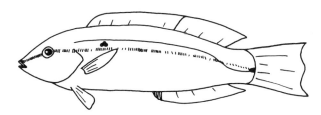

D. IX,11; A. III,12; Ll. 27 (all our species). Caudal fin truncate to doubly emarginate. Tan to pinkish, the fins blue and yellow. A dark brown to black spot on body between lateral line and upper edge of pectoral fin, the spot sometimes bi- or trilobed. A narrow dark greenish stripe sometimes present from tip of snout through eye to middle of caudal base. A small black spot often present at middle of caudal base. Five to eight inches in length.
A rare or uncommon species in deep water (fifteen to eight-five fathoms) from the Florida panhandle south.

337. SLIPPERY DICK
Halichoeres bivittatus (Bloch)

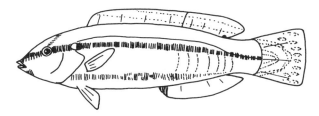

167a. *Holocentrus ascensionis.* J.E. Randall photo.

172. *Aulostomus maculatus.* W.A. Starck photo.

167b. *Holocentrus ascensionis.* From Evermann & Marsh, *Fishes of Porto Rico.*

175. *Hippocampus erectus.* W.A. Starck photo.

168. *Holocentrus bullisi.* W.A. Starck photo.

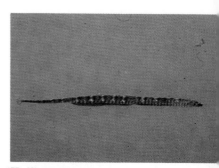

177. *Micrognathus crinigerus.* W.A. Starck photo.

169. *Holocentrus vexillarius.* J.E. Randall photo.

181. *Syngnathus fuscus.* A. Norman photo.

270

87. *Centropomus undecimalis.* W.A. Starck photo.

195. *Epinephelus adscensionis.* W.A. Starck photo.

1. *Centropristis striata* (juv.). A. Norman photo.

198a. *Epinephelus guttatus.* J.E. Randall photo.

93. *Diplectrum bivittatum.* W.A. Starck photo.

198b. *Epinephelus guttatus.* From Evermann & Marsh, *Fishes of Porto Rico.*

94. *Diplectrum formosum.* W.A. Starck photo.

199. *Epinephelus itajara.* W.A. Starck photo.

271

Caudal fin round to truncate. Greenish and silvery, with blue and yellow touches in the fins. Two scalloped or regularly broken black lines, the upper one most distinct. Upper line runs from upper snout through eye to caudal base. Lower stripe from lower corner of operculum above pelvic base to posterior edge of anal fin. A pale-bordered spot, green anteriorly and black posteriorly, in top stripe at upper edge of opercle. Broad salmon lines in front and above eye and on chin. Area between dark stripes whitish. Four to nine inches long.

Offshore reefs from Pensacola south; also scattered records from other more westerly points in our area. Rare.

338. PAINTED WRASSE
Halichoeres caudalis (Poey)

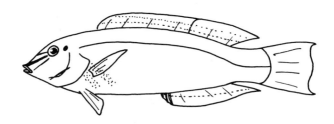

Caudal doubly emarginate. A dark spot (green, bordered with blue in life) slightly behind eye. Greenish, blue below, with rows of olive spots along sides. Narrow blue lines from eye and a pair of oblique diffuse blue parallel lines at pectoral base. Four to seven inches long.

A rare species of offshore reefs from Pensacola south and also from the central Texas coast. Generally in fifteen to forty fathoms.

339. PEARLY RAZORFISH
Hemipteronotus novacula (Linnaeus)

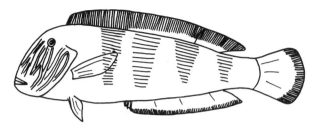

Body deep, the forehead rising at a sharp angle to axis of body. Dorsal fin long, beginning on nape; D. IX,12; A. III,12. Lateral line interrupted, about 19 to 22 + 5 or 6. Caudal peduncle very deep. Greenish above, orangish below, the fins red and green. Alternating vertical blue and orange lines on head below eye. Six to ten inches long.

A rare species in our area, but a few records from relatively shallow sandy and hard bottoms. The *Xyrichthys psittacus* of older literature.

340. HOGFISH
Lachnolaimus maximus (Walbaum)

D. XIV,11; A. III,10; Ll. 32-34. Body deep, compressed. First three dorsal spines very long, even in small juveniles longer than remaining spines. Caudal lunate in adults. Soft dorsal and anal fins with long pointed lobes. Usually a small black spot below the last few dorsal rays. Caudal fin with dark bars or fused spots. Body brownish,

200a. *Epinephelus morio*. W.A. Starck photo.

205. *Hypoplectrus chlorurus*. J.E. Randall photo.

200b. *Epinephelus morio*. From Evermann & Marsh, *Fishes of Porto Rico*.

206. *Hypoplectrus puella*. J.E. Randall photo.

202. *Epinephelus niveatus*. U.E. Friese photo.

206Xa. *Liopropoma mowbrayi*. J.E. Randall photo.

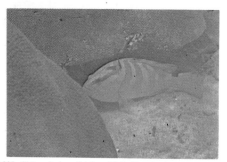

203. *Epinephelus striatus*. W.A. Starck photo.

206Xb. *Liopropoma rubre*. J.E. Randall photo.

274

207. *Mycteroperca bonaci.* W.A. Starck photo.

211. *Mycteroperca venenosa.* J.E. Randall photo.

208. *Mycteroperca microlepis.* W.A. Starck photo.

212. *Paranthias furcifer.* J.E. Randall photo.

209. *Mycteroperca phenax.* W.A. Starck photo.

213. *Petrometopon cruentatum.* W.A. Starck photo.

210. *Mycteroperca rubra.* J.E. Randall photo.

216. *Serranus phoebe.* W.A. Starck photo.

275

red, or silvery, usually with vague bars or mottling. Adult males sometimes with distinct black band from snout over nape to caudal peduncle. One to three feet long.

This distinctive fish seems to be rare in our area, but divers report it to be present on offshore reefs and oil rigs. One of the few fishes which eats sponges.

341. BLUEHEAD
Thalassoma bifasciatum (Bloch)

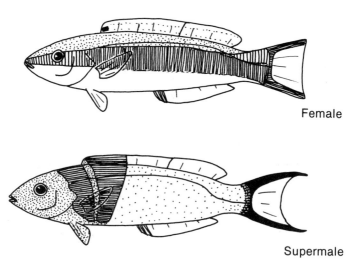

Female

Supermale

D. VIII,13; A. III,11. Ll. continuous, with twenty-six pored scales. Color highly variable with age and sex. *Small:* A black midlateral stripe continued as red blotches on head; back with yellow or white stripe, the venter white; black spots at front of dorsal and at upper pectoral base. *Intermediate:* Black lateral stripe broken into squarish blotches. *Large (supermales):* Head blue, followed by two broad black bands separated by a blue interspace; remainder of body green. Caudal fin shallowly concave to deeply lunate. Two to six inches long.

This common tropical reef fish is rare in our area, there being few reliable records.

Family SCARIDAE — parrotfishes

Wrasse-like fishes with the teeth fused into a coral-crushing beak. Scales large, 22 to 24 in lateral line. D. IX,10; A. III,9. Five species.

The following key will distinguish the genera:

Teeth still distinct, not completely fused ....
    Depth about 4 or more in standard length......
       ....*Cryptotomus*
    Depth about 3 in standard length ...*Nicholsina*
Teeth fused, their edges giving a bumpy appearance to the plates; lower plate overlapping upper.............................*Sparisoma*
Teeth completely fused; upper plate overlapping the lower.............................*Scarus*

Beaks of: a, *Cryptotomus* and *Nicholsina*; b, *Sparisoma*; c, *Scarus*.

a   b   c

342. BLUELIP PARROTFISH
Cryptotomus roseus Cope

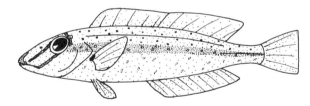

Teeth still distinct in both jaws although partially fused. Snout long and pointed. Body very slender, its depth 4 to 4.6 in standard length. Yellowish brown to green or salmon with reddish and yellow tinges. Blue lines from eye to upper lip. Midlateral salmon band. Body with pink spots. Three or four inches.

An inhabitant of shallow weedy bottoms. In our area seemingly restricted to the west coast of Florida.

218. *Rypticus saponaceus.* A. Norman photo.

221. *Apogon aurolineatus.* W.A. Starck photo.

219a. *Priacanthus arenatus.* W. Hoppe photo.

222. *Apogon maculatus.* J.E. Randall photo.

219b. *Priacanthus arenatus.* From Evermann & Marsh, *Fishes of Porto Rico.*

223. *Apogon pseudomaculatus.* W.A. Starck photo.

220. *Pristigenys alta.* A. Norman photo.

224. *Astrapogon alutus.* W.A. Starck photo.

278

25. *Phaeoptyx conklini.* J.E. Randall photo.

236. *Alectis crinitus* (juv.). S. Shen photo.

227. *Malacanthus plumieri.* W.A. Starck photo.

237a. *Caranx bartholomaei.* J.E. Randall photo.

229. *Rachycentron canadum.* S. Shen photo.

237b. *Caranx bartholomaei* (juv.). A. Norman photo.

230. *Echeneis naucrates.*
O. Terver (Nancy Aquarium) photo.

238a. *Caranx crysos.* W.A. Starck photo.

279

343. EMERALD PARROTFISH
Nicholsina usta (Valenciennes)

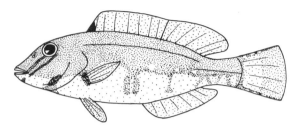

Teeth only partially fused, still distinct. Snout shorter, anterior profile angled. Body deeper, 3 to 3.2 in standard length. Greenish, yellowish below with darker mottling. Dark spots at pectoral base, lower angle of preopercle, and first two dorsal spines. Two orangish lines from eye. Six to twelve inches in length.

West coast of Florida in grass beds.

344. STRIPED PARROTFISH
Scarus croicensis Bloch

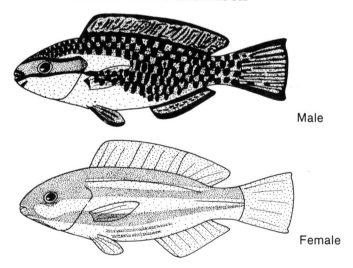

Male

Female

Teeth completely fused, the upper beak overlapping the lower. Body deep. Caudal rounded to truncate with produced corners. *Male:* Blue green dorsally with orange scale edges; pinkish below; two greenish bands through eye; broad pinkish band above pectoral fin. Tail with numerous blue streaks on orange. *Female:* Silvery with three brownish or bluish stripes on sides and two short, narrow reddish stripes very low on body. Ten inches long.

An uncommon fish on offshore reefs from Pensacola south.

345. BUCKTOOTH PARROTFISH
Sparisoma radians (Valenciennes)

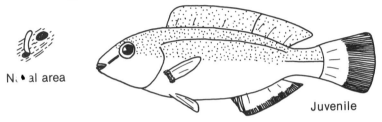

Nasal area

Juvenile

Tooth plates knobby, the lower plate overlapping the upper. Flap of anterior nostril not divided into cirri. Pale tan with reddish brown scales, reddish above. Dark stripe at pectoral base. Male with broad black margins to anal and caudal fin. Orange and blue bands from eye to mouth in males. Four to seven inches long. Caudal rounded.

Rare in our area, the few records being of young individuals mostly from shallow water.

346. STOPLIGHT PARROTFISH
Sparisoma viride (Bonnaterre)

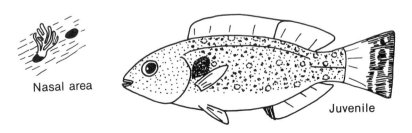

Nasal area

Juvenile

238b. *Caranx crysos.* From Evermann & Marsh, *Fishes of Porto Rico.*

244. *Decapterus punctatus.* W.A. Starck photo.

239. *Caranx hippos* (juv.). A. Norman photo.

245a. *Elagatis bipinnulata.* S. Shen photo.

240. *Caranx latus.* J.E. Randall photo.

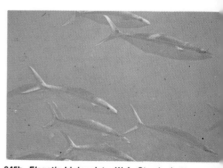

245b. *Elagatis bipinnulata.* W.A. Starck photo.

242. *Caranx ruber.* J.E. Randall photo.

247. *Naucrates ductor* (juv.). S. Shen photo.

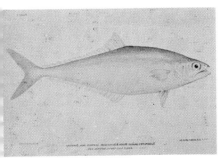

248. *Oligoplites saurus.* From Evermann & Marsh, *Fishes of Porto Rico.*

253. *Seriola rivoliana* (6-inch). W.A. Starck photo.

249. *Selar crumenophthalmus.* A. Norman photo.

255a. *Trachinotus carolinus* (juv.). A. Norman photo.

250. *Selene vomer* (juv.). A. Norman photo.

255b. *Trachinotus carolinus.* From Evermann & Marsh, *Fishes of Porto Rico.*

251. *Seriola dumerili* (10-inch). W.A. Starck photo.

256. *Trachinotus falcatus.* J.E. Randall photo.

Tooth plates knobby, the lower plate overlapping the upper. Flap of anterior nostril divided into four to seven cirri. *Male:* Greenish blue with three diagonal orange bars on head, large yellow spot at caudal base, and a yellow crescent in the caudal fin; dorsal and anal fins yellow and blue. *Female* and *young:* Brown, the fins and venter red; juvenile with the caudal white basally and three rows of pale spots on body and large black spot over pectoral base. Caudal fin rounded to lunate depending on age. Ten to twenty inches long.

Rare in the northern Gulf, usually not distinguished from the bucktooth parrotfish.

Family **MUGILIDAE** — mullets

Silvery fishes with large scales. Dorsal fins widely separated, IV-I,8. Anal fin III,8 or 9. Mouth small, weak, inferior. Pectoral fin set high on body. Pelvic under posterior part of pectoral. Three species.

347. MOUNTAIN MULLET
Agonostomus monticola (Bancroft)

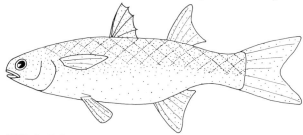

A. III,9. Ll. 40 to 42. Eye not partially covered by a thick, transparent eyelid. Snout longer than eye, projecting over lower jaw, especially in large specimens. Forehead somewhat concave. Olive above with black scale edgings, silver below. Fins yellow. Six to twelve inches.

A tropical species occurring in southern Florida and Texas and reported as juveniles from Louisiana. Enters freshwater.

348. STRIPED MULLET
Mugil cephalus Linnaeus

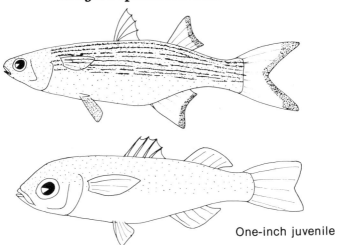

One-inch juvenile

A. III,8. Ll. 38 to 42. A thick, gelatinous adipose eyelid over eye. Soft dorsal and anal without scales or nearly so. Grayish green above, silvery below. Operculum without yellow blotches. Fins dusky yellowish. Sides with dusky lateral stripes. One to two feet long.

An abundant fish in bays to moderately deep water. Penetrates freshwater for many miles.

Juveniles are plain silvery, with anal fin II,9, without visible scales.

349. WHITE MULLET
Mugil curema Valenciennes

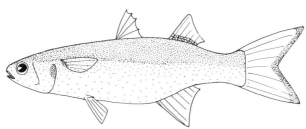

A. III,9. Ll. 35 to 41. Adipose eyelid present. Soft dorsal and anal densely scaled almost to edge. Greenish above, silvery laterally and be-

263a. *Lutjanus analis.* J.E. Randall photo.

263b. *Lutjanus analis.* From Evermann & Marsh, *Fishes of Porto Rico.*

264a. *Lutjanus apodus.* J.E. Randall photo.

264b. *Lutjanus apodus.* From Evermann & Marsh, *Fishes of Porto Rico.*

265. *Lutjanus buccanella.* J.E. Randall photo.

266. *Lutjanus campechanus.* From Evermann & Marsh, *Fishes of Porto Rico.*

267. *Lutjanus cyanopterus.* W.A. Starck photo.

268a. *Lutjanus griseus.* J.E. Randall photo.

286

68b. *Lutjanus griseus.* From Evermann & Marsh, *Fishes of Porto Rico.*

271a. *Lutjanus synagris.* J.E. Randall photo.

69a. *Lutjanus jocu.* W.A. Starck photo.

271b. *Lutjanus synagris.* From Evermann & Marsh, *Fishes of Porto Rico.*

69b. *Lutjanus jocu.* From Evermann & Marsh, *Fishes of Porto Rico.*

272. *Lutjanus vivanus.* W.A. Starck photo.

270. *Lutjanus mahogoni.* J.E. Randall photo.

273a. *Ocyurus chrysurus.* W.A. Starck photo.

287

low. No dusky striping. Prominent yellow blotch at upper edge of operculum when living or freshly dead. Fins yellowish. Young silvery, A. II,10. One to two feet long.

A common fish which seems to prefer somewhat higher salinity than the striped mullet, but the two overlap broadly in ecology.

Mugil trichodon may occur on the west coast of Florida. The fins are densely scaled like those of *Mugil curema*, but the anal count is III,8.

Family SPHYRAENIDAE — barracudas

Elongate, long-jawed fishes with strong teeth. Scales small. Pelvics abdominal. Dorsal fins widely separated, V-I,9; anal I,8. Three species.

350. GREAT BARRACUDA
Sphyraena barracuda (Walbaum)

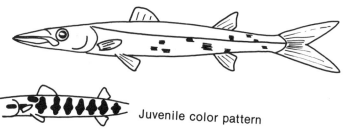

Juvenile color pattern

Over five inches: Origin of first dorsal fin behind pelvic origin; pectoral fin reaches to pelvic origin. Lower jaw without fleshy tip. Scales in Ll. 75 to 87. Anterior soft rays of dorsal and anal extending beyond the posterior rays when depressed. Greenish above, silvery laterally, white below; 18 to 22 dark oblique backwardly directed bars on sides; also some inky irregular blotches on lower sides. *Young:* Fins similar to adults, but anterior rays equal to or longer than posterior rays. Seven to twelve vertical bars, closest in very young, becoming further apart with growth. Opercle with little or no silvery reflection. Reaches three to six feet in length.

The common barracuda throughout our area.

351. NORTHERN SENNET
Sphyraena borealis DeKay

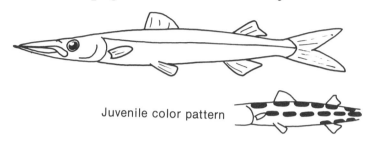

Juvenile color pattern

Over five inches: Origin of first dorsal fin above or slightly in front of pelvic origin; pectoral not reaching pelvics. Lower jaw with fleshy tip. Ll. 110 to 135. Silvery. *Young:* Silvery, with squarish blotches along lateral line. Ten to fifteen inches long.

Found throughout our area, but not common.

352. GUAGUANCHE
Sphyraena guachancho Cuvier

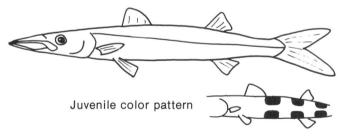

Juvenile color pattern

Over five inches: Origin of first dorsal fin behind the pelvics. Pectoral long. No fleshy tip on lower jaw. Ll. 108 to 114. Anterior fin rays shorter when depressed than posterior rays. Silvery olive with a yellow longitudinal stripe; three encircling black bands in smaller specimens. *Young:* Similar to larger specimens. Three broken dark bands on body forming dorsal and ventral saddles. One to two feet long.

Common throughout our area.

273b. *Ocyurus chrysurus.* From Evermann & Marsh, *Fishes of Porto Rico.*

277. *Eucinostomus argenteus.* W.A. Starck photo.

274. *Pristipomoides* sp. J.E. Randall photo.

278. *Eucinostomus gula.* W.A. Starck photo.

275. *Rhomboplites aurorubens.* J.E. Randall photo.

280. *Gerres cinereus.* W.A. Starck photo.

276. *Lobotes surinamensis.* A. Power photo.

281. *Anisotremus surinamensis.* J.E. Randall photo

290

83. *Haemulon aurolineatum.* J.E. Randall photo.

287. *Haemulon striatum.* W.A. Starck photo.

4. *Haemulon flavolineatum.* W.A. Starck photo.

290. *Archosargus probatocephalus.*
W.A. Starck photo.

5. *Haemulon plumieri.* J.E. Randall photo.

292a. *Calamus bajonado.* W.A. Starck photo.

. *Haemulon sciurus.* J.E. Randall photo.

292b. *Calamus bajonado.* From Evermann & Marsh,
Fishes of Porto Rico.

291

Reference: DeSylva, D.P., 1963(*Stud. Trop. Oceanogr.*, #1).

Family **POLYNEMIDAE** — threadfins

A single common species in the northern Gulf.

353. ATLANTIC THREADFIN
Polydactylus octonemus (Girard)

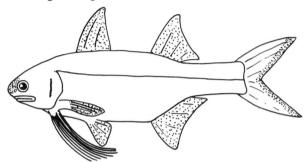

Body compressed, oblong. Dorsal fins widely separated, D. VIII-I,12. Anal fin III,13. Mouth inferior, large, overhung by conical, translucent snout. Caudal fin large, deeply forked. Pectoral fin in two parts, the upper part normal, the lower of eight long free rays. Silvery, fins dusky. Four to twelve inches in length.

Small specimens are common in estuaries and shallow water in spring and summer. Adults are somewhat less common and found in deeper water.

Sometimes still placed in the genus *Polynemus*.

Family **OPISTOGNATHIDAE** — jawfishes

Small fishes with small scales and an incomplete lateral line. Caudal fin rounded or lanceolate. Three anal spines. Dorsal fins continuous. Snout very short; eye large. Maxillary very long. Three species.

354. SWORDTAIL JAWFISH
Lonchopisthus lindneri Ginsburg

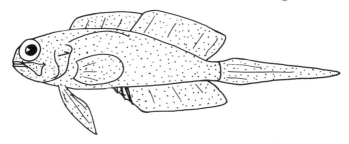

D. XI,19; A. III,16. Lateral scale rows about sixty. Caudal fin long, lanceolate, the rays not branched. Tan, without an opercular spot; fins dusky, narrowly margined with black; a few vague light vertical bars sometimes present anteriorly. Two to four inches long, plus the caudal fin about half as long as the body.

An apparently uncommonly taken species found off Louisiana and Texas in thirty to forty fathoms. May be associated with offshore rubble bottoms.

355. MOUSTACHE JAWFISH
Opistognathus lonchurus Jordan & Gilbert

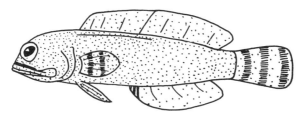

D. X,15; A. III,13. Snout shorter than pupil. Maxillary narrow, extending beyond eye. Caudal fin about as long as head. Lateral scales very small, number variable. Pronounced naked area behind pectoral base. Uniform olive, the fins dusky; caudal with three indistinct bars. A dark brown or black line above upper jaw. Three to four inches long.

294. *Calamus nodosus.* W.A. Starck photo.

305. *Equetus umbrosus.* W.A. Starck photo.

297a. *Lagodon rhomboides.* W.A. Starck photo.

307. *Leiostomus xanthurus.* A. Norman photo.

297b. *Lagodon rhomboides* (juv.). A. Norman photo.

316a. *Mulloidichthys martinicus.* J.E. Randall phot

304. *Equetus lanceolatus.* R. Straughn photo.

316b. *Mulloidichthys martinicus.* From Evermann & Marsh, *Fishes of Porto Rico.*

294

a. *Pseudupeneus maculatus*. W.A. Starck photo.

321b. *Chaetodipterus faber* (subadult). A. Norman photo.

b. *Pseudupeneus maculatus*. From Evermann Marsh, *Fishes of Porto Rico*.

322. *Chaetodon aya*. G.C. Miller photo.

Kyphosus sectatrix. W.A. Starck photo.

323a. *Chaetodon capistratus*. W.A. Starck photo.

. *Chaetodipterus faber*. W.A. Starck photo.

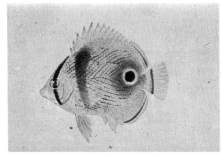

323b. *Chaetodon capistratus* (subadult). From Evermann & Marsh, *Fishes of Porto Rico*.

A very rare species known from thirty to fifty fathoms off Pensacola and the Florida Keys, plus Haiti and Surinam. Obviously more widespread.

The width and shape of the maxillary varies in this species, apparently with sex. *Gnathypops mystacinus* represents the alternate sex with the maxillary extending beyond the operculum.

356. MOTTLED JAWFISH
Opistognathus maxillosus Poey

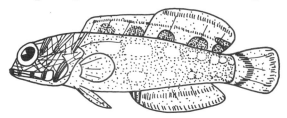

D. XI,15; A. III,15. Lateral scales about 90 to 100. Snout very short. Caudal fin shorter than head. Maxillary relatively short and wide. Body brown, mottled with whitish or tan areas, especially ventrally and on head. Large black spots in base of dorsal fin. Five inches long.

In our area straying northward along the west coast of Florida. Shallow water, rare.

References: Bohlke, J.E. and L.P. Thomas, 1961 (*Bull. Mar. Sci.*, 11(4):503-516); Mead, G.W. 1959 (*Stud. Fauna Suriname*, 2(5):104-112; *Lonchopisthus*).

Family **DACTYLOSCOPIDAE** — sand stargazers

A single rare species in the northern Gulf.

357. SAND STARGAZER
Dactyloscopus tridigitatus Gill

D. XII,28, starting on nape; spines short, graduated. A. II,31-32. Pelvic fin short, I,3, hidden at base under enlarged operculum. Upper edge of operculum with prominent ctenii. Upper lip fringed. Mouth oblique. Eyes small, dorsal, on long and retractile stalks. Scales about forty-five. Translucent with brown mottling above, whitish below. Two to three inches.

Occurs buried in loose sand bottoms in shallow water. Rare in our area, but there are scattered reports from most states. Probably just hard to collect in even the proper habitat.

Family **URANOSCOPIDAE** — stargazers

Mouth very oblique, dorsal, very large; lips generally fringed. Pelvics large, strong, jugular. Eyes dorsal. Top of head bony. Dorsal spines low, few or absent; soft dorsal and anal similar. Three species.

358. SOUTHERN STARGAZER
Astroscopus ygraecum (Cuvier)

Head
(dorsal)

324a. *Chaetodon ocellatus.* J.E. Randall photo.

326a. *Chaetodon striatus.* W.A. Starck photo.

324b. *Chaetodon ocellatus* (prejuv.).
W.A. Starck photo.

326b. *Chaetodon striatus* (subadult). From Everman
& Marsh, *Fishes of Porto Rico.*

325a. *Chaetodon sedentarius.* J.E. Randall photo.

327a. *Holacanthus bermudensis.* J.E. Randall phot

325b. *Chaetodon sedentarius* (subadult).
H.R. Axelrod photo.

327b. *Holacanthus bermudensis* (juv.).
H.R. Axelrod photo.

298

328a. *Holacanthus ciliaris.* W.A. Starck photo.

329b. *Pomacanthus arcuatus* (subadult). W.A. Starck photo.

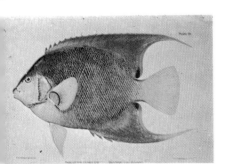

328b. *Holacanthus ciliaris.* From Evermann & Marsh, *ishes of Porto Rico.*

330a. *Pomacanthus paru.* J.E. Randall photo.

328c. *Holacanthus ciliaris* (juv.). H.R. Axelrod photo.

330b. *Pomacanthus paru* (juv.). J.E. Randall photo.

329a. *Pomacanthus arcuatus.* W.A. Starck photo.

331. *Abudefduf saxatilis.* J.E. Randall photo.

299

D. IV-I,12, separate, the first dorsal with very low and strong spines. A. 13. Body with small and embedded scales. Head large, body strongly tapered. Raised skinfold along middle of belly. A Y-shaped area behind and between the eyes. Electric organs behind eyes. Preopercle without spines. Black above, with numerous white spots, especially on head. Venter white. Chin black. Caudal and soft dorsal fin with black and white patterns. Pectoral black with broad white margin. Ten to fifteen inches in length.

A common fish in shallow and moderate depths; especially in sandy bottoms. Burrows in bottom with just the eyes exposed. Two-inch young are common in estuaries in the spring.

359. FRECKLED STARGAZER
Gnathagnus egregius (Jordan & Thompson)

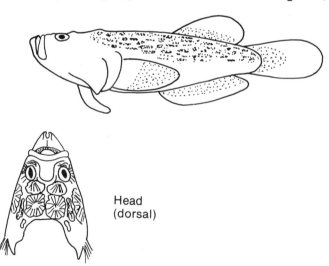

Head
(dorsal)

D. 12-14, spines absent; A. 16-17. Body with scales, these small and embedded in young specimens. Head large, body elongate. Top of head covered with exposed bony plates. Lower jaw with two heavy bony ridges converging anteriorly to form a deep median channel. Head of young with bony knobs. Lower edge of preopercle a long flattened wing-like structure lacking spines. Very young blackish with light fins, the body then becoming brownish with age and developing white specks which tend to form short lateral stripes, especially dorsally. Three to twelve inches in length.

This is a rare deepsea fish whose young (up to about four inches) are rarely found as shallow as thirty fathoms. Adults in one hundred to two hundred and forty fathoms.

As now used, this name includes the *Execestides egregius* of Jordan & Thompson, representing the juvenile, and *Benthoscopus laticeps* Longley & Hildebrand, representing the adult.

360. LANCER STARGAZER
Kathetostoma albigutta (Bean)

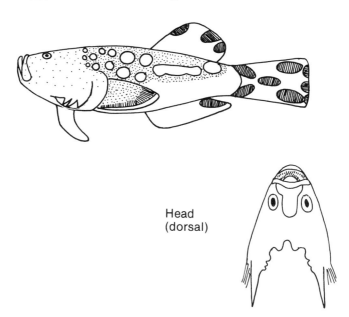

Head
(dorsal)

D. 10, the spines absent; A. 12. Scales absent. Preopercle with three large spines on the lower margin. No bony ridges on lower jaw or Y-shaped area on top of the head. Brownish, the top of the head with small white spots and the body with

331x. *Abudefduf taurus.* A. Norman photo.

334b. *Eupomacentrus leucostictus* (juv.). From Evermann & Marsh, *Fishes of Porto Rico.*

332. *Chromis enchrysura.* W.A. Starck photo.

335. *Eupomacentrus variabilis* (juv.). W.A. Starck photo.

333. *Chromis scotti.* W.A. Starck photo.

337a. *Halichoeres bivittatus* (male). J.E. Randall photo.

334a. *Eupomacentrus leucostictus.* J.E. Randall photo.

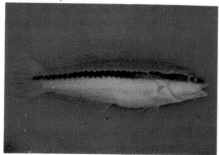

337b. *Halichoeres bivittatus* (female). W.A. Starck photo.

9. *Hemipteronotus novacula.* J.E. Randall photo.

341b. *Thalassoma bifasciatum* (female).
J.E. Randall photo.

0a. *Lachnolaimus maximus.* W.A. Starck photo.

342. *Cryptotomus roseus.* J.E. Randall photo.

40b. *Lachnolaimus maximus* (juv.).
V.A. Starck photo.

344a. *Scarus croicensis* (male). J.E. Randall photo.

341a. *Thalassoma bifasciatum* (male).
W.A. Starck photo.

344b. *Scarus croicensis* (female). J.E. Randall photo.

303

large white spots. Dorsal and caudal fins with black spots. Five to eight inches long.

A deep water fish generally found in over thirty fathoms. Common in deeper water but uncommon in our depth range.

Reference: Berry, F.H. and W.W. Anderson, 1961 (*Proc. U.S. Nat. Mus.*, 112(3448):563-586).

Family **CLINIDAE** — scaled blennies or clinids

Dorsal and anal fins long, the dorsal spines fifteen or more and the rays twelve or less in our species. Pelvics reduced to I,3 or less and inserted in front of the pectorals. Mouth large, terminal. Scales present. Cirri present over eyes and nostrils, at least in males. Three species.

361. HAIRY BLENNY
Labrisomus nuchipinnis (Quoy & Gaimard)

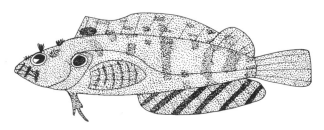

D. XVIII,12; A. II,17-19. Scales small, over sixty in lateral line. Dorsal fin spines rather even in height, highest at middle. Brownish with darker bars and dark and light mottling. Underside of head of males reddish. A large ocellated black spot on upper edge of operculum, very conspicuous. Three to eight inches in length.

A tropical species which in our area seems restricted to rocky jetties and similar habitats. Central and southern coast of Texas.

362. BANDED BLENNY
Paraclinus fasciatus (Steindachner)

D. XXVIII to XXXI, with no segmented rays. A. II,17-20. Lateral line scales large, thirty-two to thirty-eight. Front of dorsal fin with a low lobe followed by a somewhat higher and rounded lobe. Brownish with indistinct darker bars; mottled with dark and light. Posterior part of dorsal fin with large ocellated black spot. Two inches long.

Rare in our area, if it occurs at all. West coast of Florida, hard bottoms.

363. CHECKERED BLENNY
Starksia ocellata (Steindachner)

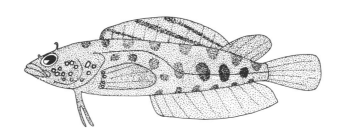

D. XX to XXII,7-9; A. II,16-19, the first two spines enlarged and separate in males, functioning as a copulatory organ. Anterior dorsal spines highest. Lateral line interrupted, with about 35 to 45 scales total. Light tan with variable dark spots over body, most dorsally and behind eye. One-and-a-half inches long.

A sponge dweller reported from the southwest coast of Florida.

345a. *Sparisoma radians* (male). J.E. Randall photo.

348. *Mugil cephalus*. G.R. Allen photo.

345b. *Sparisoma radians* (female). J.E. Randall photo.

349. *Mugil curema*. A. Norman photo.

346a. *Sparisoma viride* (male). J.E. Randall photo.

350. *Sphyraena barracuda*. W.A. Starck photo.

346b. *Sparisoma viride* (female). J.E. Randall photo.

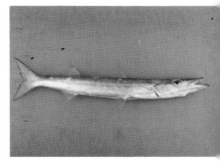

351. *Sphyraena borealis*. W.A. Starck photo.

306

355. *Opistognathus* cf. *lonchurus*. W.A. Starck photo.

363. *Starksia ocellata*. W.A. Starck photo.

361a. *Labrisoma nuchipinnis*. W.A. Starck photo.

365. *Blennius marmoreus*. W.A. Starck photo.

361b. *Labrisoma nuchipinnis*. From Evermann & Marsh, *Fishes of Porto Rico*.

368. *Chasmodes saburrae*. A. Norman photo.

362. *Paraclinus fasciatus*. W.A. Starck photo.

369. *Hypleurochilus geminatus*. A. Norman photo.

307

Family **BLENNIIDAE** — naked blennies

Small fishes which lack scales and have long dorsal fins with more rays than spines. Pelvic fins reduced to I,2 or 3, the elements usually hard to count, inserted before the pectoral. Mouth small to large, usually subterminal. Cirri sometimes present over eyes and nostrils. Dorsal spines flexible. Nine species.

364. MOLLY MILLER
Blennius cristatus Linnaeus

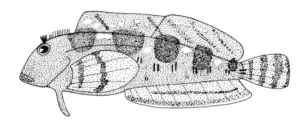

D. XII,14-15; A. II,16-17. Gill membranes free from chest. A cluster of cirri over eye and a long row of median cirri from behind eye to dorsal fin origin. Color variable, usually with rectangular dark blotches above midside and continuing into the dorsal fin base. Rest of body generally olive green, often with numerous small white spots. Two to four inches long.

A tropical species generally uncommon in our area. Generally on shallow hard bottoms.

365. SEAWEED BLENNY
Blennius marmoreus Poey

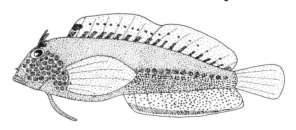

D. XII,17-18; A. II,19-20. Gill membranes free from chest. Tentacles above eye a cluster of four or more. No median nape cirri. Variable, generally darkish above and lighter below, with numerous small dark spots forming distinct clusters. Sometimes much orange or yellow in pattern. Gill covers often look honeycombed with dark and light. Dark spot at dorsal origin. Three inches long.

Not uncommon on west coast of Florida at least north to Pensacola, more scattered and rare over rest of our range. Occurs on both shallow and offshore hard bottoms.

Synonyms are currently thought to include *Blennius fucorum, B. stearnsi*, and *B. favosus*, but one or more of these may be valid species.

366. HIGHFIN BLENNY
Blennius nicholsi Tavolga

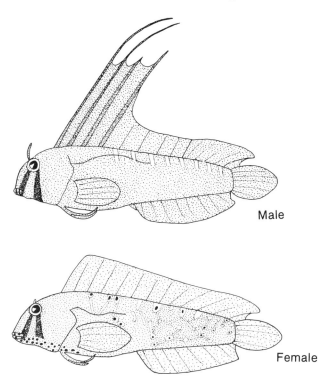

Male

Female

372a. *Ophioblennius atlanticus.* H.R. Axelrod photo.

375. *Eleotris pisonis.* A. Norman photo.

372b. *Ophioblennius atlanticus* (head).
H.R. Axelrod photo.

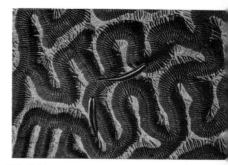

389. *Gobiosoma oceanops.* P. Colin photo.

373. *Callionymus bairdi.* J.E. Randall photo.

390. *Gobiosoma prochilos.* P. Colin photo.

374. *Dormitator maculatus.* H. Schultz photo.

391. *Gobiosoma robustum.* A. Norman photo.

310

392. *Ioglossus calliurus*. W.A. Starck photo.

399b. *Acanthurus coeruleus*. From Evermann & Marsh, Fishes of Porto Rico.

393. *Microgobius carri*. W.A. Starck photo.

405. *Euthynnus pelamis*. S. Shen photo.

398. *Acanthurus chirurgus* (Juv.). A. Norman photo.

407. *Scomber japonicus*. S. Shen photo.

399a. *Acanthurus coeruleus* (yng.). W.A. Starck photo.

410. *Scomberomorus regalis*. W.A. Starck photo.

311

Sexually dimorphic. Gill membranes free from chest. A single tentacle over the eye, none on nape. Soft dorsal fin joined to caudal. Male with first four dorsal spines greatly elongate, over half length of body. Female dorsal fin high anteriorly, but no rays elongated. Two dark stripes below eye. Brownish olive with vague pattern of light stripes dorsally. Female with more distinct pattern of light lines connecting dark spots; dark spots on lower margin of head and chest. Four inches.

An uncommon species of rocky bottoms of the southwest coast of Florida.

367. STRIPED BLENNY
Chasmodes bosquianus (Lacepede)

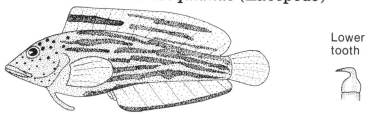

Lower
tooth

Gill membranes fused to chest. Gill opening restricted to area from upper edge of operculum to opposite lower edge of pectoral base. D. XI,18-19; A. II,18-19. Interorbital region flat. Pectoral rays twelve. Teeth in lower jaw slender, pointed, strongly recurved. Maxillary longer at any size than in Florida blenny, giving head a more pointed shape. Body brownish with light lines of mottling, giving appearance of irregular lateral stripes. Dorsal fin of male with bright blue band anteriorly. Females more mottled. Head with small spots above and on sides. Two to four inches long.

A common species on hard bottoms of bays out to about five fathoms. Ranges from southern Texas to the Mobile Bay area or perhaps a bit more eastward. Sympatric with the Florida blenny from Mississippi Sound to the Florida panhandle area.

368. FLORIDA BLENNY
Chasmodes saburrae Jordan & Gilbert

Lower
tooth

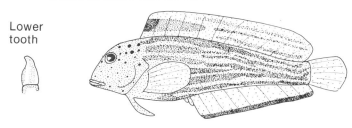

Identical in color and morphology to the striped blenny, differing only in the teeth and maxillary. Teeth in lower jaw stout, blunt, little or not at all recurved. Maxillary shorter at all sizes than in striped blenny, so head appears more blunt at similar sizes.

Ranges from Mississippi Sound east along the west coast of Florida. This species does not occur in Texas and, probably, Louisiana.

369. CRESTED BLENNY
Hypleurochilus geminatus (Wood)

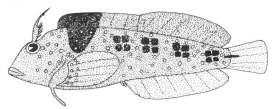

Gill membranes fused to chest. Gill opening restricted. Interorbital region concave. Pectoral rays fourteen. Canines present posteriorly in jaws. D. XI,15 to XIII,14; A. II,18. Male with large supraorbital cirrus with an additional four small cirri at base. Female with a short, many branched cluster over eye. Olive, plain or with orange spots arranged in irregular rows along sides. Four clusters of dark blotches forming distinct squares. Front of dorsal fin black. Two to three inches in length.

A moderately uncommon species in bays with shells and other hard substrates.

423. *Nomeus gronovii.* J.E. Randall photo.

433. *Peristedion* sp. From Evermann & Marsh, *Fishes of Porto Rico.*

428. *Scorpaena brasiliensis.* J.E. Randall photo.

444. *Dactylopterus volitans.* J.E. Randall photo.

429. *Scorpaena calcarata.* W.A. Starck photo.

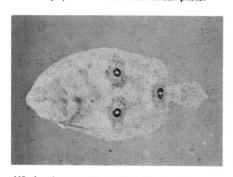

445. *Ancylopsetta dilecta.* W.A. Starck photo.

431. *Scorpaena plumieri.* J.E. Randall photo.

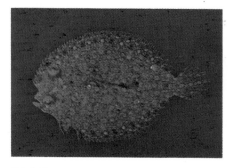

447. *Bothus ocellatus.* W.A. Starck photo.

314

469. *Trinectes maculatus.* A. Norman photo.

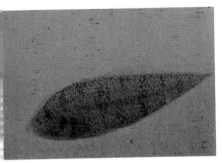

474. *Symphurus plagiusa.* A. Norman photo.

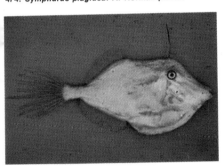

478. *Aluterus schoepfi.* W.A. Starck photo.

479. *Aluterus scriptus.* W.A. Starck photo.

480. *Balistes capriscus.* W.A. Starck photo.

481a. *Balistes vetula.* J.E. Randall photo.

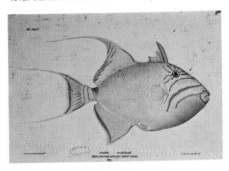

481b. *Balistes vetula.* From Evermann & Marsh, *Fishes of Porto Rico.*

482. *Cantherhines pullus.* J.E. Randall photo.

315

370. FEATHER BLENNY
Hypsoblennius hentzi (Lesueur)

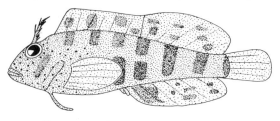

Gill membranes fused to chest. Gill opening restricted. Interorbital concave. Pectoral rays fourteen. Jaws without canines. D. XII,15; A. II, 16. Head very blunt. Supraorbital cirrus long or short, but with numerous small branches extending from origin to near tip. Olive, sometimes with about five brown crossbars or blotches. Head with many small brown spots, especially on sides. No dark lines from eye to mouth, nor is the dark blotch behind the eye bordered anteriorly by a darker line. Fins dark, variable. Two to four inches long.

A species of soft bottoms such as muddy oyster beds. Often not as common as the freckled blenny.

371. FRECKLED BLENNY
Hypsoblennius ionthas (Jordan & Gilbert)

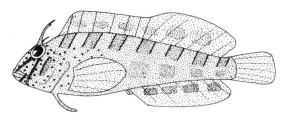

Similar to feather blenny except in details of cirrus and color. Supraorbital cirrus long or short (long in males), simple, with a division only near tip and perhaps one small branch basally. Two dark lines from eye to the mouth. Dark blotch behind the eye with a crescentic dark line anteriorly.

Common throughout our area, often on oyster reefs.

372. REDLIP BLENNY
Ophioblennius atlanticus (Valenciennes)

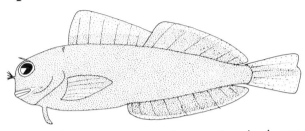

Gill membranes free from chest. A small cirrus on each side of nape just before the dorsal fin origin. Face very blunt. A simple cirrus over eye. Brown, the lips and edge of dorsal fin red. A black spot behind the eye. Two to four inches long.

A tropical species rather dubiously reported from our area. To be expected on west coast of Florida and southern Texas coast. Hard bottoms.

Family CALLIONYMIDAE — dragonets

Only one species in our area.

373. LANCER DRAGONET
Callionymus bairdi Jordan

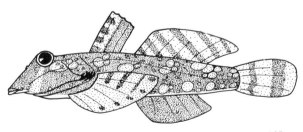

Small goby- or blenny-like fishes with very strong preopercular spines bearing strong hooks. Gill opening reduced to a rounded pore high on side. Body elongate, head depressed with protrud-

317

483. *Canthidermis sufflamen.* W.A. Starck photo.

483x. *Canthidermis maculatus.* S. Shen photo.

484. *Melichthys niger.* H.R. Axelrod photo.

485a. *Monacanthus ciliatus* (male). W.A. Starck photo.

485b. *Monacanthus ciliatus* (female). W.A. Starck photo.

486. *Monacanthus hispidus.* W.A. Starck photo.

488. *Xanthichthys ringens.* D.L. Savitt & R.B. Silver photo.

489a. *Lactophrys quadricornis.* W.A. Starck photo.

318

39b. *Lactophrys quadricornis* (juv.).
*.A. Starck photo.

91. *Canthigaster rostrata.* W.A. Starck photo.

96. *Sphoeroides spengleri.* W.A. Starck photo.

497. *Sphoeroides testudineus.* From Evermann
& Marsh, *Fishes of Porto Rico.*

498a. *Chilomycterus schoepfi* (lateral). W.A. Starck
photo.

498b. *Chilomycterus schoepfi* (dorsal).
W.A. Starck photo.

499. *Diodon hystrix.* W.A. Starck photo.

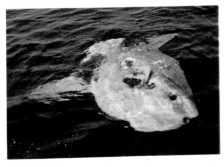

501. *Mola mola.* A. Norman photo.

319

ing eyes and a small, ventrally directed mouth. Scaleless. D. IV-9, the spines elongate in males; A.8. Pinkish to tan, the dorsal spines with orange; variable. Two to three inches long.

A reef dweller which is rare in our area and seemingly found only on the west coast of Florida. Should be looked for on hard offshore bottoms. Other species may occur in deeper water.

Family **GOBIIDAE** — gobies and sleepers

Generally small to medium sized fishes which lack a lateral line. Pelvics I,5, either connected by a basal membrane or separate. Dorsal fins long or short, continuous or separate, the spines flexible. Scales present or absent. Caudal fin rounded or lanceolate.

This family is often treated as two, the Eleotridae for those species with the pelvic fins separate, and the Gobiidae for those with the pelvics fused to form a ventral sucking disk. There are now known to be several intermediate conditions and the family Eleotridae as usually defined would have to contain species obviously derived from ancestors with fused pelvics and species whose ancestors had separate pelvics. It is still convenient to treat this complex family as two groups, however. Twenty-two species, four of eleotrids and eighteen of gobiids.

374. FAT SLEEPER
Dormitator maculatus (Bloch)

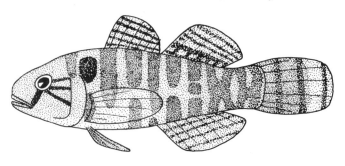

Pelvics separate. D. VII-9; A. 10. Lateral scales large, 33 to 36. Preopercle unarmed. Body stout, the eyes lateral. Mouth inferior. Snout blunt. Nape profile ascending. Brown, variously mottled or banded with brown, blue or green. A large blue spot over the pectoral fin base. Fins streaked. Six to twelve inches long.

A common species in brackish water, penetrating coastal freshwater as well.

375. SPINYCHEEK SLEEPER
Eleotris pisonis (Gmelin)

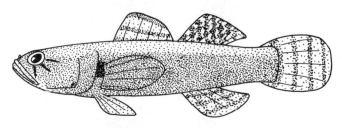

Pelvics separate. D. VI-9; A. 9. Lateral scales 53 to 60. Preopercle with a concealed spine dorsally. Mouth oblique, the eyes somewhat dorsal. Pectoral fin reaches anal fin. Caudal fin short, rounded, its rays not continued onto edges of peduncle for any great length. Dorsal profile nearly flat. Brownish, lighter below and under head. Fins streaked. Four to eight inches in length.

A common species in brackish water.

376. EMERALD SLEEPER
Erotelis smaragdus (Valenciennes)

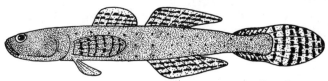

Pelvics separate. D. VI-12; A. 10. Scales very small, somewhat embedded, about 100 or more in lateral series. Body slender, elongate. Eyes dorsal, the mouth very oblique. Pectoral fin not reaching anal. Caudal long, lanceolate, its anterior rays continued onto edges of peduncle for about half head length. Brown, with small black spots in irregular rows laterally. Fins heavily streaked, the caudal blackish brown. Adults are said to have chevron stripes laterally. Two to eight inches in length.

The young are rare to locally common in shallow estuarine bays. Adults are very rare in our area and have been taken from more than ten fathoms.

This species is probably not uncommon in shallow brackish bays along the northern Gulf, but such areas are seldom collected seriously.

377. BIGMOUTH SLEEPER
Gobiomorus dormitor Lacepede

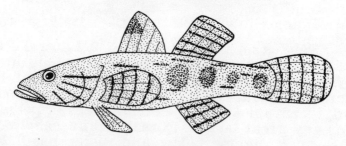

Pelvics separate. D. VI-9 or 10; A. 9. Lateral scales about 55 to 57. Body rather elongate, the eyes lateral. Mouth large, extending well beyond eye and with a projecting lower jaw. Brownish to olive, lighter below. Black margin to dorsal fin. Head sometimes spotted; body variously mottled. To one foot in length.

A brackish to freshwater species found in our area in extreme southern Texas.

The remaining species are true gobies, with the pelvic fins united to form a sucking disk, except in Ioglossus.

378. FRILLFIN GOBY
Bathygobius soporator (Valenciennes)

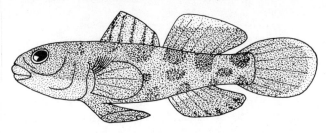

D. VI-10; A. 9. Scales forty-two. Cheek and opercle naked. Body stout, mouth small, with very thick lips. Pectoral large, the upper four or five rays simple, short, and free from the membrane for most of their length. Brownish, the fins dusky. Three to five inches in length.

Not common in our area. Generally on rocky bottoms but sometimes in shallow bays.

379. RAGGED GOBY
Bollmannia communis Ginsburg

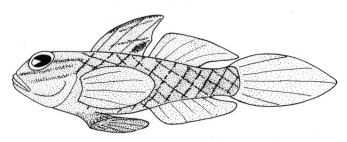

D. VII-14; A. 14. Scales about thirty, deciduous and easily lost. Head large, the body elongate. Eyes large, dorsal, the mouth oblique. Caudal fin long, lanceolate. Brownish, the fins clear or dusky, with a black spot at the posterior base of the first dorsal. Sides of preserved specimens with a darker brown open meshwork representing the bases of the deciduous scales. Three inches.

An abundant goby in water fifteen to thirty fathoms deep, but not easily collected because of its small size.

380. SPONGE GOBY
Evermannichthys spongicola (Radcliffe)

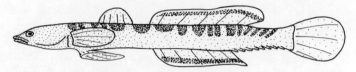

An elongate goby with the dorsal fins widely separated, the soft dorsal and anal similar; caudal broadly rounded. Mouth large, with heavy lips. Body naked except for a few scales on caudal peduncle, those on lower edge of peduncle projecting beyond the ventral profile of the fish. Tan with vague darker oblique bars, usually paired or in triplets. Fins sometimes with dark spots. One to two inches long.

A sponge dweller dubiously reported from the west coast of Florida. Probably not really within our area, but should be looked for in tubular and massive sponges on offshore reefs.

381. LYRE GOBY
Evorthodus lyricus (Girard)

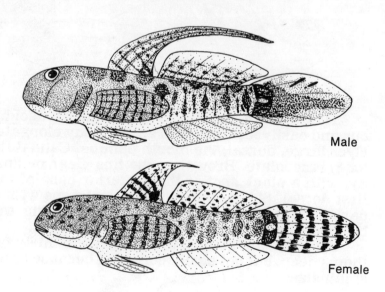

Male

Female

D. VI-11; A. 12. First dorsal with the spines very elongate in adult males, the spines shorter but still elongate in females. Head blunt, the mouth small and with thin lips; the lower jaw is included. Lateral scales thirty to thirty-five. Brownish to gray, with irregular lateral bars or blotches. Caudal base with two dark blotches separated by a light area. Fins streaked with brown, the caudal of the male with two elongate black spots at the upper edge. Two to three inches in length.

Locally common in shallow water that is brackish or of low salinity.

382. VIOLET GOBY
Gobioides broussonneti Lacepede

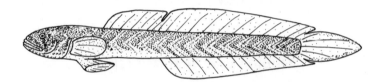

D. VII,15; A. 16. Dorsal fins continuous and of nearly even height. Anal fin very long. Body elongate, the head very large for a goby, the mouth large. Eyes small, lateral. Scales very small, embedded, giving the sides a granular appearance. Caudal fin lanceolate. Brownish purple with a series of pale chevrons on sides pointed anteriorly. Body iridescent in life. One to one-and-a-half feet long.

This bizarre and impressive goby is locally common in brackish water marshes throughout our area and less common in deeper water of moderate salinity. Specimens less than three or four inches long are rare.

383. DARTER GOBY
Gobionellus boleosoma (Jordan & Gilbert)

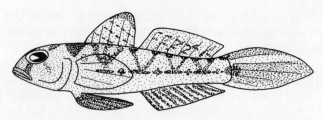

D. VI-11; A. 12. Scales twenty-nine to thirty-three, the predorsal area naked. Snout blunt, the body elongate. Caudal fin lanceolate. A large brown spot over the pectoral base. Body pale brown with dark brown lateral blotches joining the dark dorsal saddles to produce V-shaped mid-lateral bars. Fins of males with red marginal bars and a red line through the caudal fin. Fins otherwise dusky. Two inches long.

A common goby of shallow water, including estuaries.

384. SHARPTAIL GOBY
Gobionellus hastatus Girard

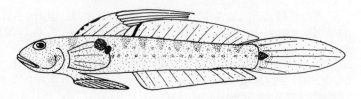

D. VI-14; A. 15. Scales seventy-three to ninety-two. Body greatly elongated, the caudal fin long and lanceolate. Dorsal spines very high. Mouth large, eyes relatively small. Body light straw brown with vague lateral banding. A prominent large dark brown, often divided, spot above and under the pectoral fin. Four to eight inches long.

This elongate goby is a common fish in both estuarine and shallow high salinity waters. It is also found to a considerable distance offshore.

The similar *Gobionellus oceanicus* is probably not found within our area, being more tropical. It has only sixty-one to seventy-two lateral scales.

Gobionellus gracillimus cannot be recognized as a distinct species, as its counts and measurements broadly overlap those of *G. hastatus*, with which it is supposed to be fully sympatric.

385. FRESHWATER GOBY
Gobionellus shufeldti (Jordan & Eigenmann)

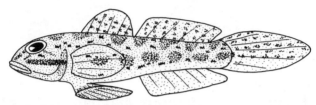

D. VI-12; A. 13. Scales thirty-five to forty, the predorsal area naked or with up to seven embedded scales. Body elongate, the caudal fin long. Pale brown with dark lateral blotches not connected to dorsal saddles. No shoulder spot. A dark horizontal line across the cheek, sometimes broken or indistinct. Two to three inches long.

A moderately common fish in shallow brackish and low salinity water.

This species lacks a large canine in the lower jaw and does not have elongated dorsal spines.

386. MARKED GOBY
Gobionellus stigmaticus (Poey)

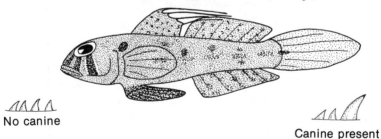

No canine

Canine present

Similar to the freshwater goby in fin counts and general color pattern. The predorsal area is consistently naked, and the lower jaw has a large outwardly curved canine. The dorsal spines are somewhat elongated and there is a dark spot above the pectoral fin. Two inches.

Rare along the northern Gulf, most records from the west coast of Florida.

387. NAKED GOBY
Gobiosoma bosci (Lacepede)

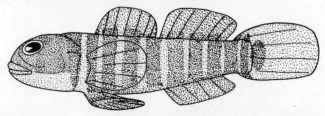

D. VII-13; A. 11. Body and caudal fin without scales. Body stout, the head large and blunt. Pale gold or straw with broad black lateral bands, these wider than their interspaces. Some individuals may be almost entirely black. One to two inches long.

An abundant little fish in shallow bays and brackish water. Enters freshwater.

388. TWOSCALE GOBY
Gobiosoma longipala Ginsburg

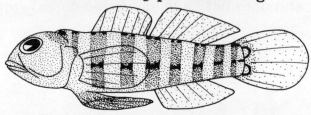

D. VII-12; A. 10. Body naked, but the caudal fin base with a ctenoid scale near each corner. Body stout. Straw brown with seven to eight dark vertical bars not much wider than the interspaces. Bars darkest at middle and at dorsal profile of body, sometimes forming small dark dumbell-shaped areas. Fins light. One to one-and-a-half inches long.

An uncommon fish generally found in five or more fathoms over hard bottoms.

389. NEON GOBY
Gobiosoma oceanops (Jordan)

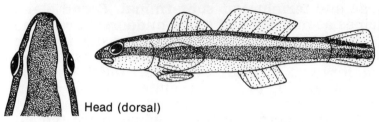

Head (dorsal)

D. VII-12 or 13; A. 11-12. Body naked, as is caudal fin. Body slender, the blunt snout overhanging the inferior mouth. Black stripes over snout and through middorsal area and a wide black stripe from snout through eye into caudal fin; light below. The light band between the dark dorsal and lateral bands is iridescent blue, the blue stripe continued only slightly beyond eye anteriorly and not joined with light line of other side on snout. Fins light. Brooding males may be uniform black. Two inches long.

A coral dwelling species famous for its habit of picking parasites off other reef fishes. Very rare in our area, reported from only the southwestern coast of Florida and the coral heads off Texas. Shore to fifteen fathoms.

A member of the distinctive subgenus *Elacatinus*.

390. WHITELINE GOBY
Gobiosoma prochilos Bohlke & Robins

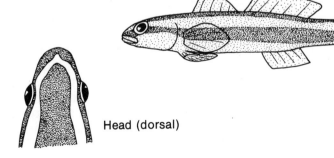

Head (dorsal)

D. VII-12; A. 11. Body and caudal fin naked.
Body slender, the snout pointed; the mouth is
large and terminal or subterminal. Broad black
stripes at midside and along middorsal area, the
snout dark. Light stripe along upper side is white
to bluish white and continues into the caudal fin
and forward through the eyes, meeting stripe
from other side to form a white V on the snout.
One inch long.

Another coral dwelling cleaner more typical
of tropical reefs. One record of what is probably
this species from the coral heads off Texas. Perhaps this species and the neon goby are more
widely distributed on the offshore coral heads and
snapper banks of the northern Gulf.

Belongs to the subgenus *Elacatinus*.

391. CODE GOBY
Gobiosoma robustum Ginsburg

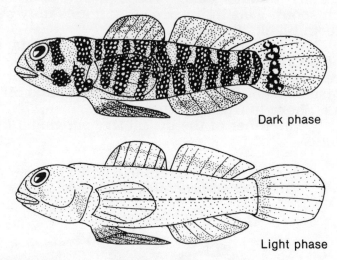

Dark phase

Light phase

D. VII-12; A. 10. Body and caudal fin scaleless. Body stout, the head blunt. Pale tan either
unmarked or with ten to twelve irregular dark
vertical bars which seem to be made of light-cen-
tered dark spots. There is usually a series of midlateral dark dashes, one in each vertical bar. Fins
dusky or light. One to two inches long.

A common species usually found in shallow to moderate depths and moderate to high salinity. In contrast, the similar naked goby is usually restricted to low salinity water.

392. BLUE GOBY
Ioglossus calliurus Bean

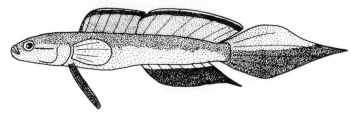

D. VI-I,23; A. 22. The pelvic fins are separate as in the eleotrids, but this genus is definitely related to the more typical gobiids and not eleotrids. Body slender, the mouth somewhat oblique. Caudal fin very large, over half the body length, wide basally and very pointedly lanceolate. Median fins high and flowing. Bluish, the dorsal fin with a broad black margin, the soft dorsal with a black submarginal band. Anal fin dark, as is the lower half of the caudal fin. Three to four inches, plus another inch or two for the caudal fin.

A poorly known goby seemingly restricted to the west coast of Florida from Pensacola south. Four to thirty fathoms over hard to sandy bottoms.

393. SEMINOLE GOBY
Microgobius carri Fowler

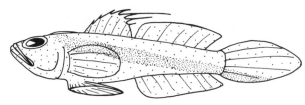

D. VII-16; A. 16. Lateral scales over fifty, deciduous. Dorsal spines elongated in larger specimens. Body slender, the head large and with a low crest on the nape in large specimens. Mouth very large and oblique. Caudal fin long, roundly lanceolate. Silvery to straw brown, with a broad golden stripe from the nape to the lower caudal rays. This golden stripe is lost in preservative. Three inches long.

Locally common on the west coast of Florida almost to the Mobile Bay area. Shallow water.

394. CLOWN GOBY
Microgobius gulosus (Girard)

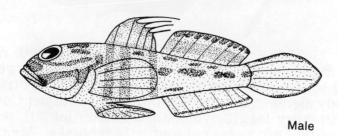

Male

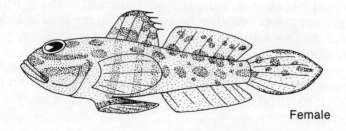

Female

D. VII-16; A. 17. Scales deciduous, forty-five to fifty-two in a lateral series. Body slender, the head very large, the mouth large and oblique. Body dark brown with large or small brown spots. The male has iridescent vertical violet bands anteriorly on the body, these fading on death. Soft dorsal fin spotted. Male anal fin with a dark border, that of the female plain. First dorsal fin of the male dusky, that of the female spotted. One to three inches long.

A common fish in estuarine to moderately deep water.

395. GREEN GOBY
Microgobius thalassinus (Jordan & Gilbert)

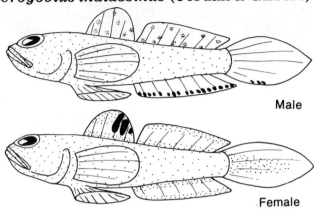

Male

Female

D. VII-16; A. 16. Lateral scales about fifty. Body plain, without spotting or stripes. Fins lightly dusky and without prominent markings with two exceptions: anal fin of male with a series of marginal black spots, and the dorsal of females with large black spots posteriorly toward the margin. One to two inches. Very delicate.

A moderately uncommon little goby usually found in shallow water of high salinity and with sand bottoms. However, it is also not uncommon with the clown goby in shallow estuarine waters as well.

References: Colin, P.L., 1973(Unpubl. Ph.D. dissertation, Univ. of Miami; *Gobiosoma* (*Elacatinus*)); Dawson, C.E., 1969(*Publ. Gulf Coast Res. Lab.*, #1); Randall, J.E., 1968(*Ichthyologica*, 39 (3/4):107-118; *Ioglossus*).

Family MICRODESMIDAE — wormfishes

Elongate, eel-like goby relatives with the very small pelvics I,3. The lower jaw is large, oblique, and projecting; eye very small. Dorsal and anal fins both very long, the spines not easily distinguishable from the rays. Two species.

396. LANCETAIL WORMFISH
Microdesmus lanceolatus Dawson

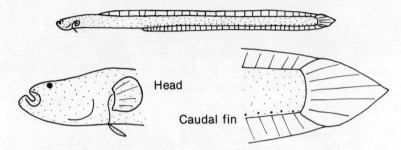

Head

Caudal fin

Gill opening restricted laterally. D. XII,56; A. 55. Caudal fin short but lanceolate. Brownish. Four inches.

A rare species apparently known from a single specimen taken in twenty fathoms off Grand Isle, Louisiana.

397. PINK WORMFISH
Microdesmus longipinnis (Weymouth)

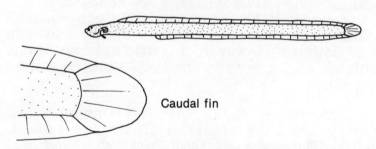

Caudal fin

Gill opening restricted laterally. D. XX or XXI,50; A. 44. Caudal fin short, rounded. Brownish. Six to ten inches in length.

This is a common but very secretive burrower in sandy and muddy bays and sounds. Found to depths of thirty feet, but most commonly in only a foot or two of water.

The AFS *Checklist* common name pink wormfish is a totally inappropriate name (see Dawson, 1969, under Gobiidae) which should be replaced with tan wormfish or something similar.

Family ACANTHURIDAE — surgeonfishes

Oval fishes with forked tails and an unnotched dorsal fin. Mouth small, terminal, the teeth slender and with lateral lobes. The caudal peduncle of our species bears a single sharp and retractile spine in a special pouch on each side. Three species, one questionably distinct.

Acronurus larva of
Acanthurus.

398. DOCTORFISH
Acanthurus chirurgus (Bloch)

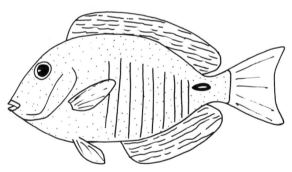

D. IX,24-25; A. III,22-23. Body relatively elongate. Caudal spine outlined in dark brown and blue. Body brownish, with about ten narrow darker vertical bars on lower sides. Dorsal and anal fins dark, only vaguely banded, with blue margins. Ten to fourteen inches long.

A tropical species found in our area only as strays. Rare.

399. BLUE TANG
Acanthurus coeruleus Bloch & Schneider

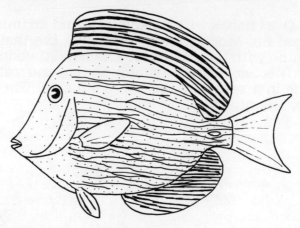

D. IX,26-28; A. III,24-26. Body nearly round. Caudal spine white. Brown to gray with grayish longitudinal lines which are very irregular. Dorsal and anal fins blue with definite brownish bands. Ten to fourteen inches long.

Another tropical straggler, rare in our area but sometimes seen on the west coast of Florida.

400. GULF SURGEONFISH
Acanthurus randalli Briggs & Caldwell

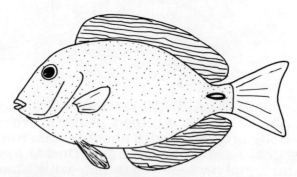

A questionably distinct species which is almost identical with the doctorfish. Caudal fin more shallowly forked, the lobes broadly rounded. Pectoral fin shorter than snout length (longer than snout length in *A. chirurgus*). Dark vertical bars apparently consistently absent. Ten inches.

Seems to be restricted to the west coast of Florida, especially the area when the panhandle joins the peninsula. The doctorfish is said to be absent from this area, although it occurs in southern Florida.

Considering the wide range of many of the acanthurids and their pelagic acronurus larvae, it seems unlikely that two species as closely related as *A. chirurgus* and *randalli* could remain isolated enough to retain their identity. Perhaps there is a weakly differentiated resident population of *Acanthurus chirurgus* in the "bend" of Florida, but it would, on published information, certainly not seem to be distinct to the species level.

Family **TRICHIURIDAE** — cutlassfishes

A single species in the northern Gulf.

401. ATLANTIC CUTLASSFISH
Trichiurus lepturus Linnaeus

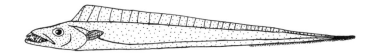

D. 133 to 140; A. 97 to 108. Body greatly compressed, high anteriorly and tapering to a pointed caudal end. Dorsal and anal very long. Pelvic fins absent, caudal fin absent; tail a thin filament. Head large, with long, bony jaws bearing irregular, barbed teeth. Silvery, the color easily rubbing off. Two to five feet long.

A common fish from shallow bays to deep water, usually preferring higher salinities.

Family SCOMBRIDAE — mackerels, tunas, wahoo

Unusually large fusiforme fishes with small scales which are often absent over much of the body or enlarged in the pectoral region. Caudal peduncle slender, very strong, with two lateral keels. Caudal fin large, lunate. Dorsal and anal fins followed by isolated finlets. Fourteen species, most of them found only offshore in blue waters.

Larval tuna.

Although the species are often difficult to identify because of changes with growth and the great importance of osteology and internal anatomy in their classification, the genera are relatively simple to tell apart.

Dorsal fins separated by more than snout length; body fully scaled .... *Scomber*

Dorsal fins separated by more than snout length; scaled anteriorly, along the lateral line and back, and in the region of the pectoral (the corselet) .... *Auxis*

Dorsal fins contiguous; snout as long as rest of head; fully scaled; body slender; spinous dorsal fin outline nearly straight, with 24 to 26 spines .... *Acanthocybium*

Dorsals contiguous; snout shorter; fully scaled; 15 to 18 dorsal spines, the fin outline straight or convex; s nder .... *Scomberomorus*

Dorsals contiguous; deep-bodied; fully scaled except top of head; first dorsal fin outline straight, the second spine longer than the first .... *Sarda*

Dorsals contiguous; body deep; fully scaled; first dorsal fin concave in outline, the first spine higher than the second .... *Thunnus*

Dorsal fins contiguous; deep bodied; scales only anteriorly, along lateral line and back and in corselet .... *Euthynnus*

402. WAHOO
Acanthocybium solanderi (Cuvier)

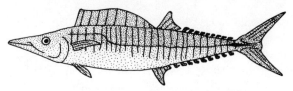

Body slender, elongate. Snout about as long as rest of head. Dorsal fins contiguous, the spinous dorsal fin with twenty-four to twenty-six spines. First dorsal outline nearly straight. Body fully scaled. Silvery, with faint indications of vertical lines. Three to six feet in length.

A popular but uncommon offshore game fish.

403. BULLET MACKEREL
Auxis rochei (Risso)

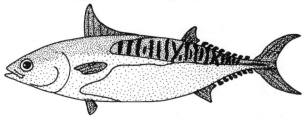

Dorsal fins separated by more than snout length. Body scaled along lateral line and back, in corselet area, and anteriorly. Corselet extension along lateral line under second dorsal fin origin six or more scales wide. Pectoral short, its tip failing to reach a vertical at the front of the scaleless dorsal area. Silvery, the posterior dorsal portion of body with dark nearly vertical bars on a blue background. Reaches about two feet in length.

A rare fish in our area, known mostly by young specimens taken in deep water.

The very similar *Auxis thazard* might also occur in our area. The corselet extension along the lateral line is only one to five scales wide, the pectoral fin is longer, and the dark bars on the back are wavy and oblique.

404. LITTLE TUNNY
Euthynnus alletteratus (Rafinesque)

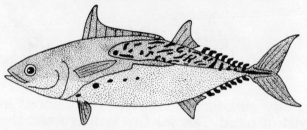

Snout short; dorsal fins close together. Body scaled anteriorly, along lateral line and on back. Corselet well developed. Dorsal spines fourteen to sixteen. Anal finlets six or seven. Pectoral long, reaching to under tenth to twelfth dorsal spines. Silvery blue with wavy horizontal lines on back. Several irregular black blotches below the pectoral fin. Two to three feet long.

A common sportsfish throughout our area. Many fishermen seem to think this a small specimen of one of the true tunas.

405. SKIPJACK TUNA
Euthynnus pelamis (Linnaeus)

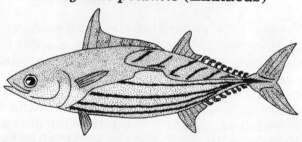

Dorsals close together; snout short. Body partially scaled as in little tunny, the corselet present. Dorsal spines fifteen to sixteen. Pectoral fin reaches to under eight or nine dorsal spines. Silvery blue above, silver below with three dark longitudinal stripes on lower sides, these converging on caudal peduncle. One to two feet long.

Common offshore fish. Often placed in the genus *Katsuwonus*.

406. ATLANTIC BONITO
Sarda sarda (Bloch)

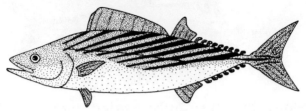

Snout short, fins contiguous. Body fully scaled. Outline of first dorsal fin straight, the first spine shorter than the second. No scales on top of head or on opercle. Corselet present. Silvery and blue, with many narrow dark stripes above running downward and forward. Twenty to twenty-two dorsal spines. One to two feet long.

A rare fish in the northern Gulf, although fishermen commonly call other tunas (especially *Euthynnus*) bonito.

407. CHUB MACKEREL
Scomber japonicus Houttuyn

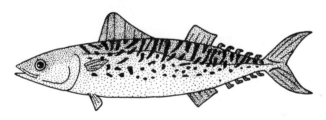

Dorsal fins separated by more than snout length. Body fully scaled. Five dorsal and five anal finlets. Snout short. Silvery, with wavy lines and spots on bluish dorsum, these dark markings extending to midside. About one foot long.

Rare in the northern Gulf and found only in water deeper than fifteen fathoms.

408. KING MACKEREL
Scomberomorus cavalla (Cuvier)

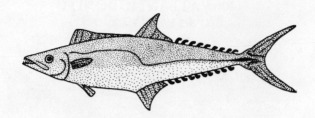

Body slender, fully scaled including head. First dorsal straight to convex in outline. Snout short; dorsal fins contiguous. Dorsal spines fifteen to sixteen. Anal finlets nine or ten. Lateral line abruptly decurved below second dorsal fin. Adults plain silvery, the dorsal fin without black anteriorly. Young with rows of yellow spots on sides and black on first dorsal membranes. Three to five-and-a-half feet long.

This, our largest Spanish mackerel, is a common sportsfish throughout our area.

409. SPANISH MACKEREL
Scomberomorus maculatus (Mitchill)

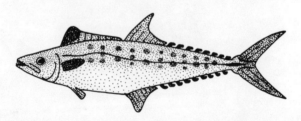

Body slender, fully scaled including the head. Snout short. Dorsal fins close together, the spinous dorsal outline straight to convex. Seventeen to eighteen spines in the dorsal fin. Anal finlets eight or nine. Lateral line not abruptly decurved under second dorsal, only gently so. Pectoral fin without scales. Bluish silvery, the sides with yellow spots. First dorsal fin black anteriorly. Two to four feet long.

A common sportsfish in the northern Gulf. The young are often abundant in shallow water near shore.

410. CERO
Scomberomorus regalis (Bloch)

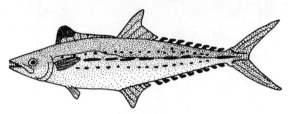

Body slender, fully scaled, as is head. Snout short. Dorsal fins close together, the spinous dorsal straight or convex in outline. Dorsal with seventeen to eighteen spines. Eight anal finlets. Lateral line not sharply decurved. Pectoral fin scaled. Silvery blue, the first dorsal fin black anteriorly. Sides with yellow spots and one or two narrow yellow horizontal lines usually broken into dashes. Two to four feet long.

A more tropical species which is uncommon or rare in our area.

411. ALBACORE
Thunnus alalunga (Bonnaterre)

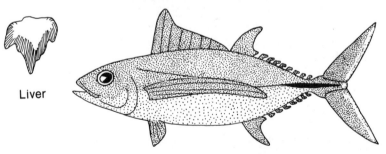

Liver

Body fully scaled. Spinous dorsal concave, the first spine longer than the second. Dorsal spines thirteen to fourteen. Seven or eight dorsal and anal finlets. Pectoral fin very long, strap-like, extending well beyond second dorsal fin. Greatest depth of body at about midbody or slightly more posteriorly. Liver with the ventral surface heavily striated. Caudal margin whitish. Bluish above, silvery below. To five feet long.

No current records from the northern Gulf, but this species is likely to occur here. To be expected offshore.

412. YELLOWFIN TUNA
Thunnus albacares (Bonnaterre)

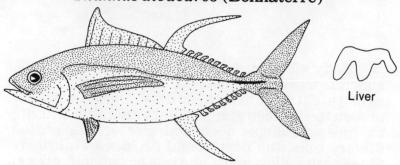

Liver

Body fully scaled. Spinous dorsal fin concave, the first spine longer than the second. Dorsal spines thirteen to fifteen, usually fourteen. Dorsal finlets eight to eleven, anal finlets eight to ten. Pectoral fin reaching to second dorsal fin or beyond. Dorsal and anal fin lobes very long in the adult, pointed, reaching to seventh finlet or beyond when depressed. Corselet indistinct. Bluish above, silvery below. Reaches a length of six feet and a weight of over four hundred pounds. The ventral surface of the liver lacks striations.

A popular sportsfish, moderately common off the Mississippi delta.

413. BLACKFIN TUNA
Thunnus atlanticus (Lesson)

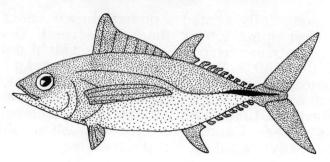

Body fully scaled. Spinous dorsal fin concave, the first spine longer than the second. Dorsal spines thirteen to fourteen. Dorsal finlets seven to nine, anal finlets seven or eight. Pectoral fin reaches to somewhere between the twelfth dorsal spine and the origin of the second dorsal. Dorsal and anal fin lobes short, not extending beyond third finlet when depressed. Corselet well developed. Bluish above, silvery below. A small tuna, reaching only two to two-and-a-half feet in length.

A common little tuna in deep water.

414. BIGEYE TUNA
Thunnus obesus Lowe

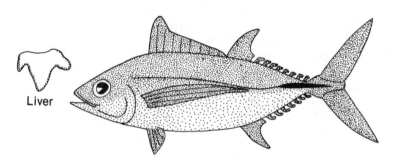

Liver

Body fully scaled. Spinous dorsal fin concave, the first spine longer than the second. Dorsal spines fourteen to sixteen. Dorsal finlets eight to ten, anal finlets eight or nine. Pectoral fin variable, usually reaching to or beyond second dorsal. Greatest depth of body anterior to midbody. Only edges of ventral surface of liver striated. Caudal margin dark. Bluish above, silvery below. Six to seven feet long.

This large species seems to be generally rare and there are no records from the Gulf. It may be present and confused with other species, however.

415. BLUEFIN TUNA
Thunnus thynnus (Linnaeus)

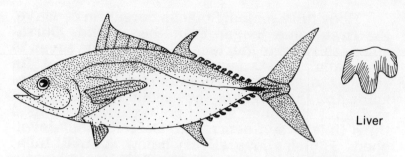

Liver

Body fully scaled. Spinous dorsal fin concave, the first spine longer than the second. Dorsal spines fourteen or fifteen. Anal finlets variable, usually nine dorsal and eight anal. Pectoral fin short, reaching only to the twelfth dorsal spine. Lobes of soft dorsal and anal fins short. Corselet well developed. Blue above, silvery below. Eight to fifteen feet in length, very rare at small sizes. Ventral surface of liver heavily striated.

An offshore sportsfish found in deep waters.

Although the tunas are often hard to distinguish, the following key may be of use in our area:

1a. Pectoral fin short, ending about under twelfth dorsal spine; 8-15 feet; common ....
........................bluefin—*T. thynnus*
1b. Pectoral longer, usually at least reaching second dorsal; adults less than eight feet 2
2a. Dorsal and anal lobes very long in adults, at least as long as height of first dorsal in juveniles; 6 feet; common ....
....................yellowfin—*T. albacares*
2b. Soft fin lobes short, length in large adults only as long as height of first dorsal..............3
3a. Pectoral ending near second dorsal; 1½-2½ feet; common ....blackfin—*T. atlanticus*
3b. Pectoral usually longer; over 3 feet; rare in northern Gulf 4

4a. Greatest body depth at or behind midbody; liver heavily striated; caudal margin light ...
...................albacore—*T. alalunga*
4b. Greatest depth anterior to midbody; only edges of liver striated; caudal margin dark ..
...................bigeye—*T. obesus*

Family XIPHIIDAE — swordfish

Only one species in our area.

416. SWORDFISH
Xiphias gladius Linnaeus

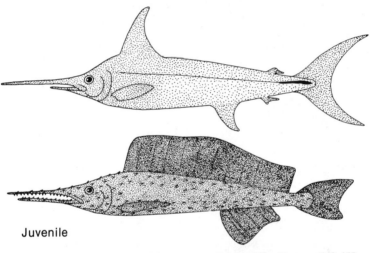

Juvenile

Upper jaw prolonged into a flattened bill or sword. No scales. Pelvic fins absent. Caudal peduncle with a single large lateral keel. Dorsal fin short, the first of about forty rays, second of four. First dorsal very high, concave posteriorly. Anal fins with eighteen and four rays, the first very high and concave posteriorly. Caudal deeply lunate, strong. Young with continuous dorsal fin and continuous anal fin; body covered with large spines. Blue-black, whitish below. Ten to sixteen feet in length.

A pelagic fish seldom seen or caught in our waters.

Family ISTIOPHORIDAE — billfishes

Upper jaw a rounded bill. Body with thornlike scales. Filamentous pelvic fins present. Caudal peduncle with two lateral keels. Caudal very strong, lunate. Four species.

417. SAILFISH
Istiophorus platypterus (Shaw & Nodder)

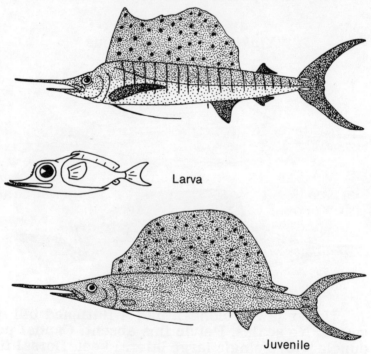

Larva

Juvenile

First dorsal fin very long, the longest spines in posterior third of fin. Vent located just anterior to first anal fin. Blue above, silvery below, with indications of narrow dark vertical bars. Sail dark blue with many small black spots. Five to eight feet long.

Young with dorsal fin convex, the middle rays longer than the anterior ones. Dorsal with dark spots. Vent just before anal fin.

A famous sportsfish not uncommon offshore.

418. BLUE MARLIN
Makaira nigricans Lacepede

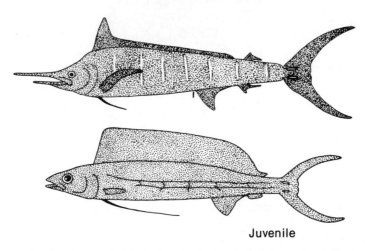

Juvenile

Anterior lobe of first dorsal low and pointed, its height less than the body depth at fin origin. Lateral line complex, forming hexagons, hard to see in adult fish. Pelvics short. Vent close to anal fin. Flesh pale. Blue-black with vaguely indicated pale vertical bars. Six to ten feet long.

Young with the fin of moderate height, profile straight. Bill short or absent. Lateral line forming hexagons.

Uncommon in the open Gulf.

419. WHITE MARLIN
Tetrapturus albidus Poey

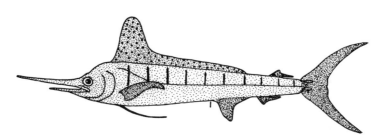

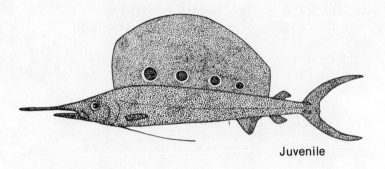

Juvenile

Lobe of first dorsal fin high, rounded, its height as great as depth of body. Vent close to anal fin, separated from it by less than fin height. Dorsal profile strongly arched over and behind eyes. Flesh red. Dark blue, the body with prominent dark vertical bars. Dorsal with small blackish spots. Three to six feet long.

Young with the dorsal very high and convex, with four large black ocellated spots near base.

Moderately uncommon in the open Gulf.

420. LONGBILL SPEARFISH
Tetrapturus pfluegeri Robins & deSylva

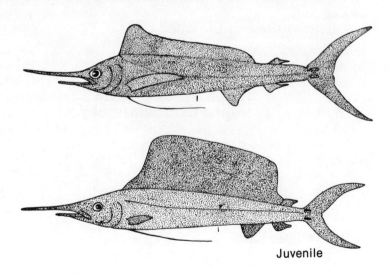

Juvenile

Spinous dorsal relatively high throughout, the middle rays almost equal to the anterior rays. Anterior lobe low and rounded. Vent separated from the anal fin by more than the fin height. Dorsal profile above and behind eye straight. Flesh red. Body blue with indistinct silvery bands. Dorsal fin unspotted. Four to six feet long.

Young with a high dorsal with small black spots. Vent widely separated from the anal fin.

Uncommon offshore. Often confused by fishermen with the sailfish.

References: Robins, C.R. and D.P. deSylva, 1960(*Bull. Mar. Sci.*, 10(4):383-413); same, 1963 (*Bull. Mar. Sci.*, 13(1):84-122); deSylva, D.P., 1963(*Bull. Mar. Sci.*, 13(1):123-132).

STROMATEOIDEI — butterfishes and relatives.

A complex group of families or subfamilies sharing the common character of pouches in the posterior part of the pharynx, the pouches usually bearing various ridges and teeth. In our forms the body scales are small or absent and the caudal peduncle is slender and usually bears a forked caudal fin. These groups are commonly considered to form the single family Stromateidae, but recent work indicates that the different body forms and generic groups should be accorded family rank. Four familes are found within our area.

Family **ARIOMMIDAE** — driftfishes

One species.

421. SPOTTED DRIFTFISH
Ariomma regulus (Poey)

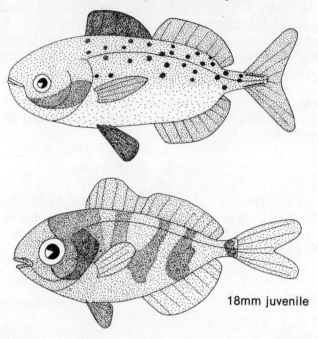

18mm juvenile

Vomer and palatines without teeth. Spinous dorsal fin of adults strong, separated from soft dorsal by a deep notch. Anal III,15. Head bluntly rounded. Silvery blue with small black spots dorsally; spinous dorsal and pelvic black. Caudal peduncle small, with two keels. Juvenile moderately elongate, the dorsal fins shallowly notched. Broad black blotch anteriorly, plus about three oblique bars on body. Larger juveniles with numerous large black spots. Ten inches long.

Pelagic, the young sometimes found near shore. Rare.

Family **CENTROLOPHIDAE** — ruffs

A single species.

422. BLACK DRIFTFISH
Hyperoglyphe bythites (Ginsburg)

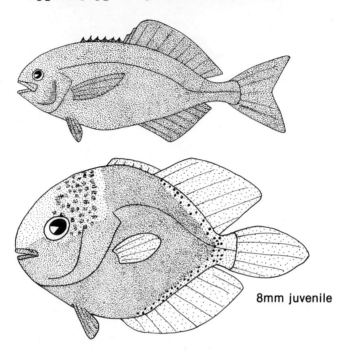

8mm juvenile

Vomer and palatines without teeth. Spinous dorsal fin of low, uniform spines much lower than the long soft dorsal. Anal III,17. Body deep. Young very deep-bodied, almost round. Dorsal spines very low, the soft fins high; caudal rounded. Generally dark with large melanophores on head and fin bases. Adults uniform brownish. About one foot long.

Adults are generally found in about two hundred fathoms, but the juveniles are sometimes found in inshore waters.

Family **NOMEIDAE** — cigarfishes

Vomer and palatines with teeth. Spinous dorsal fin separated from soft dorsal by a deep notch. Anal III,26 or more. Two species.

423. MAN-OF-WAR FISH
Nomeus gronovii (Gmelin)

Mouth about reaching to eye. Body moderately elongate, less so in young. Caudal fin deeply forked. Pelvics large, black, connected to body by a membrane for their entire length, fitting into a groove in the chest. Blue and silver, usually with about four or five broad broken dark saddles or bands on body and smaller blue spots below. Caudal and anal fins with spots. Six to eight inches long.

Adults pelagic, usually associated with Portuguese man-of-war siphonophores. Juveniles not uncommonly found inshore.

424. FRECKLED DRIFTFISH
Psenes cyanophrys Valenciennes

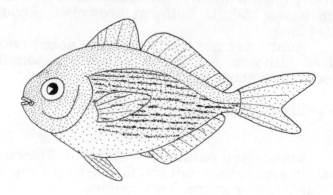

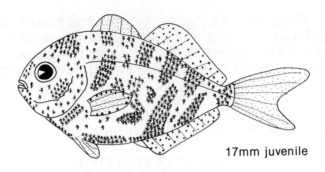

17mm juvenile

Mouth small, not reaching to eye. Body deep. Caudal fin shallowly forked, the upper lobe longer than the lower. Adults silvery with vague darker horizontal stripes on sides. Fins lightly dusky. Juveniles with large blotches formed of large black pigment cells. Six inches.

Adults pelagic offshore, rare. Juveniles rarely found in inshore waters.

Family **STROMATEIDAE** — butterfishes

Rounded silvery fishes with the scales so small and embedded that the body appears naked. Spinous dorsal fin absent, as are pelvics. Anal III,36 or more. Two species.

425. GULF BUTTERFISH
Peprilus burti Fowler

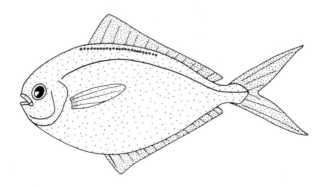

Body oval-elongate. Dorsal and anal fins low, the lobes not long and pointed. Mouth small. Caudal deeply forked. A row of conspicuous pores below the dorsal fin base. Silvery, the fins dusky. Six to twelve inches long.

Common in shallow to moderate depths, the largest specimens from deepest water. Formerly known as *Poronotus triacanthus*.

426. HARVESTFISH
Peprilus alepidotus (Linnaeus)

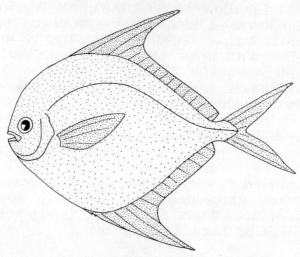

Body round. Mouth small; caudal deeply forked. Dorsal and anal low, but the anterior lobes of each fin very high and pointed. No pores below the dorsal fin base. Silvery, the fins dusky. Six to twelve inches in length.

A common fish in shallow to moderate water. As is commonly found, the smallest fish are most common inshore, the largest offshore.

Recent work indicates that the proper name of the harvestfish should be *Peprilus paru, P. alepidotus* being unrecognizable as a distinct species.

Reference: Haedrich, R.L., 1969(Mimeo. publ. Woods Hole Biol. Lab).

Family **SCORPAENIDAE** — scorpionfishes

Chunky, round-bodied fishes with large spiny heads and a short anal fin of three spines and five or six rays. Caudal rounded. Scales small, the lateral line distinct. Head with many spines, those of taxonomic interest being especially those on the preopercle and on the preorbital over the maxillary. There is normally a shallow to deep depression (occipital pit) on the midline of the head behind the eyes; this is absent in the smoothhead scorpionfish and the juveniles of other species. Dorsal fin IX-I,9, not variable. Five species.

The reader should be warned that other genera and species of scorpionfishes occur commonly in water beyond about forty fathoms out to the continental shelf. These may occasionally wander into our range, but there are no definite records.

427. LONGFIN SCORPIONFISH
Scorpaena agassizi Goode & Bean

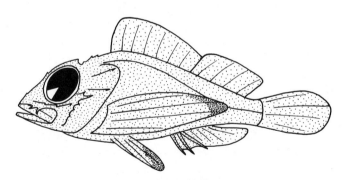

Two free preorbital spines over the maxillary. Supplemental preopercular spine present. Occipital pit moderately developed. The snout is conspicuously short and the eye very large. Uniform pale reddish brown, the fins dusky, without a definite pattern of dark; the caudal fin lacks black spots. There is sometimes a dark spot behind the eye. Five inches maximum.

This is a species characteristic of the continental shelf and deeper waters; it has rarely been recorded from depths of as little as twenty-five fathoms.

428. BARBFISH
Scorpaena brasiliensis Cuvier

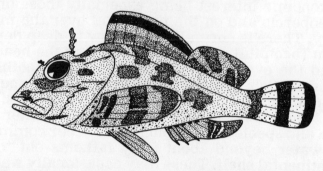

Two free spines on preorbital bone. Supplemental preopercular spine present but small. Occipital pit well developed. Brown, the body with darker bands and spots including several spots on the lower sides between the pectoral and anal fins. Two larger dark spots near the lateral line behind the head. Axilla of pectoral fin pale, with several small but distinct brown spots. Seven inches in length.

This is a bay and shore species not at all common in our area. Synonyms include *Scorpaena stearnsi* and *S. colesi.*

429. SMOOTHHEAD SCORPIONFISH
Scorpaena calcarata Goode & Bean

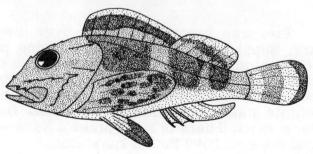

Preorbital bone with two free spines. The first preopercular spine lacks a supplemental spine. The occipital area is flat and lacks a distinct pit at all sizes. Brownish, heavily overlaid with red. The body may be variably spotted and mottled with dark and light. The fins are mostly red, the pectoral fin brown. Five inches long.

The smoothhead is the only scorpionfish likely to be found commonly in our area. It is most abundant at the ten to thirty fathoms range. *Scorpaena russula atlantica* is a synonym.

430. HUNCHBACK SCORPIONFISH
Scorpaena dispar Longley & Hildebrand

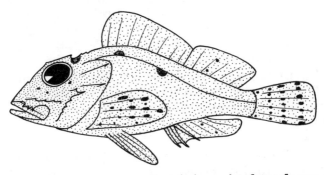

Specimens over about two inches long with three or four free spines on the preorbital bone. Supplemental preopercular spine present. Occipital pit well developed. Uniform red, the pectoral and caudal fins with rows of brown spots. There are sometimes two small brown spots on the body. The pectoral axilla is unmarked. Eight inches in length.

Moderately common in deeper water, twenty to sixty-five fathoms, off the coast of the northern Gulf. *Scorpaena similis* Gunter is a synonym.

431. SPOTTED SCORPIONFISH
Scorpaena plumieri Bloch

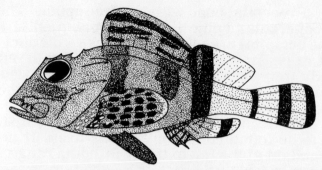

Preorbital bone of specimens over two inches long with three free spines. A supplemental preopercular spine is present and the occipital pit is well developed. Brownish, the fins with brown lines. The caudal peduncle is distinctly lighter than the anterior part of the body, especially in juveniles. Axilla of pectoral fin black with large black spots. Our largest scorpionfish, reaching fourteen inches in length.

An uncommon species in our area, usually found on rocky bottoms out to a few fathoms. *Scorpaena ginsburgi* Gunter is a commonly seen synonym.

Reference: Eschmeyer, W.N., 1965(*Bull. Mar. Sci.*, 15(1):84-164).

Family TRIGLIDAE — searobins

Generally slender fishes, the head bony and with strong spines and ridges. Dorsal fins separate; one anal spine. Pectoral fins divided into a normal upper portion and two or three free, thickened, unbranched lower rays. Upper jaw wide, flat, bony. Twelve species.

432. HORNED SEAROBIN
Bellator militaris (Goode & Bean)

Head
(ventral)

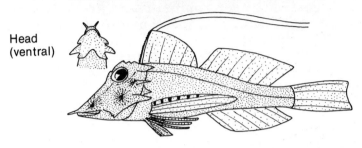

D. XI-11; A. I,10; Pect. 12 + 3. Head heavily armored, the snout steep. Lacrymal plates produced into sharp horns easily visible from below. Venter scaled anteriorly and posteriorly, naked in the middle. Body scales comparatively large and heavy. First two dorsal spines elongated, filamentous in adults but shorter in young; these filaments are often broken. The pectoral fin has the longest rays in the middle, is wedge shaped, and reaches from about the fifth anal ray to beyond the anal base. Plain reddish brown, sometimes with irregular dark spots. Usually less than five inches in length.

Although common in the deeper part of its range, the horned searobin is seldom found as shallow as twenty fathoms and ranges to sixty fathoms.

433. ARMORED SEAROBIN
Peristedion spp.

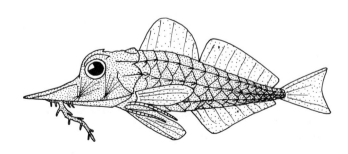

This genus is sometimes placed in its own family, the Peristediidae, and is certainly distinct from the rest of our sea robins. There are only two free lower pectoral rays, three in our other genera. The body is heavily plated with large modified scales, these overlapping and bearing strong median spines in most species. The caudal peduncle is very thin compared to the wide head. There are two long maxillary barbels, each bearing numerous fringes. The head is very heavy and broad, and preserved specimens sometimes break apart behind the head. Generally reddish or pale brown. Some species large, exceeding eight inches, others much smaller.

Although there are several species of this genus found in the waters of the northern Gulf, they are poorly known and greatly confused. Also, the genus is rarely found as shallow as twenty or thirty fathoms, being most common near the continental shelf. For this reason no species is included here. The genus is considered very rare in our depth range, and usually only juveniles are taken.

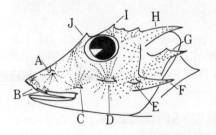

Sea robin head spines.

A, nasal; B, maxillary; C, lacrymal; D, subocular; E, supplemental preopercular; F, preopercular; G, opercular; H, occipital; I, postocular; J, preocular.

434. SPINY SEAROBIN
Prionotus alatus Goode & Bean

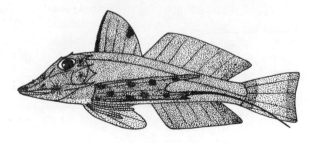

D. X-12(13); A. I,11(10-12); Pect. 13 + 3. Nasal spine present. Preopercular spine very long. Chest in front of pelvics naked. Pectoral deeply emarginate between fourth and eighth rays from top. Ninth ray very long, usually 58 to 78 percent of standard length in larger specimens; longest pectoral ray above notch 39 to 48 percent of standard length. Uniformly light colored; pectoral fin barred with irregular dark areas. Spinous dorsal spot present. Eight inches in length.

A widely distributed offshore species which occurs only on the lower edge of our depth range. Often common in thirty-six to one hundred fathoms. Most records are from east of the Mississippi delta.

435. BARRED SEAROBIN
Prionotus martis Ginsburg

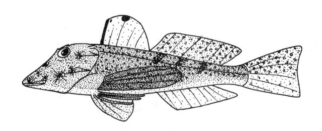

D. X-13; A. I,11; Pect. 14 + 3. Head spines moderately developed. The supplemental preoperclar spine is weak and disappears with growth. Chest completely scaled in specimens over an inch or so long, naked in specimens under one inch. Pectoral fin truncate to rounded, the fourth ray longest, reaching about to fifth to eighth anal ray. Brown, upper half of body with many small diffuse spots. Pectoral mostly dark with irregular small spots. Spinous dorsal fin with an elongate spot behind the first spine and a round spot between the fourth and fifth spines. Reaches six inches long, but generally much smaller.

A shallow water species found in two to eigh-teen fathoms. It seems to be widely distributed along the northern Gulf coast but is spotty and never very common. Prefers shallow sandy bays and similar areas.

It is likely that this species is simply a weakly differentiated Gulf subspecies of *Prionotus caroli-nus*, a common Atlantic seaboard species.

436. BANDTAIL SEAROBIN
Prionotus ophryas Jordan & Swain

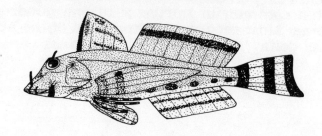

D. X-12; A. I,10; Pect. 14 + 3. Head short, the profile steep. A long filament behind the anterior nostril and a shorter, thicker tentacle on the pos-terior part of the eyeball. Supplemental preoper-cular spine absent; other head spines small or ab-sent. Pectoral fin long, reaching to about the end of the anal fin or beyond and ending in a rounded point. Generally dark brown with red bands on the lips and chin. Spinous dorsal fin without a distinct spot; soft dorsal and anal with horizontal red stripes. Caudal fin with three dark reddish brown vertical bars. Pectoral fin dark with an indication of lighter spotting and banding near its base and a reddish spot on the rays of the upper half. Some specimens have a row of large red spots on the ventrolateral margin of the body. Ten inches in length.

This prettily patterned searobin is a common species in waters of about ten to fifty fathoms. It is commonly taken by trawlers.

437. MEXICAN SEAROBIN
Prionotus paralatus Ginsburg

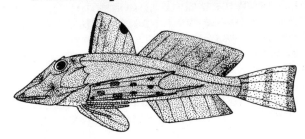

D. X-12; A. I,11; Pect. 13 + 3. Nasal spine absent. Preopercular spine very long. Chest without scales anterior to pelvics. Pectoral deeply emarginate between the fourth and eighth rays. The longest ray above the notch is 34 to 41 percent of the standard length, while the long ray below the notch is forty to fifty-two percent of the standard length. Light brown, the pectoral fin dusky with irregular barring. Spinous dorsal fin with a black spot between the fourth and fifth spines. Six inches long.

A common deepwater species ranging from twenty-four to ninety fathoms. Known only from off the coast of Louisiana and Texas in our area.

438. BLUESPOTTED SEAROBIN
Prionotus roseus Jordan & Evermann

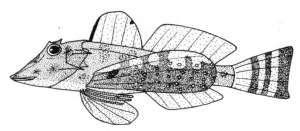

D. X-12; A. I,10; Pect. 13 + 3. Supplemental preopercular spine absent or very weak; all head spines weakly developed. Chest variably scaled. First three dorsal spines serrated. Pectoral fin truncate, extending beyond the anal fin base in adults but shorter in specimens less than three inches long. Brownish red with irregular dorsal spotting or mottling. Pectoral fin dark with well defined brown-circled blue spots, the spots remaining in preserved specimens. An elongated black spot near the pectoral base between the fifth or sixth and seventh upper rays. Nine inches long.

This is an uncommon offshore searobin generally found in twenty-two to thirty-eight fathoms. Rare inshore. *Prionotus microlepis* is a synonym.

439. BLACKFIN SEAROBIN
Prionotus rubio Jordan

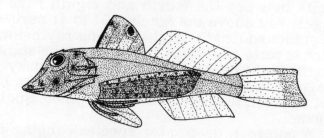

D. X-12; A. I,10; Pect. 13 + 3. Head short. Head spines moderately strong, the supplemental preopercular spine present in most specimens. Chest scaled with only a small naked area. Dorsal spines smooth or weakly granular. Pectoral fin obliquely rounded, the upper rays longer than the lower and extending over the base of the posterior anal rays in most specimens. Uniformly pale brown, rarely mottled. Pectoral fin dark, with small blue spots which fade in preservative. A persistent dark dorsal fin spot. At least twelve inches maximum length.

This is a very common searobin in shallow waters of our area. In Louisiana it is second only to the bighead searobin in abundance in bays and other inshore waters. Young specimens are generally the ones found in estuaries, while adults occur in deeper water, usually fifteen to ninety fathoms.

366

440. BLACKWING SEAROBIN
Prionotus salmonicolor Fowler

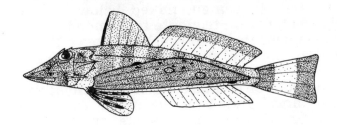

D. X-12; A. I,10; Pect. 13 + 3. Head low, long. Head spines weak, the supplemental preopercular disappearing at six inches or so. Chest mostly scaled, but a variable small portion naked. Pectoral oblique, the lower rays longer than the upper. Pectoral in most specimens reaches beyond the posterior anal base. Brownish with reddish brown spots and mottling. Pectoral fin black with lighter marbling or banding above. Spinous dorsal fin mottled, without a distinct spot. Nine inches in length.

A common species in six to thirty-five fathoms off our coast, but sometimes found in shallower water. Some populations resemble the leopard searobin in having thirteen dorsal and eleven anal rays, but differ in pectoral length and other characters. *Prionotus pectoralis*, a synonym, is a much more familiar name for this species.

441. LEOPARD SEAROBIN
Prionotus scitulus Jordan & Gilbert

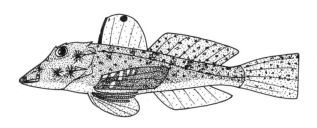

D. X-13; A. I,11; Pect. 13 + 3. Head spines moderately developed, the supplemental preopercular weak and disappearing with growth. Chest only partially scaled, naked below two inches long. Pectoral fin truncate to rounded, the upper rays longest. Pectoral reaches to over the anterior half of the anal fin, usually to about the eighth ray. Brown, the upper half of the body with small round spots of two sizes. Pectoral mostly black, lighter and banded on the upper rays. Spinous dorsal fin with two black spots, one between the fourth and fifth spines (rounded), the other behind the first spine (vertically elongate). Eight inches long.

A moderately common inshore species ranging out to about twenty-five fathoms. Our subspecies has been described as *P.s. latifrons*.

442. SHORTWING SEAROBIN
Prionotus stearnsi Jordan & Swain

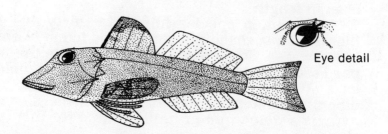

Eye detail

D. X-12; A. I,10; Pect. 13 + 3. Body less searobin-like than other species, shaped more like a "normal" fish. Mouth terminal, the jaws about subequal. Head spines moderately or weakly developed, the supplemental preopercular spine absent. Upper posterior corner of eyeball with several papillae or tabs, some slender and of moderate length; this cluster is sometimes hard to detect. Pectoral fin very narrow and short, not reaching beyond second anal ray; tip of pectoral rounded or pointed. Body and fins dark brown. Under six inches long.

This searobin is an offshore species not uncommon beyond forty fathoms. Rare in water as shallow as twenty fathoms.

443. BIGHEAD SEAROBIN
Prionotus tribulus Cuvier

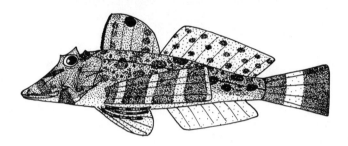

D. X-12(11); A. I,11; Pect. 13 + 3. Head broad, the interorbital area wider than the eye diameter (narrower in all other species). Head spines well developed and with broad bases, especially in the young. Postocular and supplemental preopercular spines both very large. Pectoral fin truncate or nearly so, not reaching end of anal fin. Brown, usually with greenish or pearly spots presenting a mottled appearance. Usually a few dark bars under the dorsal fin base. Pectoral fin mostly dark, usually banded with darker. Dorsal fin spot at margin of fin. Over one foot long.

A common and sometimes abundant estuarine and shallow water species throughout the northern Gulf. It ranges out to about fifteen fathoms, where the largest specimens occur; young generally found in estuaries. The gigantic heads of large specimens are striking. The subspecies in our area is *P.t. crassiceps.*

References: Ginsburg, I., 1950(*Texas Journ. Sci.*, 4:489-527); Miller, G.C., 1967(*Bull. Mar. Sci.*, 17(1):16-41; *Peristedion*); Miller, G.C. and D.M. Kent, 1972(*Quart. Jour. Florida Acad. Sci.*, 34(3): 223-242).

Family **DACTYLOPTERIDAE** — flying gurnards

Only one species in the northern Gulf.

444. FLYING GURNARD
Dactylopterus volitans (Linnaeus)

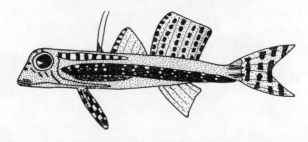

Elongate fishes with a dorsal formula of II-IV or V-8, the first two isolated spines longer than those of the spinous dorsal. Pectoral fin divided into two parts, the anterior of short rays and the posterior of greatly elongate rays extending to or beyond the base of the shallowly forked caudal. Head covered with bone, with a long flattened keel on each side of the nape before the dorsal fin and a long preopercular spine. Snout short, eyes large. Scales keeled; two keels on caudal base. Brownish, the fins mostly clear and with dark spots; pectoral fins blackish with small blue spots. Juveniles with shorter pectoral fins and longer, more protuberant head spines. About one foot long.

An uncommon fish in the northern Gulf, usually seen as small juveniles in shallow water, the adults being in deep offshore water. Another tropical stray. *Cephalacanthus* is an old generic name for this fish.

ORDER PLEURONECTIFORMES — flounders

Oval or elongate greatly flattened fishes with the eyes, fins, and jaws asymmetrical. In larval specimens the eyes and mouth are more normal, shifting to one side or the other at metamorphosis. Easily recognized fishes represented in our area by three families and thirty-one species, many very common and commercially important fishes.

The user should keep in mind the fact that juvenile specimens of most of the larger flounders are not at all common, especially in shallow water. Many small flounders considered by trawlers and some fisheries people to be small *Paralichthys* are in reality adults of *Citharichthys* and other genera with small adults.

Family **BOTHIDAE** — lefteye flounders

Small to large flatfishes with the eyes and color on the left side. Pectoral fin of ocular (left) side well developed, often elongate. Preopercle with a free edge not covered by skin and scales. Lateral line well developed on ocular side and usually also on blind side. Teeth present in jaws. Twenty-one species, many very common.

In the following discussions, all statements refer to the ocular side unless otherwise indicated.

445. THREE-EYE FLOUNDER
Ancylopsetta dilecta (Goode & Bean)

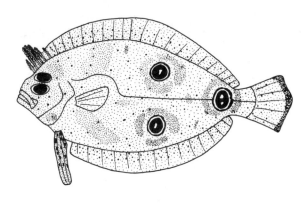

Anterior part of lateral line strongly curved. Ocular pelvic fin inserted above the ventral profile. D. 68-79; A. 53-60, Ll. 73-82. Anterior dorsal and ocular pelvic rays distinctly elongated. Pale brownish to grayish with three large ocellated spots often having light centers. Basal pair of spots located at middle of straight part of lateral line, the third spot just before the caudal peduncle. Often several other dark spots in background color, but never as prominent as principal three. Twelve inches long.

This beautiful little species is common in water from thirty to at least two hundred fathoms and is seldom found in our depth range except for occasional wandering juveniles.

446. OCELLATED FLOUNDER
Ancylopsetta quadrocellata Gill

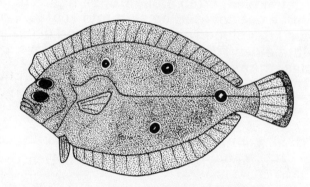

Anterior part of lateral line strongly curved; ocular pelvic fin above ventral profile. D. 67-76, A. 54-61, Ll. 80-90. Pectoral rays not elongated, but some anterior dorsal rays may be slightly longer than the others. Brown, with four dark ocellated spots, the anterior one over the lateral line arch and often weak or absent. Other three spots in form of a backwardly directed triangle, the basal pair about at middle of straight lateral line, the apex just before the caudal peduncle. Less than ten inches in length.

Moderately common, adults generally found beyond the three fathom mark out to about twenty-five fathoms. Occasional juveniles can be found in less than a fathom.

447. EYED FLOUNDER
Bothus ocellatus (Agassiz)

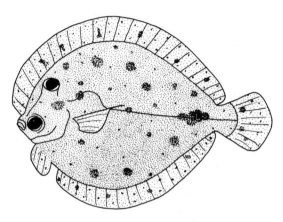

A very round-bodied flounder with a small mouth. Lateral line strongly arched. The eyes are widely separated in males. Ocular pelvic fin with its base on the ventral midline and much wider at its base than the fin of the blind side. D. 76-91; A. 58-68; Ll. 70-78. Brownish to grayish with lighter and darker mottling and spotting, including two large clusters of spots on the lateral line. A vertical pair of round dark spots on proximal caudal rays. Six inches long.

A mostly tropical species, in our area found only near sandy or coralline bottoms off Florida and Texas, usually in ten to fifty fathoms.

A similar species, currently undescribed, occurs with the eyed flounder. It differs in having the caudal spots horizontal instead of vertical.

448. GULF STREAM FLOUNDER
Citharichthys arctifrons Goode

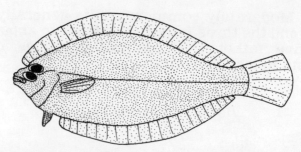

Lateral line weakly curved anteriorly; mouth large. D. 75-86; A. 58-67; Ll. 37-43; gill rakers 5 + 6 to 8. Body slender, its depth usually less than forty percent (34-43%) of standard length. Teeth in both jaws uniserial. A horizontally projecting bony protuberance on the snout, often inconspicuous in smaller specimens. Uniformly brownish. Four to five inches long.

An offshore Atlantic seaboard species rarely found on the west coast of Florida. Usually in more than fifty fathoms, but sometimes in fifteen to twenty-five fathoms.

449. HORNED WHIFF
Citharichthys cornutus (Gunther)

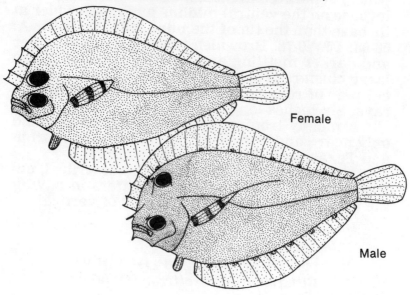

Female

Male

Lateral line weakly curved anteriorly; mouth large; teeth in both jaws uniserial. D. 74-83; A. 59-66; Ll. 40-45. Body depth 44 to 50 percent of standard length. Pectoral fin long, over twenty percent of standard length, much longer and elongated in males. In all other *Citharichthys* the pectoral is less than 20% of SL. Pectoral fin with dark crossbars and a dark spot in the axilla. Males with a widened interorbital and prominent spines on the orbital rims. A horizontally directed spine on the snout, not projecting through the skin in females and juveniles. Brownish. Four inches in length.

A truly deepwater species, seldom found in water less than seventy-five fathoms deep. A few records from as little as fifteen fathoms permit it to be included here.

450. SPOTTED WHIFF
Citharichthys macrops Dresel

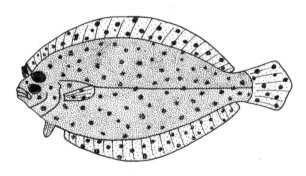

Lateral line weakly curved anteriorly; mouth large; teeth in both jaws uniserial. D. 80-85; A. 56-64; Ll. 37-44; gill rakers long and slender, 5 to 6 + 13 to 16. Brownish, the body and fins with numerous small darker spots, often very densely placed. Six inches long.

An uncommon species in our area, usually found in water over ten fathoms deep, but occasionally in shallower areas.

451. BAY WHIFF
Citharichthys spilopterus Gunther

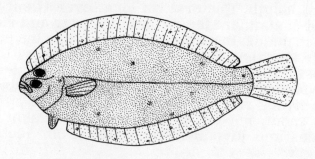

Lateral line weakly curved anteriorly; mouth large; teeth in both jaws uniserial. Highly variable in counts, proportions, and color. D. 75-84; A. 56-63; Ll. 41-49; Gill rakers 4 to 5 + 9 to 15, shorter and stouter than in the spotted whiff. Coloration variable, light sandy brown to deep brown with darker and lighter spots; never as densely and distinctly spotted as the spotted whiff. Body depth varies from 41 to 51 percent of standard length. Seldom exceeds six inches in length.

Abundant from brackish water to estuaries and out to at least twenty-five fathoms. In deeper water it is often with and practically indistinguishable from *Syacium gunteri* and *S. papillosum* except by teeth and gill rakers.

452. MEXICAN FLOUNDER
Cyclopsetta chittendeni Bean

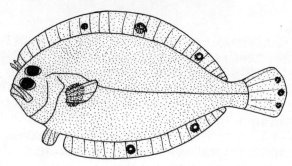

Lateral line nearly straight anteriorly; mouth very large, over 48% of head length; forehead convex. D. 82-90; A. 63-69; Ll. 74-80. Pectoral fin with oblique distal edge, hyaline with a large brown spot on the body under its basal half. Brownish, fins with large spots; caudal fin with three small spots distally but lacking large spot at center. One foot long.

Very common in ten to seventy-five fathoms; edible.

453. SPOTFIN FLOUNDER
Cyclopsetta fimbriata (Goode & Bean)

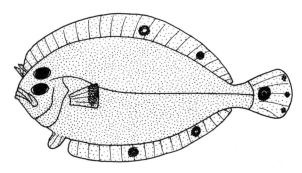

Lateral line slightly curved or straight anteriorly; mouth very large, over 48% of head length; forehead convex. D. 78-87; A. 59-67; Ll. 65-75. Pectoral fin with a truncate distal margin; hyaline basally but with a large brown spot on its distal third. Body and fins brownish, vaguely mottled and spotted. Two or three large dark spots in dorsal and anal fins and a large central spot in the caudal. One foot long.

Relatively common in the northern Gulf in from ten to seventy-five fathoms, but not as common as the Mexican flounder.

A third species, *Cyclopsetta decussata* Gunter, is currently considered a synonym of the Mexican flounder, *C. chittendeni*, but with reservations. *C. decussata* was based on a single mounted specimen from off Texas that has five or six dark vertical bars running across the fins and body; the dorsal, anal, caudal, and pectoral fins lack spots. Occasional specimens of *C. chittendeni* can be found with indications of body banding, but never to the extent of the type of *C. decussata*. Also, *C. decussata* is supposed to have twelve pectoral rays, as in *C. fimbriata*, not the fourteen to sixteen of *C. chittendeni*. It is probably best to consider *C. decussata* to have been based on an abnormal *C. chittendeni* which was perhaps damaged and then incorrectly painted by the taxidermist. However, our offshore fauna is so poorly known that the possibility that a third and very distinctive species exists off Texas should not be ignored.

454. SPINY FLOUNDER
Engyophrys senta Ginsburg

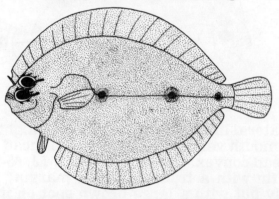

Lateral line strongly curved anteriorly; pelvic fin on ventral profile. Mouth very small, extending only to anterior margin of lower eye. D. 74-83; A. 60-67; Ll. 50. Posterior part of eyeball with a long tentacle, shorter in males at larger body lengths; usually three to five interorbital spines, most prominent in males. Brown, with darker blotches along the lateral line and the dorsal and ventral profiles; usually three blotches on straight part of lateral line. Three inches.

Locally common in water fifteen to one hundred fathoms deep, but its small size makes it very difficult to collect in average nets.

455. FRINGED FLOUNDER
Etropus crossotus Jordan & Gilbert

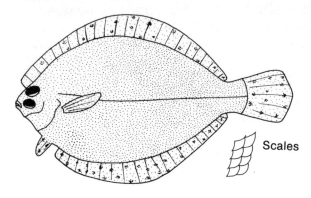

Scales

Lateral line weakly curved anteriorly; mouth very small. D. 75-87; A. 58-68; Ll. 41-47. Body depth usually over half of standard length, about 50-58%. Scales of ocular side simple, weakly ctenoid, without secondary scales; no scales anterior to eyes. Uniformly brownish, without darker spots; fins may be spotted. Five inches in length.

The common shallow water *Etropus*. Small specimens not uncommon in estuaries, but adults come mostly from water five to thirty-five fathoms deep.

456. SMALLMOUTH FLOUNDER
Etropus microstomus (Gill)

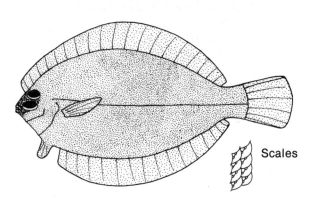

Scales

Lateral line weakly curved anteriorly; mouth very small. D. 67-82; A. 50-63; Ll. 37-45. Body slender, depth 43 to 51% of standard length. Scales with a single row of secondary scales; snout with scales, which can easily be rubbed off; a row of scales before eyes. Body and fins nearly uniform brown, not spotted or mottled; sometimes darker around eyes and mouth. Under four inches long.

An uncommon species seemingly restricted to waters east of the Mississippi delta. Estuarine to fifty fathoms.

457. GRAY FLOUNDER
Etropus rimosus Goode & Bean

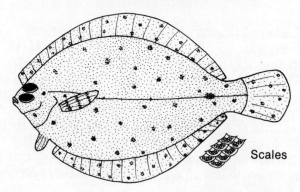

Scales

Lateral line weakly curved anteriorly; mouth very small. D. 74-83; A. 57-63; Ll. 37-43. Body depth about half of standard length, 48-57%. Scales of ocular side strongly roughened and covered with many secondary scales; snout scaled. Body brownish with distinct dark spots; ocular pelvic fin with three or four dark vertical bars. Five inches long.

Uncommon in waters ten to twenty fathoms deep, mostly in the extreme northeastern Gulf; not recorded west of the Mississippi delta.

458. SHRIMP FLOUNDER
Gastropsetta frontalis Bean

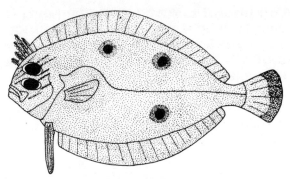

Lateral line strongly arched anteriorly; pelvic fin above ventral profile; mouth large. Forehead prominently convex. D. 58-65; A. 46-53; Ll. 95-112. Some anterior dorsal rays elongated, as are some ocular pelvic rays. Brown, with three large ocellated spots on the ocular side, none on the lateral line, the first over the pectoral and the other two over the middle of the straight lateral line. Usually less than a foot in length.

This is a deep water species which seldom occurs in less than twenty fathoms, but is often common just beyond our depth range.

459. GULF FLOUNDER
Paralichthys albigutta Jordan & Gilbert

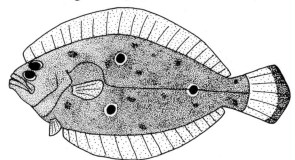

Lateral line strongly curved anteriorly; pelvic fin above ventral profile; mouth large. D. 71-85; A. 53-63; Ll. 78-81. No elongated dorsal or pectoral rays. Forehead concave. Brownish, with three relatively small ocellated dark spots, the first two paired just behind lateral line arch, the third on lateral line about one pectoral fin length anterior to caudal peduncle. One foot long.

A deepwater species, the adults uncommon in ten to fifty fathoms. Occasional juveniles may be taken in shallower water, including estuaries.

460. SOUTHERN FLOUNDER
Paralichthys lethostigma Jordan & Gilbert

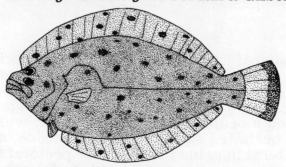

Lateral line strongly curved anteriorly; pelvic fin above ventral profile; mouth large; forehead concave. D. 80-95; A. 63-74; Ll. 85-100. Body relatively slender, the depth 39 to 47 percent of standard length. Brownish, with many small light and dark spots, irregular in size and sharpness, over ocular side; blind side of juveniles dusky or white. Commonly over two feet long.

Abundant in water only a few inches deep in estuaries out to several fathoms.

461. BROAD FLOUNDER
Paralichthys squamilentus Jordan & Gilbert

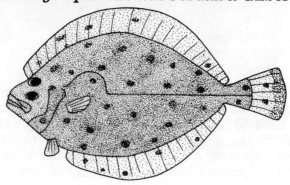

Lateral line strongly curved anteriorly; pelvic fin above ventral profile; mouth large; forehead concave. D. 76-85; A. 59-65; Ll. 104-117. Body deep, 48 to 59 percent of standard length; difference in depth easily seen when compared to typical southern flounders. Brownish with indistinct small darker and lighter spots over ocular side. About one foot long.

An uncommon flounder in our depth limits, usually seen as juveniles taken in ten or more fathoms. Adults seldom venture into water shallower than sixty fathoms. Occasional juveniles may be found in estuaries, but only rarely.

462. SHOAL FLOUNDER
Syacium gunteri Ginsburg

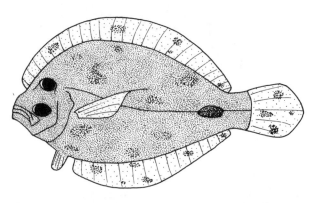

Lateral line weakly curved anteriorly; mouth large; upper teeth in two rows, lower in one row. D. 74-85; A. 59-68; Ll. 43-50 pored, 46-55 total; gill rakers 2 to 3 (rarely 4) + 6 to 8. The interorbital area is relatively wide but varies with size and sex. Male upper pectoral rays elongated. Brownish, with vague spots and mottling; usually a diffuse dark blotch on lateral line just anterior to caudal peduncle. Five inches in length.

Common in ten to fifty fathoms.

Easily distinguished from the other *Syacium* by the lower counts and deeper body, the depth 48 to 55 percent of standard length.

463. CHANNEL FLOUNDER
Syacium micrurum Ranzani

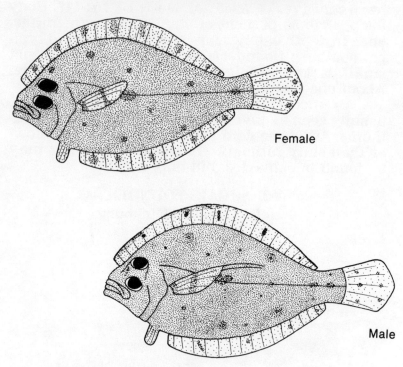

Female

Male

Lateral line weakly curved anteriorly; mouth large; upper teeth biserial, lower uniserial. D. 82-94; A. 47-60; Ll. 57-68 pored, 62-73 total. Body depth 38 to 45 percent (usually 42%) of standard length. Interorbital of large males commonly half or less of diameter of lower eye, not exceeding 75%; females 20 to 25%. Juveniles with snout length 80% or more of lower eye (less than 75% in dusky flounder juveniles). Brownish, variably spotted or not; males without dark lines on snout and under anterior dorsal fin. Nine inches long.

Apparently a tropical species which is either very rare in our area or does not occur at all. Easily confused with the dusky flounder and requires a series of specimens of both sexes for proper identification.

464. DUSKY FLOUNDER
Syacium papillosum (Linnaeus)

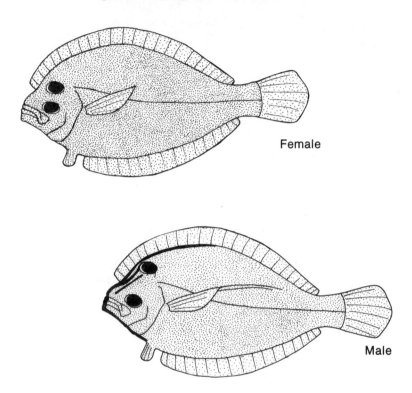

Female

Male

Lateral line weakly curved anteriorly; mouth large; upper teeth biserial, lower uniserial. D. 82-94; A. 64-75; Ll. 50-61 pored, usually 54 or 55. Body depth 44 percent (40-47%) of standard length. Interorbital wide, in males of six or more inches equal to 50-90% of diameter of lower eye; in large females, commonly 25-35%. Brownish, variably spotted and mottled or not. Males with dark line (blue in life) from snout to eye and along anterior dorsal profile. Eight to nine inches in length.

Common in ten to fifty or more fathoms throughout the northern Gulf. The only *Syacium* likely to be found in our area are *S. gunteri* and *S. papillosum*.

465. SASH FLOUNDER
Trichopsetta ventralis (Goode & Bean)

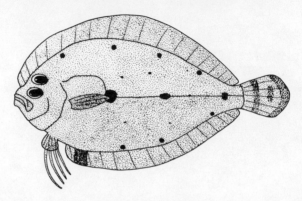

Lateral line strongly arched anteriorly; mouth large; pelvic fin on ventral profile. D. 89-95; A. 69-75; Ll. 63-68. Pelvic fin of blind side greatly elongated in males. Brown, usually with vague spots and mottlings; usually a dark blotch on lateral line arch and three spots along straight lateral line; males with a dark blotch on anterior anal fin rays. To about a foot long.

An uncommon deepwater flounder that just enters our range at twenty fathoms; extends to at least sixty fathoms depth.

References: Fraser, T.H., 1971(*Bull. Mar. Sci.*, 21(2):491-509; *Syacium*); Gutherez, E., 1967 (*Circular Fish & Wild. Serv.*, Washington, #263); Moe, M.A. and G.T. Martin, 1965 (*Tulane Stud. Zool.*, 12(4):129-151).

Family SOLEIDAE — soles

Broadly oval flatfishes with caudal peduncle very short; the eyes and color on the right side; pelvic fin of the ocular (right) side attached to the anal fin. Dorsal fin begins on snout. Preopercle covered with skin, its edge not free. Mouth small, toothless or nearly so. Lateral line straight and well developed. Pectoral fin of eyed side small or absent. Four species.

466. LINED SOLE
Achirus lineatus (Linnaeus)

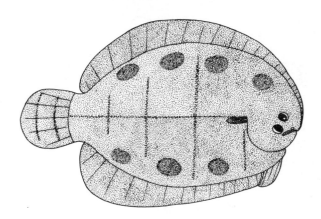

Head and body fully scaled, rough to touch; skin firmly attached to body. Small pectoral fin present at upper edge of operculum, usually longer than eye and consisting of four to six rays. Grayish brown, usually with indications of narrow cross bars and a darker lateral line; several round dark spots along dorsal and ventral profiles. Fins dark. Blind side in juveniles dark posteriorly, light anteriorly. Commonly four inches long, but reaches five.

Rather common in bays and shallow water throughout the northern Gulf, but usually confused with the hogchoker, which it closely resembles in color.

467. NAKED SOLE
Gymnachirus melas Nichols

Skin very loose, scaleless, easily torn. Pectoral fin absent; gill opening restricted. Dark lines few and wide, about twenty to thirty stripes and partial stripes originating on dorsal fin; dark stripes about as wide as lighter interspaces. Juveniles almost solid dark until over two inches long. Reaches six inches in length. Cream to brownish, the lines black.

The *Gymnachirus* of the Florida west coast, extending west only as far as the Florida panhandle. Although reported from one to over fifty fathoms, it is most common in fifteen to twenty-five fathoms.

Nodogymnus is a synonym of *Gymnachirus*. *Nodogymnus nicholsi* and *N. williamsoni* are both synonyms of *G. melas*, as are most Gulf records of *G. nudus*, a tropical species.

468. FRINGED SOLE
Gymnachirus texae Gunter

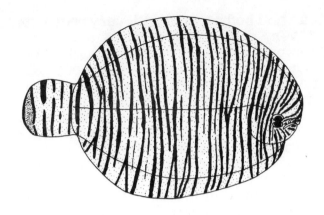

Skin scaleless, very loose and easily torn. Pectoral fin absent. Gill slit smaller than in *Achirus* and *Trinectes*. Background color cream to brownish with many (twenty-five to forty-nine, usually over thirty) narrow dark stripes and partial stripes beginning on the dorsal fin. Dark stripes about half width of light interspaces. Juveniles over one inch long with a striped pattern. Blind side pale, fins dusky. Four inches.

An abundant sole in the western Gulf of Mexico from Alabama to Mexico. Found in water from fifteen to fifty fathoms deep, occasionally in less than five fathoms.

469. HOGCHOKER
Trinectes maculatus (Bloch & Schneider)

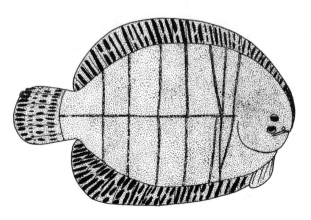

Head and body scaled with very rough ctenoid scales; very difficult to remove the living fish from a smooth surface; scales rougher than in lined sole; skin firmly attached to body. No pectoral fin on eyed side (rarely a short one- or two-rayed rudiment may be present). Gray to brown, with six to eight narrow dark vertical bars and a dark lateral line; fins dark; no large round spots along dorsal and ventral profiles. Blind side usually immaculate, sometimes mottled with darker. Six to eight inches long.

A very common fish in estuaries, ascending rivers and coastal streams to at least 100 miles inland; also very common in deeper water out to twenty fathoms.

Achirus fasciatus and *Achirus browni* are synonyms.

Reference: Dawson, C.E., 1964(*Copeia*, 1964 (4):646-665; *Gymnachirus*).

Family **CYNOGLOSSIDAE** — tonguefishes

Elongated left-eyed flatfishes which taper to a point posteriorly; caudal fin continuous with dorsal and anal. Pectoral fin of eyed side absent; lateral line absent; pelvic fin separate from anal on eyed side. Six species, only two common.

470. OFFSHORE TONGUEFISH
Symphurus civitatus Ginsburg

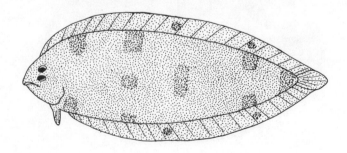

D. 87-92; A. 70-77; caudal rays normally 12, sometimes 11. Lower jaw of eyed side with few or no teeth. Color brownish, mottled with darker; fins dusky posteriorly; variable. Operculum brownish, without a dark spot posteriorly. Six inches.

The common tonguefish in moderately deep water, most common in fifteen to twenty-five fathoms, but extending shoreward to at least six fathoms.

The offshore tonguefish differs from the blackcheek principally in having 12 caudal rays and lacking a dark opercular spot; both these characters vary, and it is possible to find estuarine specimens of the blackcheek which are indistinguishable from the offshore tonguefish. Although listed here as a distinct species, it seems likely that *Symphurus civitatus* is just a deepwater form of the normally shallow water *S. plagiusa*. Tonguefishes from depths between six and ten fathoms could be either form, and specimens from this depth range are sometimes not certainly identifiable as either "species."

471. SPOTTEDFIN TONGUEFISH
Symphurus diomedianus (Goode & Bean)

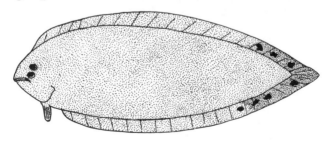

Lower jaw with no teeth or a few near the middle. D. 89-93; A. 73-78; caudal 10. Body brownish, vaguely banded or mottled. Dorsal and anal fins dusky posteriorly, usually with one to four rounded, irregular, very dark spots in posterior fifth; in some specimens these dark spots are obscured by the intensity of the dark background pigment of the fins. Caudal fin dusky, not spotted. Eight inches in length.

Collected in eight to fifty fathoms, usually near snapper banks and other hard bottoms; this preference for hard bottoms may be the reason it is seldom collected.

472. PYGMY TONGUEFISH
Symphurus parvus Ginsburg

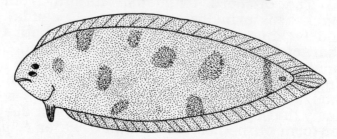

Teeth present over greater part of lower jaw, very small. D. 78-84; A. 56-61; caudal 10-11. Body depth and caudal fin of normal proportions. Body pale brown, mottled with darker. Two to three inches long.

Most common in waters more than twenty fathoms deep out to fifty fathoms or more. Apparently not found west of the Mississippi delta.

473. LONGTAIL TONGUEFISH
Symphurus pelicanus Ginsburg

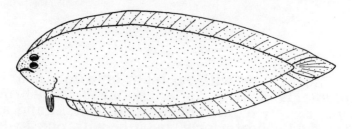

Teeth present over greater part of the lower jaw, very small. D. 80-81; A. 63-67; caudal 12. Body relatively slender for the genus in our waters, with the caudal fin comparatively long. Yellowish, with fine melanophores over sides, the appearance very pale. Three inches in length.

Common and widely distributed in the twenty-five to fifty fathom zone over muddy bottoms.

474. BLACKCHEEK TONGUEFISH
Symphurus plagiusa (Linnaeus)

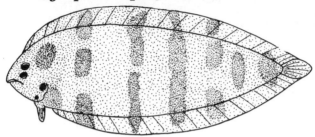

Lower jaw of eyed side with few or no teeth. D. 85-92; A. 69-78; caudal 10, sometimes 11, rarely 9. Brownish, very variably patterned with darker mottling, spots, or bands, sometimes almost plain; fins clear or dusky, sometimes with faint spots. Posterior ventral portion of operculum with a large dusky spot in most specimens, lacking in some or broken into two smaller spots. Four to six inches long, rarely eight.

The most common tonguefish in the northern Gulf, found in estuarine and shallow coastal water commonly out to ten fathoms, rarely to twenty fathoms. Compare closely with the offshore tonguefish.

475. SPOTTAIL TONGUEFISH
Symphurus urospilus Ginsburg

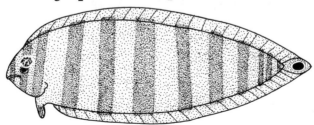

Teeth mostly absent on lower jaw. D. 84-86; A. 68-71; caudal 11. Body with wide regular dark bands, about three on head and nine on body. Posterior dorsal and anal fins without distinct dark spots, but a large ocellated dark spot on the posterior part of the caudal fin. Six inches.

Found in relatively shallow water (ten fathoms or deeper) on the eastern edge of our range.

Reference: Ginsburg, I., 1951(*Zoologica, N.Y.*, 36(3):185-201).

ORDER TETRAODONTIFORMES (PLECTOGNATHI) — triggerfishes, puffers, molas

An easily recognized group of fishes with the gill opening reduced to a slit anterior to the pectoral fin. Pelvic fins generally absent or reduced to a large spine and a few rays on each side. Scales absent, plate-like, or modified into cilia, prickles, or spines. Mouth small and terminal, the jaw elements indistinct externally. Teeth conical, incisors, or fused into plates. Six families, twenty-seven species.

Family **TRIACANTHODIDAE** — spikefishes

This is a small family of normally deepwater species (found in more than sixty fathoms) which will probably occasionally be found on the outer edges of our depth range. Although shaped much like the filefishes, they are readily recognized by the presence of six or more dorsal spines and long, strong pelvic spines. Most are small fishes only two to five inches long, silvery or brownish in color and often with spots or stripes. One species is illustrated as an example of the family.

476. JAMBEAU
Parahollardia lineata (Longley)

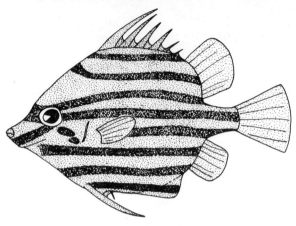

Described from sixty fathoms off the Tortugas and not uncommon. It or a similar species may be found in our area.

Family **BALISTIDAE** — triggerfishes and filefishes

Compressed, rather rhomboidal fishes with terminal mouths containing conical teeth. A distinct pelvic expansion or "flap" is often present. Soft dorsal preceded by a spinous dorsal fin of two or three spines. Pelvic fins absent. Twelve species.

This family is commonly broken into two, the Balistidae for the triggerfishes and Monacanthidae for the filefishes. These two groups are very similar in form, the major differences being that the triggerfishes have three dorsal spines forming a locking mechanism and have plate-like scales, while the filefishes have only two spines, the second very short, and the scales are usually ciliate. Only one family is recognized here in keeping with most modern thinking.

477. DOTTEREL FILEFISH
Aluterus heudeloti Hollard

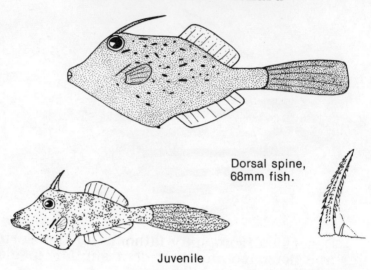

Dorsal spine,
68mm fish.

Juvenile

D. II - 36-41; A. 39-44. Relatively deep-bodied with a caudal peduncle longer than deep. A distinct pelvic flap is present, bearing a small immoveable spine which just penetrates the skin; this spine is absent in specimens over five inches long. Eye relatively close to dorsal spine. Mottled olive-brown in life with numerous blue or purple scrawls and spots. After preservation most dark pigment is concentrated on the dorsolateral part of the body. Juvenile with a well developed pelvic flap and pelvic spine; first dorsal spine relatively shorter and stouter than in orange filefish and more heavily armed. Reaches at least eighteen inches, possibly more.

Not uncommon in waters ten fathoms or more deep. Poorly known.

This genus is sometimes placed in a distinct family, Aluteridae, and the genus spelled *Alutera*. *Aluterus ventralis* is a synonym.

478. ORANGE FILEFISH
Aluterus schoepfi (Walbaum)

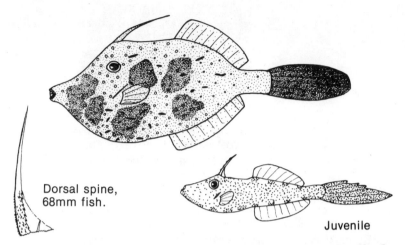

Dorsal spine,
68mm fish.

Juvenile

D. II - 32-39; A. 35-41. Relatively deep-bodied, with the snout oblique and short, terminating well below the eye. The pelvic flap is well developed in large specimens; pelvic spine absent. Caudal peduncle longer than deep. Eye usually about one diameter below first dorsal spine. In life, whitish anteriorly with grayish mottling and blotches. Many orange spots over the body. In preservative the colors fading, but many dark blotches appear, usually concentrated along the ventrolateral surface of the body. Juvenile slender, with caudal fin long and lighter above than below as in other juvenile *Aluterus*; first dorsal spine relatively long and slender with only a few weak barbs. Reaches three feet, but commonly much smaller.

Adults most common in water deeper than twenty fathoms. Juveniles often found inshore with wind-blown *Sargassum*.

479. SCRAWLED FILEFISH
Aluterus scriptus (Osbeck)

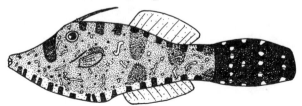

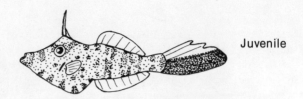

Juvenile

D. II 43-49; A. 46-52. Relatively elongate, slender, with a poorly developed pelvic flap; pelvic spine absent. First dorsal spine long and slender, inserted over middle or posterior part of eye; gill slit very oblique, usually at a 45° angle to the horizontal (all *Aluterus*). Snout long, concave above, its tip only slightly below level of eye. Caudal peduncle deeper than long. Pale olive brown, mottled with darker, especially along dorsal and ventral profiles; numerous blue, green, and black spots and lines in life. Three feet long.

Adults are offshore fishes not very common in the northern Gulf. Juveniles may be associated with floating *Sargassum*.

480. GRAY TRIGGERFISH
Balistes capriscus Gmelin

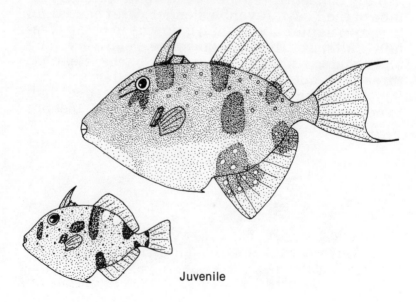

Juvenile

D. III - 26-29; A. 23-26. Deep-bodied, with a long third dorsal spine and enlarged plates behind the gill slit. Dorsal and anal fins high anteriorly, no rays prolonged; caudal fin moderately lunate in adults. Caudal peduncle scales without keels. Grayish with darker mottling; no blue bands on snout or from eye. Young with four dark dorsal saddles below soft dorsal, separated by distinct light spots; saddles fading in adult but often still recognizable. Twelve inches in length.

The common triggerfish of the northern Gulf and apparently the only one which is resident. Although seldom found in bays and water less than a fathom deep, it is common on hard bottoms in deeper water and is often a nuisance to snapper fishermen. *Balistes carolinensis* is a synonym.

481. QUEEN TRIGGERFISH
Balistes vetula Linnaeus

Juvenile

D. III - 29-31; A. 26-28. Deep bodied, with a long third dorsal spine about equal to the eye diameter. Enlarged plates behind gill slits; caudal peduncle without keels. Soft dorsal and anal fins high anteriorly, some anterior rays prolonged; caudal fin deeply lunate in adults. Grayish to bluish above, yellowish below; two broad blue stripes on snout and about six short blue stripes from eye. Young grayish with darker streaks arranged in a diagonal fashion; blue stripes indistinct. Two feet long.

A tropical straggler occasionally reaching the northern Gulf during the summer in the form of juveniles.

482. ORANGESPOTTED FILEFISH
Cantherhines pullus (Ranzani)

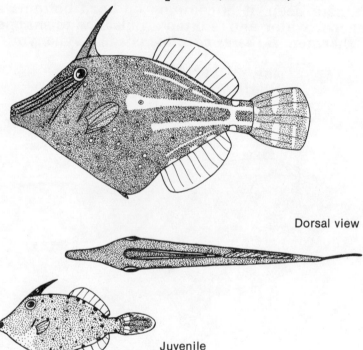

Dorsal view

Juvenile

D. II - 33-37; A. 29-32. Dorsal spine stout, almost smooth, and inserted over the anterior part of the eye. A deep groove between the spinous and soft dorsal fins into which first dorsal spine can be retracted. Pelvic spine not moveable (if not broken by too much pressure). Caudal peduncle of females plain, that of males with a large setose patch extending onto the body. Color variable, usually dark with scattered orange and white spots; usually several white lines converging on caudal peduncle and distinct white spots on edges of peduncle behind the last dorsal and anal rays. Juveniles similar in morphology but with several rows of small black spots on sides. Maximum length probably under eight inches.

A rare straggler in our area, usually in the form of juveniles associated with floating debris offshore. Often referred to as *Amanses pullus*.

483. OCEAN TRIGGERFISH
Canthidermis sufflamen (Mitchill)

Juvenile

D. III - 25-28; A. 23-25. An elongated, high-finned triggerfish with normal scales behind the gill slit and a third dorsal spine which extends beyond the dorsal profile. Soft dorsal and anal very high, anterior rays often as long as the head. Cheeks fully scaled. Grayish brown with a large brown spot at base of pectorals; fins dark. Young with high fins; color pattern of several horizontal stripes on a lighter brown background, these stripes broken into streaks and bars. Two feet or more in length.

A pelagic triggerfish which is probably widely distributed in the Gulf but seldom seen near shore. The young have occasionally been collected under floating debris. *Canthidermis sobaco* is a synonym.

The rough triggerfish, *Canthidermis maculatus*, is similar but has a pattern of pale spots on the body, rougher scales, and fewer fin rays (dorsal 24, anal 21). Pelagic in the central Gulf but not yet recorded near land.

484. BLACK DURGON
Melichthys niger (Bloch)

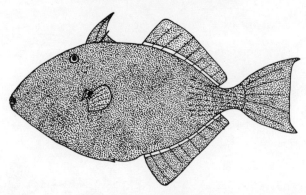

D. III - 31-35; A. 29-31. A slender fish with enlarged plates behind the gill slit and a third dorsal spine which barely projects beyond the dorsal profile. Scales on caudal peduncle and posterior part of the body with strong lengthwise keels. Body uniformly deep black, as are the fins. A narrow pale blue line along the bases of the dorsal and anal fins. Juvenile similar to adult. Fourteen inches long.

An omnivorous species (other triggerfishes are carnivorous) usually found on deeper reefs.

Very rare in the northern Gulf, reported only from an offshore reef in Texas.

Genus Monacanthus: First dorsal spine inserted over posterior part of eye, barbed; no groove between dorsal fins; pelvic spine moveable up and down with little pressure.

485. FRINGED FILEFISH
Monacanthus ciliatus (Mitchill)

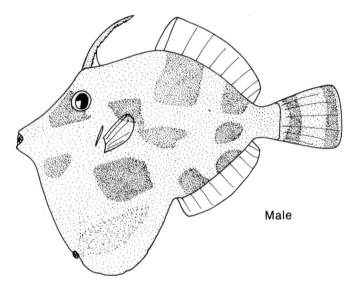

Male

D. II - 29-37; A. 28-36. Pelvic flap of both sexes very deep, its ventral edge extending well below a line drawn through the tips of the anal rays and much deeper than the caudal peduncle. Pelvic spine not terminal, greatly exceeded by the edge of the pelvic flap. At least two pairs of spines (small except in mature males) on caudal peduncle, more in males. Posterior edge of pelvic flap black in males. Grayish, mottled with brown, often with white spots. Five inches long.

A species of shallow grassy bays, not common in the northern Gulf.

486. PLANEHEAD FILEFISH
Monacanthus hispidus (Linnaeus)

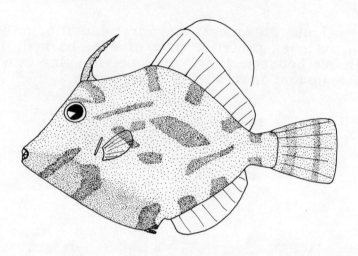

D. II - 29-35; A. 30-35. Pelvic flap small, not deeper than caudal peduncle, with a terminal pelvic spine. No spines on caudal peduncle of either sex, but the second dorsal ray elongated in males. Brownish, with irregular and poorly defined darker dashes and blotches on sides; breast light or dark, but lacking distinct dark spots; caudal fin with one or two indistinct dark bars. Reaches ten inches in length.

The most common filefish in our area which has a pelvic spine. The young are often common in grassy bays, but adults are found in depths to twenty fathoms or more.

487. PYGMY FILEFISH
Monacanthus setifer Bennett

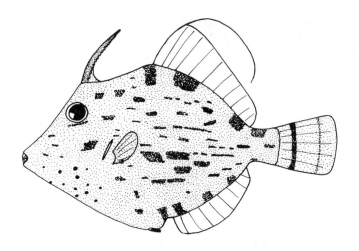

D. II - 27-30; A. 26-30. Pelvic flap not much deeper than caudal peduncle; spine terminal. No spines on caudal peduncle of either sex. Males with elongated second dorsal ray. Brownish, with sharply defined dark dashes on the sides, arranged in more-or-less regular lines; breast with distinct dark spots. Caudal fin with two distinct bars, the proximal one darker. Maximum length about seven inches, but generally smaller.

Uncommon in the northern Gulf and usually in water over ten fathoms deep.

This species and the planehead filefish are often referred to the genus *Stephanolepis* as distinct from *Monacanthus*. In these species the scales each have one to three small spines and each spine is branched many times. In *Monacanthus* there are more spines per scale and each spine is simple or nearly so.

488. SARGASSUM TRIGGERFISH
Xanthichthys ringens (Linnaeus)

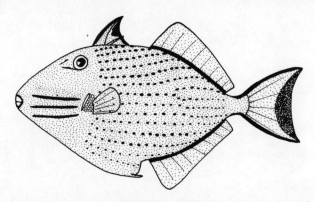

D. III - 26-30; A. 23-27. Cheek with modified
scales, forming three naked grooves that are horizontal or slightly oblique and separated by rows of
fused scales. The naked grooves are dark brown
and stand out sharply from the paler background
color. Scales behind gill slit normal; keels on caudal peduncle absent; third dorsal spine short, not
extending above dorsal profile. Median fins low;
caudal fin with stout but prolonged outer edges.
Light grayish brown with many rows of blackish
spots on the body; caudal fin pale, with orange
edges and a terminal crescent mark; median fins
pale. Juvenile similar to adult. Seldom reaches
ten inches in length.

A tropical species common on deep reefs but
seldom reaching our shores. Juveniles are rare
but more common than adults and are usually associated with masses of *Sargassum*.

Family OSTRACIIDAE — boxfishes

Scales fused into a rigid armor (carapace)
enclosing the entire trunk except for the eyes,
mouth, gill slits, fins, and caudal peduncle. Carapace roughly triangular with ventrolateral keels
ending in strong spines. Dorsal, anal, and caudal
rays ten. Teeth in a single row in each jaw, 8-12
above, 6-10 below; conical to incisor-like in shape.
Two species.

489. SCRAWLED COWFISH
Lactophrys quadricornis (Linnaeus)

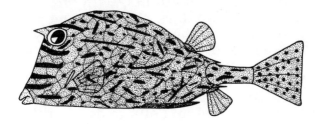

Carapace with the dorsal profile evenly curved and continuous behind the dorsal fin, ending in a short spine. Prominent flattened spines or "horns" projecting anteriorly from the upper edge of the carapace above each eye. Pectoral rays usually eleven. Color variable, usually brownish to grayish with blue scrawls and spots; about three parallel horizontal lines below the eye. Eighteen inches long, but rarely over a foot.

A common species occurring in waters of higher salinity in five to forty fathoms. Often dried as souvenirs by trawlers. The genus *Acanthostracion* is often used for this species, and *Lactophrys tricornis* is a synonym.

490. TRUNKFISH
Lactophrys trigonus (Linnaeus)

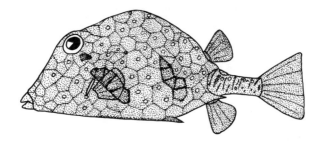

Dorsal profile of the carapace distinctly humped just behind the middle, sloping rapidly downward to the dorsal fin. A distinct gap in the carapace behind the dorsal fin, often with one or two small plates within the gap. No "horns" over eyes. Pectoral rays usually twelve. Olive green, often with bluish highlights, with white spots on the carapace. Two dark blotches, one behind the pectoral and the other on side midway between the pectoral and dorsal fins. Eighteen inches in length.

Although common in more tropical waters, the trunkfish is rare in our area and usually found east of the Mississippi delta in five to fifteen fathoms.

Reference: Tyler, J.C., 1965(*Proc. Acad. Nat. Sci., Phila.*, 117(8):261-287).

Family **TETRAODONTIDAE** — puffers

Body moderately elongate, the dorsal and anal fins set far to back. Body smooth or with small prickles. Teeth fused into beaks, each with a median division at the front, producing two plates in each jaw. Seven species.

 Beaks

491. SHARPNOSE PUFFER
Canthigaster rostrata (Bloch)

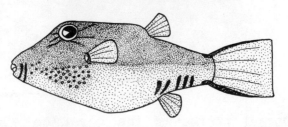

Dorsal profile convex, much more ridge-like than the normally flat back of other puffers. A midventral skin fold present. Dorsal rays usually ten, anal rays nine. Body smooth dorsally. Lateral line absent. Tan with dark upper and lower caudal rays, this banding continued onto caudal peduncle. Blue lines and spots on snout and blue lines radiating from eye. Less than four inches in length.

A tropical reef fish rarely recorded from our area. An old record from the snapper banks off Pensacola indicates that it occurs on the northeastern edge of the Florida coral reefs, presumably in deep water.

This genus is sometimes given its own family, Canthigasteridae.

492. SMOOTH PUFFER
Lagocephalus laevigatus (Linnaeus)

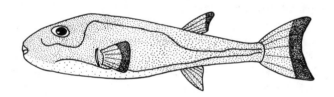

Body more elongate than in other puffers, ending in a distinctly concave caudal fin. Dorsal and anal fins relatively high and pointed, with thirteen to fourteen dorsal and thirteen anal rays. Lateral line conspicuous against the smooth, shiny body skin, continued forward under eye. A strongly developed fleshy lateral keel on ventrolateral margin of body, running from snout to caudal fin. Grayish green above, whitish below. Fins dusky, the caudal often with a distinct terminal band. Commonly a foot long, but reaches about two feet in length.

A common fish in the northern Gulf, found mostly in water two to forty fathoms deep and rarely inshore.

Genus Sphoeroides: Dorsal rays eight to nine, anal rays six to nine. Dorsum flat or nearly

409

so; body with small prickles at least on sides. Lateral line indistinct, no fleshy lateral folds.

493. MARBLED PUFFER
Sphoeroides dorsalis Longley

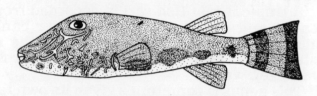

A single black lappet, conspicuous against the light body, on each side above the pectoral fin and just below the dorsal profile. Ventrolateral spots most regular anteriorly, becoming one to five irregular blotches behind the pectoral, often not distinct from the dorsal color. Olive above with vague darker blotches, white below. Caudal fin with dark bands against a dusky background; caudal sometimes dark enough to obscure banding. Snout and cheeks with blue marbling in the form of lines and spots. Under eight inches in length.

A tropical deepwater species found in our area mostly off southern Texas and Florida in ten to fifty fathoms.

494. SOUTHERN PUFFER
Sphoeroides nephelus (Goode & Bean)

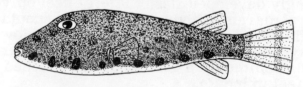

Body without lappets. Green to brown above, with small orange spots concentrated laterally. Several black spots in a regular row along the ventrolateral edge of the body, the one in pectoral axilla most intense. Bony interorbital narrow and concave, more than four in snout length. Reaches twelve inches in length and not mature until at least five inches.

The common inshore puffer of western Florida, rarely extending west to Alabama and Mississippi; not recorded from Louisiana and Texas. Bays to several fathoms. *Sphoeroides harperi* is a synonym.

495. LEAST PUFFER
Sphoeroides parvus Shipp & Yerger

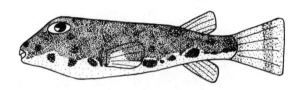

Body without lappets. Brownish to gray above, with vague black blotches and white dots. Sides often golden; venter white. Ventrolateral row of black blotches of irregular size and arrangement. No spot in the pectoral axilla or, if a spot is present, it is weaker than the other spots. Caudal plain or dusky. The bony interorbital is broad and flat, its width going less than four in the snout length. Very small, adults seldom four inches long.

This is the only common inshore puffer in Louisiana and Texas; it is also commonly found in Mississippi and Alabama and in Florida east to Pensacola. Common in bays and occasionally out to thirty-five fathoms.

496. BANDTAIL PUFFER
Sphoeroides spengleri (Bloch)

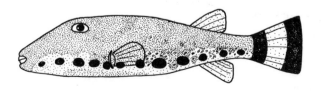

Body with many small tan lappets, especially concentrated on the posterior ventrolateral surface. Pale yellowish above, white below. Dorsum with many small black blotches and dots, none as distinct as the ventrolateral spots. A regular ventrolateral line of round black spots, some as large as the eye, extending in an unbroken series from the snout to the caudal peduncle. Cheeks without blue marbling. Caudal fin orange with two broad black bands. Reaches at least one foot in length.

Widely distributed along the northern Gulf but nowhere common. Most records are from ten or more fathoms, usually near hard bottoms, but the species also occurs inshore.

497. CHECKERED PUFFER
Sphoeroides testudineus (Linnaeus)

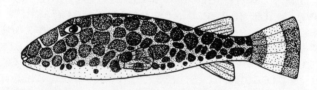

Body without fleshy lappets. Olive to green above, with numerous small blackish spots; venter whitish. Dorsal color broken into large, roughly circular dark areas by whitish reticulations. Two white interorbital bars, these often connected by a white line to the reticulated dorsal pattern. Cheeks and snout not marbled with blue. Caudal often with two dusky bars, but these are often indistinct. To about ten inches long.

A tropical straggler usually taken in Texas or Florida waters. Although a shore species, it is also recorded down to twenty fathoms.

Reference: Shipp, R.L. and R.W. Yerger, 1969(*Proc. Biol. Soc. Washington*, 82:477-488; *Sphoeroides*).

Family **DIODONTIDAE** — porcupinefishes

Puffers with two- or three-rooted spines and large eyes equal to or longer than the snout length. The teeth are fused into a single dental plate in each jaw, there being no median suture or gap like that found in the family Tetraodontidae. Two species.

Beaks

498. **STRIPED BURRFISH**
Chilomycterus schoepfi (Walbaum)

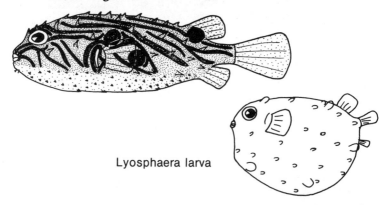

Lyosphaera larva

Body box-like when uninflated, covered with short, continually erect three-rooted spines. Greenish yellow above with narrow, curved parallel black lines and large black blotches, one over and one behind each pectoral, one at dorsal fin base, and one at anal fin base. Very young specimens have the spines absent or inconspicuous, but have fleshy lobes instead; these were once referred to the "genus" *Lyosphaera*. Reaches about ten inches in length, but usually about six.

Common in high salinity water throughout our range, from shore to at least fifteen fathoms. Large numbers are killed in shrimp trawls.

413

499. PORCUPINEFISH
Diodon hystrix Linnaeus

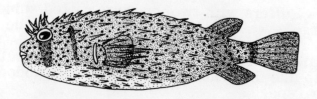

Body box-shaped when not inflated. Spines long compared to those of the striped burrfish, erect only when the fish is inflated; spines with two roots. Spines on forehead shorter than those behind the pectoral fin. Greenish brown above, white below. Dusky vertical bars through eye and cheek. Head and body covered with small black spots, no large blotches. Reaches about three feet in length but generally much smaller.

A tropical species which rarely straggles north to southern Texas and the Florida coast.

Family MOLIDAE — headfishes

Very large pelagic fishes easily recognized by the absence of a caudal peduncle and the very high, posteriorly inserted dorsal and anal fins. The body is ovoid to elongate. The teeth are fused into solid beaks. Three species.

Mola larvae: a, 11mm; b, 32mm.

a

b

500. SHARPTAIL MOLA
Mola lanceolata Lienard

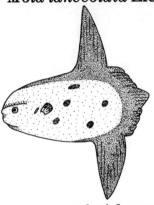

Body oval, somewhat longer than high. Dorsal and anal fins pointed, slightly lower than body depth. Caudal fin formed of eight or nine lobes, the middle lobe longer than the others and coming to a point distally. Forehead evenly rounded, not concave in front of eyes. Iridescent bluish above, lighter below, usually with dark round spots on lower sides. Skin thick, gristly, naked. Reaches eight feet in length and a weight of more than one thousand pounds.

Pelagic throughout the Gulf of Mexico but rarely found near shore. Occasional specimens are found stranded. Sometimes referred to the genus *Masturus*.

501. OCEAN SUNFISH
Mola mola (Linnaeus)

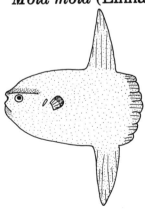

Body oval. Fins as in the sharptail mola, but the middle caudal rays form a lobe which is rounded and the same length as those above and below. The forehead in front of the eyes is distinctly concave. The skin is naked but has a rough, gristly texture. The largest mola, reaching lengths in excess of eleven feet and weights of at least a ton.

A somewhat common fish offshore, often seen floating on the surface. Occasional specimens are stranded on our coast.

502. SLENDER MOLA
Ranzania laevis (Pennant)

Body oblong, about twice as long as deep. Dorsal and anal fins pointed, about as high as body depth. Skin covered with smooth, uniform hexagonal plates. Dusky above, silvery on sides, usually with silvery or greenish bars on the body in front of the pectoral fin. Small for a mola, seldom exceeding thirty inches.

Recently recorded from the southern coast of Florida and likely to be found in our area as well. Pelagic. *Ranzania truncata* is a synonym.

References: Dawson, C.E., 1965(*Proc. Louisiana Acad. Sci.*, 28:86-89; *Mola*); Topp, R.W. and D.L. Girardin, 1972(*Quart. Journ. Florida Acad. Sci.*, 35(1):29-30; *Ranzania*).

INDEX

Page numbers in **bold** type represent color illustrations.
Page numbers in *italics* indicate a synonym or passing mention in the text.

A

Ablennes hians, 139, **266**
Abudefduf saxatilis, 261, **299**
  taurus, 264, **302**
Acanthocybium solanderi, 339
Acanthostracion, 407
ACANTHURIDAE, 335
Acanthurus chirurgus, **311**, 335
  coeruleus, **311**, 336
  randalli, 336
Achirus browni, 390
  fasciatus, 390
  lineatus, 387
Acipenser oxyrhynchus, 72, **259**
ACIPENSERIDAE, 72
ACIPENSERIFORMES, 72
acronotus, Carcharhinus, 46
aculeatus, Halieutichthys, 116
acus, Tylosurus, 141
acutirostris, Parepinephelus, *180*
Adinia xenica, 142, **267**
Adioryx, *151*, 152
adscensionis, Epinephelus, 169
Aetobatus narinari, 68, **258**
affinis, Fierasfer, *132*
affinis, Gambusia, 148
affinis, Hirundichthys, 137
affinis, Syngnathus fuscus, 160
African pompano, 196, **279**
agassizi, Scorpaena, 357
Agonostomus monticola, 284
Agu1on, 141, **267**
Ahlia egmontis, 85, **259**
Alabama shad, 92
alabamae, Alosa, 92
alalunga, Thunnus, 343
alatus, Prionotus, 362
albacares, Thunnus, 344
Albacore, 343
albidus, Tetrapturus, 349
albigutta, Kathetostoma, 301
albigutta, Paralichthys, 381
Albula vulpes, 76
ALBULIDAE, 76
Alectis ciliaris, 196
  crinitus, 196, **279**
alepidotus, Peprilus, 356
alletteratus, Euthynnus, 340
Alligator gar, 73, **259**
Almaco jack, 207, **283**
Alopias superciliosus, 42
Alopias vulpinus, 43
ALOPIIDAE, 42
Alosa alabamae, 92
  chrysochloris, 93
alta, Pristigenys, 186
Alutera, 396
ALUTERIDAE, 396
Aluterus heudeloti, 396
  schoepfi, **315**, 396
  'scriptus, **315**, 397
  ventralis, 396
alutus, Astrapogon, 188
Amanses, 401
Amberjack, greater, 205
  lesser, 206
amblyrhynchus, Hemicaranx, 201
American eel, 78, **259**

americana, Dasyatis, 64
americanus, Menticirrhus, 242
Amphelikturus dendriticus, 156
analis, Lutjanus, 215
Anchoa cubana, 100
  hepsetus, 100
  lyolepis, *101*
  mitchilli, 101
  nasuta, 101
anchovia, Sardinella, 99
Anchoviella perfasciata, 102
Anchovies, 99
Anchovy, bay, 101
  Cuban, 100
  flat, 102
  longnose, 101
  striped, 100
Ancylopsetta dilecta, **314**, 371
  quadrocellata, 372
andersoni, Pristipomoides, 221
Angel sharks, 57
Angelfish, blue, 256
  French, 260
  gray, 257
  queen, 256
Angelfishes, 255
Angelichthys, 256
  townsendi, 257
Anguilla rostrata, 78, **259**
anguillare, Dysomma, 91
ANGUILLIDAE, 78
ANGUILLIFORMES, 76
Anisotremus surinamensis, 225, **290**
Antenna codlet, 122
ANTENNARIIDAE, 112
Antennarius ocellatus, 113, **263**
  radiosus, 113
  scaber, 114, **263**
Antigonia capros, 152
aphododera, Dysomma, 92
apodus, Lutjanus, 215
Apogon aurolineatus, 187, **278**
  maculatus, 187, **278**
  pseudomaculatus, 188, **278**
APOGONIDAE, 187
Aprionodon isodon, 45
aquilonaris, Pristipomoides, 221
Archosargus probatocephalus, 231, **291**
arctifrons, Calamus, 231
arctifrons, Citharichthys, 373
arcuatus, Pomacanthus, 257
arenarius, Cynoscion, 238
arenatus, Priacanthus, 186
argalus, Platybelone, 140
argentea, Steindachneria, 123
argenteus, Eucinostomus, 223
ARIIDAE, 108
Ariomma régulus, 352
ARIOMMIDAE, 351
Ariosoma impressa, 81
Arius felis, 108
Armored searobins, **314**, 361
Arrowtooth eels, 91
ascensionis, Holocentrus, 151
Astrapogon alutus, 188, **278**
Astroscopus ygraecum, 297
ATHERINIDAE, 149
ATHERINIFORMES, 132

Atlantic angel shark, 57
  bonito, 341
  bumper, 200
  croaker, 243
  cutlassfish, 337
  flyingfish, 135
  guitarfish, 59
  manta, 70
  midshipman, 110, **263**
  moonfish, 212
  needlefish, 140
  sharpnose shark, 54
  spadefish, 249, **295**
  stingray, 65
  sturgeon, 72, **259**
  thread herring, 98
  threadfin, 292
atlantica, Megalops, 75
atlantica, Scorpaena, 359
atlanticus, Bregmaceros, 122
atlanticus, Ophioblennius, 317
atlanticus, Thunnus, 344
atrobranchus, Serranus, 183
AULOSTOMIDAE, 154
Aulostomus maculatus, 154, **270**
auratus, Mullus, 247
aurolineatum, Haemulon, 226
aurolineatus, Apogon, 187
aurorubens, Rhomboplites, 221
australis, Remora, 193
Auxis rochei, 339
  thazard, 339
aya, Chaetodon, 251
aya, Lutjanus, 217

B

Bagre marinus, 108
bairdi, Callionymus, 317
Bairdiella chrysura, 237
bajonado, Calamus, 232
Balao, 136, **266**
balao, Hemiramphus, 136
Balistes capriscus, **315**, 398
  carolinensis, 399
  vetula, **315**, 399
BALISTIDAE, 395
Ballyhoo, 137
Banded blenny, 305, **307**
  butterflyfish, 254, **298**
  drum, 240
  rudderfish, 208
Bandtail puffer, **319**, 411
  searobin, 364
Bandtooth conger, 81
Bandwing flyingfish, 134
Bank butterflyfish, 251, **295**
  cusk-eel, 129, **266**
  sea bass, 166
Bar jack, 199, **282**
barbata, Brotula, 126
Barbfish, **314**, 358
Barbier, red, 175
Barracuda, great, 288
barracuda, Sphyraena, 288
Barracudas, 288
Barred grunt, 226
  hamlet, 176
  searobin, 363
bartholomaei, Caranx, 197
Bascanichthys scuticaris, 85
  teres, 86
Bass, bank sea, 166
  black sea, 167
  blackear, 183
  pygmy sea, 182

  rock sea, 166
  striped, 164
Basslet, 177
Batfish, palespot, 118
  pancake, 116
  polka-dot, 117
  roughback, 116
  thick-tail, 120
  tricorn, 121
Batfishes, 115
Bathygobius soporator, 323
bathyphilus, Halichoeres, 269
Bathystoma rimator, 227
BATRACHOIDIDAE, 109
BATRACHOIDIFORMES, 109
Bay anchovy, 101
  whiff, 376
Bayou killifish, 146
beani, Ophidion, 128
Bearded brotula, 126, **266**
Beaugregory, 265, **302**
Bellator militaris, 361
BELONIDAE, 139
Belted sandfish, 184
Benthoscopus laticeps, 301
Bermuda chub, 248, **295**
bermudensis, Carapus, 131
bermudensis, Holacanthus, 256
BERYCIFORMES, 150
beryllina, Menidia, 150
beta, Opsanus, 109
bifasciatum, Thalassoma, 276
bigelowi, Sphyrna, 54
Bigeye, 186, **278**
  scad, 203, **283**
  short, 186
  thresher, 42
  tuna, 345
Bighead searobin, 369
Bigmouth sleeper, 322
Billfishes, 348
bipinnulata, Elagatis, 201
birostris, Manta, 70
bivittatum, Diplectrum, 168
bivittatus, Halichoeres, 269
Black driftfish, 353
  drum, 244
  durgon, **318**, 402
  grouper, 178, **275**
  jack, 199
  margate, 225, **290**
  sea bass, 167, **271**
Blackcheek tonguefish, **315**, 393
Blackear bass, 183
Blackedge cusk-eel, 127
  moray, 80, **259**
Blackfin searobin, 366
  snapper, 216, **286**
  tuna, 344
blackfordi, Lutjanus, 217
Blackline tilefish, 190
Blacknose shark, 46
Blacktip shark, 48
Blackwing searobin, 367
Blennies, naked, 308
  scaled, 304
BLENNIIDAE, 308
Blennius cristatus, 308
  favosus, 309
  fucorum, 309
  marmoreus, **307**, 308
  nicholsi, 309
  stearnsi, 309
Blenny, banded, 305
  checkered, 305

crested, 313
feather, 316
Florida, 313
freckled, 316
hairy, 304
highfin, 309
redlip, 317
seaweed, 308
striped, 312
Blotched cusk-eel, 129
snake eel, 86
Blue angelfish, 256, **298**
goby, **311**, 331
marlin, 349
runner, 197, **279**
shark, 53
tang, **311**, 336
Bluefin tuna, 345
Bluefish, 191
Bluehead, 276, **303**
Bluelip parrotfish, 277, **303**
Bluespotted cornetfish, 155
searobin, 365
Bluestriped grunt, 228, **291**
Bluntnose flyingfish, 138
jack, 201
stingray, 65
Boarfish, deepbody, 152
boleosoma, Gobionellus, 325
Bollmannia communis, 323
bonaci, Mycteroperca, 178
bonasus, Rhinoptera, 70
Bonefish, 76
Bonito, Atlantic, 341
Bonnethead, 56
borealis, Sphyraena, 289
bosci, Gobiosoma, 328
bosquianus, Chasmodes, 312
BOTHIDAE, 371
Bothus ocellatus, **314**, 373
Boxfishes, 406
brachyptera, Remora, 194
brachypterus, Parexocoetus, 138
BRANCHIOSTEGIDAE, 190
brasiliensis, Hemiramphus, 137
brasiliensis, Narcine, 60
brasiliensis, Saurida, 103
brasiliensis, Scorpaena, 358
Bregmaceros atlanticus, 122
BREGMACEROTIDAE, 122
brevibarbe, Lepophidium, 127
brevirostris, Negaprion, 53
Brevoortia gunteri, 93
patronus, 94
smithi, 95
Bridle cardinalfish, 187, **278**
Broad flounder, 382
Bronze cardinalfish, 188, **278**
broussonneti, Gobioides, 325
Brotula barbata, 126, **266**
Brotula, bearded, 126
gold, 126
Brotulas, 125
BROTULIDAE, 125
browni, Achirus, 390
buccanella, Lutjanus, 216
Bucktooth parrotfish, 281, **306**
Bull pipefish, 162
shark, 47
Bullet mackerel, 339
bullisi, Holocentrus, 151
Bullnose ray, 69
Bumper, Atlantic, 200
Burrfish, striped, 413
Burro grunt, 230

burti, Peprilus, 355
Butterfish, Gulf, 355
Butterfishes, 355
Butterflyfish, banded, 254
bank, 251
foureye, 251
reef, 253
spotfin, 252
Butterflyfishes, 250
bythites, Hyperoglyphe, 353

C

Calamus arctifrons, 231
bajonado, 232, **291**
leucosteus, 232
nodosus, 233, **294**
proridens, 234
calcarata, Scorpaena, 358
Callechelys muraena, 86
CALLIONYMIDAE, 317
Callionymus bairdi, **310**, 317
calliurus, loglossus, 331
campechanus, Lutjanus, 216
canadum, Rachycentron, 192
canis, Mustelus, 52
Cantherhines pullus, **315**, 400
Canthidermis maculatus, **318**, 402
sobaco, 402
sufflamen, **318**, 401
Canthigaster rostrata, **319**, 408
CANTHIGASTERIDAE, 409
capistratus, Chaetodon, 251
caprinus, Stenotomus, 236
capriscus, Balistes, 398
CAPROIDAE, 152
capros, Antigonia, 152
Caranx bartholomaei, 197, **279**
crysos, 197, **279**
fuscus, 197
hippos, 198, **279**
latus, 198, **279**
lugubris, 199
ruber, 199, **279**
CARANGIDAE, 195
CARAPIDAE, 131
Carapus bermudensis, 131, **266**
CARCHARHINIDAE, 45
Carcharhinus acronotus, 46
falciformis, 47
floridanus, 47
leucas, 47
limbatus, 48
longimanus, 49, **258**
maculipinnis, 49
milberti, 50
obscurus, 50
porosus, 51
Carcharias taurus, 42
carcharias, Carcharodon, 43
Carcharodon carcharias, 43
Cardinalfish, bridle, 187
bronze, 188
freckled, 189
twospot, 188
Cardinalfishes, 187
caribbaea, Saurida, 103
carolinensis, Balistes, 399
carolinus, Trachinotus, 209
Carpet sharks, 39
carpio, Floridichthys, 143
carri, Microgobius, 331
Catfish, gafftopsail, 108
sea, 108
caudalis, Halichoeres, 272
caudilimbatus, Paraconger, 83

419

Caulolatilus cyanops, 190
cavalla, Scomberomorus, 341
CENTROLOPHIDAE, 352
CENTROPOMIDAE, 163
Centropomus undecimalis, 163, **271**
Centropristis melana, 167
   ocyurus, 166
   philadelphica, 166
   striata, 167, **271**
cepedianum, Dorosoma, 95
Cephalacanthus, 370
cephalus, Mugil, 285
Cero, **311**, 343
cervinum, Lepophidium, 128
Chaetodipterus faber, 249, **295**
Chaetodon aya, 251, **295**
   capistratus, 251, **295**
   ocellatus, 252, **298**
   sedentarius, 253, **298**
   striatus, 254, **298**
CHAETODONTIDAE, 250
Chain pipefish, 160
Channel flounder, 384
Chasmodes saburrae, **307**, 313
   bosquianus, 312
Checkered blenny, 305, **307**
   puffer, **319**, 412
Chilomycterus schoepfi, **319**, 413
chirurgus, Acanthurus, 335
chittendeni, Cyclopsetta, 376
Chloroscombrus chrysurus, 200
chlorurus, Hypoplectrus, 176
CHONDRICHTHYES, 39
Chromis enchrysura, 264, **302**
   scotti, 264, **302**
chrysochloris, Alosa, 93
chrysoptera, Orthopristis, 229
chrysura, Bairdiella, 237
chrysurus, Chloroscombrus, 200
chrysurus, Ocyurus, 220
chub, Bermuda, 248
chub mackerel, **311**, 341
cigarfishes, 353
ciliaris, Alectis, 196
ciliaris, Holacanthus, 256
ciliatus, Monacanthus, 403
cinereus, Gerres, 224
cirratum, Ginglymostoma, 39
cirratus, Urophycis, 123
Citharichthys arctifrons, 373
   cornutus, 374
   macrops, 375
   spilopterus, 376
civitatus, Symphurus, 390
Clearnose skate, 61
Clearwing flyingfish, 132
Clingfish, stippled, 111
Clingfishes, 111
CLINIDAE, 304
Clinids, 304
Clown goby, 332
CLUPEIDAE, 92
CLUPEIFORMES, 92
clupeola, Harengula, 97
Cobia, 192, **279**
Cocoa damselfish, 268, **302**
Code goby, **310**, 330
Codlet, antenna, 122
Codlets, 122
Cods, 122
coeruleus, Acanthurus, 336
colesi, Scorpaena, 358
comatus, Cypselurus, 132
Comb grouper, 179, **275**
communis, Bollmannia, 323

confluentus, Fundulus, 144
Conger, bandtooth, 81
   dogface, 83
   eels, 81
   margintail, 83
   silver, 81
   threadtail, 84
   yellow, 82
Congers, pike, 80
CONGRIDAE, 81
Congrina flava, 82
   macrosoma, 83
conklini, Phaeoptyx, 189
Conodon nobilis, 226
Cornetfish, bluespotted, 155
cornutus, Citharichthys, 374
coroides, Umbrina, 246
Coryphaena equiselis, *213*
   equisetis, 213
   hippurus, 214
CORYPHAENIDAE, 213
Cottonmouth jack, 211
Cowfish, scrawled, 407
Cownose ray, 70
crassiceps, Prionotus tribulus, 369
Creole-fish, 180, **275**
Crested blenny, **307**, 313
   cusk-eel, 130
Crevalle jack, 198, **282**
crinigerus, Micrognathus, 158
crinitus, Alectis, 196
cristatus, Blennius, 308
Croaker, Atlantic, 243
Croakers, 237
crocro, Pomadasys, 230
croicensis, Scarus, 280
cromis, Pogonias, 244
crossotus, Etropus, 379
cruentatum, Petrometopon, 181
crumenophthalmus, Selar, 203
Cryptotomus roseus, 277, **303**
crysos, Caranx, 197
Cuban anchovy, 100
cubana, Anchoa, 100
cubanus, Hynnis, 196
Cubbyu, 240, **294**
Cubera snapper, 217, **286**
curema, Mugil, 285
Cusk-eel, bank, 129
   blackedge, 127
   blotched, 129
   crested, 130
   longnose, 128
   mottled, 127
   polka-dot, 130
Cusk-eels, 125
Cutlassfish, Atlantic, 337
cuvieri, Galeocerdo, 51
cyanophrys, Psenes, 354
cyanops, Caulolatilus, 190
cyanopterus, Cypselurus, 133
cyanopterus, Lutjanus, 217
Cyclopsetta chittendeni, 376
   decussata, 377
   fimbriata, 377
CYNOGLOSSIDAE, 390
Cynoscion arenarius, 238
   nebulosus, 238
   nothus, 239
Cyprinodon variegatus, 143, **267**
CYPRINODONTIDAE, 142
Cypselurus comatus, 132
   cyanopterus, 133
   exsiliens, 134
   furcatus, 134

heterurus, 135

D

DACTYLOPTERIDAE, 370
Dactylopterus volitans, **314**, 370
DACTYLOSCOPIDAE, 296
Dactyloscopus tridigitatus, 296
Damselfish, cocoa, 268
Damselfishes, 261
Darter goby, 325
DASYATIDAE, 64
Dasyatis americana, 64
  sabina, 65
  sayi, 65
Decapterus punctatus, 200, **282**
decussata, Cyclopsetta, 377
Deepbody boarfish, 152
Deepwater squirrelfish, 151, **270**
dendriticus, Amphelikturus, 156
Dermatolepis inermis, 168
desotoi, Acipenser oxyrhynchus, 73
Diamond killifish, 142, **267**
dilecta, Ancylopsetta, 371
Diodon hystrix, **319**, 414
DIODONTIDAE, 413
diomedianus, Hoplunnis, 81
diomedianus, Symphurus, 391
diplana, Sphyrna, 54
Diplectrum bivittatum, 168, **271**
  formosum, 169, **271**
Diplodus holbrooki, 234
dispar, Scorpaena, 359
Diver, sand, 105
Doctorfish, **311**, 335
Dog snapper, 218, **287**
Dogface conger, 83
Dogfish, smooth, 52
Dolphin, 214
  pompano, 213
Dormitator maculatus, **310**, 320
dormitor, Gobiomorus, 322
Dorosoma cepedianum, 95
  petenense, 96
dorsalis, Sphoeroides, 410
Dotterel filefish, 396
Dragonet, lancer, 317
Driftfish, black, 353
  freckled, 354
  spotted, 352
Drum, banded, 240
  black, 244
  red, 244
  sand, 246
  star, 245
drummondhayi, Epinephelus, 170
Drums, 237
ductor, Naucrates, 202
Dules, 184
dumerili, Seriola, 205
dumerili, Squatina, 57
Durgon, black, 402
Dusky flounder, 385
  pipefish, 159
  shark, 50
  squirrelfish, 152, **270**
Dwarf goatfish, 248
  pipefish, 160
  sand perch, 168, **271**
  seahorse, 157
Dysomma anguillare, 91
  aphododera, 92
DYSOMMIDAE, 91

E

Eagle rays, 68

ECHENEIDAE, 192
Echeneis naucrates, 193, **279**
Eel, American, 78
  blotched snake, 86
  horsehair, 86
  Key worm, 85
  palespotted, 91
  sailfin, 87
  shortbelly, 91
  shrimp, 90
  slender pike, 79
  snapper, 89
  sooty, 86
  speckled worm, 88
  spotted spoon-nose, 88
  stippled spoon-nose, 90
  thread, 87
  whip, 85
Eels, conger, 81
  freshwater, 78
  snake, 84
  spaghetti, 78
  worm, 84
eglanteria, Raja, 61
egmontis, Ahlia, 85
egregius, Gnathagnus, 300
Elacatinus, 329
Elagatis bipinnulata, 201, **282**
Electric rays, 60
ELEOTRIDAE, **320**
Eleotris pisonis, **310**, 321
ELOPIDAE, 74
ELOPIFORMES, 74
Elops saurus, 75
elucens, Syngnathus, 159
Emerald parrotfish, 280
  sleeper, 321
enchrysura, Chromis, 264
ENGRAULIDAE, 99
Engyophrys senta, 378
EPHIPPIDAE, 249
Epinephelus adscensionis, 169, **271**
  drummondhayi, 170
  flavolimbatus, 170
  guttatus, 171, **271**
  itajara, 172, **271**
  morio, 173, **274**
  nigritus, 173
  niveatus, 174, **274**
  striatus, 175, **274**
Equetus lanceolatus, 239, **294**
  umbrosus, 240, **294**
equiselis, Coryphaena, 213
equisetis, Coryphaena, 213
erectus, Hippocampus, 156
Erotelis smaragdus, 321
Etropus crossotus, 379
  microstomus, 379
  rimosus, 380
Etrumeus teres, 96
Eucinostomus argenteus, 223, **290**
  gula, 223, **290**
  lefroyi, 224
Euleptorhamphus velox, 135
Eupomacentrus leucostictus, 265, **302**
  variabilis, 268, **302**
Euthynnus alletteratus, 340
  pelamis, **311**, 340
Evermannichthys spongicola, 324
Evorthodus lyricus, 324
Execestides, 301
EXOCOETIDAE, 132
Exocoetus obtusirostris, 136
exsiliens, Cypselurus, 134
Eyed flounder, **314**, 373

F

faber, *Chaetodipterus*, 249
falcatus, Trachinotus, 210
falciformis, Carcharhinus, 47
False pilchard, 97
fasciata, Seriola, 206
fasciatus, Achirus, 390
fasciatus, Larimus, 240
fasciatus, Paraclinus, 305
Fat sleeper, **310**, 320
favosus, Blennius, 309
Feather blenny, 316
felis, Arius, 108
Fierasfer affinis, 132
Filefish, dotterel, 396
    fringed, 403
    orange, 396
    orangespotted, 400
    planehead, 404
    pygmy, 404
    scrawled, 397
Filefishes, 395
fimbriata, Cyclopsetta, 377
Finescale menhaden, 93
Finetooth shark, 45
Fistularia tabacaria, 155
FISTULARIIDAE, 155
Flamefish, 187, **278**
Flat anchovy, 102
    needlefish, 139, **266**
flava, Congrina, 82
flavolimbatus, Epinephelus, 170
flavolineatum, Haemulon, 227
Florida blenny, **307**, 313
    pompano, 209, **283**
    smoothhound, 52
floridae, Syngnathus, 159
floridanus, Carcharhinus, 47
floridanus, Urophycis, 124
Floridichthys carpio, 143
Flounder, broad, 382
    channel, 384
    dusky, 385
    eyed, 373
    fringed, 379
    gray, 380
    Gulf, 381
    Mexican, 376
    ocellated, 372
    sash, 386
    shoal, 383
    shrimp, 380
    smallmouth, 379
    southern, 382
    spiny, 378
    spotfin, 377
    three-eye, 371
Flounders, 371
Flying gurnard, **314**, 370
    halfbeak, 135
Flyingfish, Atlantic, 135
    bandwing, 134
    bluntnose, 138
    clearwing, 132
    fourwing, 137
    margined, 133
    oceanic two-wing, 136
    sailfin, 138
    spotfin, 134
Flyingfishes, 132
focaliger, Menticirrhus, 242
foetens, Synodus, 104
formosa, Heterandria, 148
formosum, Diplectrum, 169
Foureye butterflyfish, 251, **295**

Fourwing flyingfish, 137
Freckled blenny, 316
    cardinalfish, 189, **279**
    driftfish, 354
    skate, 62
    stargazer, 300
freminvillei, Myliobatis, 69
French angelfish, 260, **299**
    grunt, 227, **291**
Freshwater eels, 78
    goby, 327
Frillfin goby, 323
Fringed filefish, **318**, 403
    flounder, 379
    pipefish, 158, **270**
    sole, 388
Frogfish, ocellated, 113
    singlespot, 113
    splitlure, 114
Frogfishes, 112
frontalis, Gastropsetta, 380
fucorum, Blennius, 309
Fundulus confluentus, 144
    grandis, 145
    jenkinsi, 145
    pulvereus, 146
    similis, 146
furcatus, Cypselurus, 134
furcifer, Paranthias, 180
fuscus, Caranx, 197
fuscus, Syngnathus, 159

G

GADIDAE, 122
GADIFORMES, 121
Gafftopsail catfish, 108
Gag, 178, **275**
Galeichthys, 108
Galeocerdo cuvieri, 51
Gambusia affinis, 148, **267**
Gar, alligator, 73
Garrupa, 174
Gars, 73
GASTEROSTEIFORMES, 154
Gastropsetta frontalis, 380
geminatus, Hypleurochilus, 313
GERREIDAE, 223
Gerres cinereus, 224, **290**
gibba, Histrio, 114
gibbifrons, Prognichthys, 138
Ginglymostoma cirratum, 39, **258**
ginsburgi, Scorpaena, 360
Gizzard shad, 95
gladius, Xiphias, 347
glauca, Prionace, 53
glesne, Regalecus, 153
Gnathagnus egregius, 300
Gnathypops mystacinus, 296
Goatfish, dwarf, 248
    red, 247
    spotted, 247
    yellow, 246
Goatfishes, 246
Gobies, 320
GOBIESOCIDAE, 111
GOBIESOCIFORMES, 111
Gobiesox punctulatus, 111
    strumosus, 112, **263**
GOBIIDAE, 320
Gobioides broussonneti, 325
Gobiomorus dormitor, 322
Gobionellus boleosoma, 325
    gracillimus, 327
    hastatus, 326
    oceanicus, 326

shufeldti, 327
stigmaticus, 327
Gobiosoma bosci, 328
    longipala, 328
    oceanops, **310**, 329
    prochilos, **310**, 329
    robustum, **310**, 330
Goby, blue, 331
    clown, 332
    code, 330
    darter, 325
    freshwater, 327
    frillfin, 323
    green, 333
    lyre, 324
    marked, 327
    naked, 328
    neon, 329
    ragged, 323
    Seminole, 331
    sharptail, 326
    sponge, 324
    twoscale, 328
    violet, 325
    whiteline, 329
Gold brotula, 126
Goldspotted killifish, 143
gomesi, Ophichthus, 90
goodei, Trachinotus, 210
Gordiichthys irretitus, 86
    springeri, 87
gracillimus, Gobionellus, 327
graellsi, Lepophidium, 127
GRAMMISTIDAE, 185
grandis, Fundulus, 145
Grass porgy, 231
Gray angelfish, 257, **299**
    flounder, 380
    snapper, 217, **286**
    triggerfish, **315**, 398
grayi, Ophidion, 129
Graysby, 181, **275**
Great barracuda, 288, **306**
    hammerhead, 55
Greater amberjack, 205, **283**
    soapfish, 185, **278**
Green goby, 333
Greenband wrasse, 269
griseus, Lutjanus, 217
gronovii, Nomeus, 354
Grouper, black, 178
    comb, 179
    marbled, 168
    Nassau, 175
    red, 173
    snowy, 174
    Warsaw, 173
    yellowedge, 170
    yellowfin, 180
Groupers, 165
Grunt, barred, 226
    bluestriped, 228
    burro, 230
    French, 227
    striped, 229
    white, 227
Grunts, 225
guachancho, Sphyraena, 289
Guaguanche, 289
Guitarfish, Atlantic, 59
Guitarfishes, 59
gula, Eucinostomus, 223
Gulf butterfish, 355
    flounder, 381
    hake, 123

killifish, 145
kingfish, 243
menhaden, 94
pipefish, 161
surgeonfish, 336
toadfish, 109
Gulf Stream flounder, 373
gulosus, Microgobius, 332
gunteri, Brevoortia, 93
gunteri, Syacium, 383
Gunterichthys longipenis, 126
Gurnard, flying, 370
guttatus, Epinephelus, 171
Gymnachirus melas, 388
    texae, 388
Gymnothorax moringa, 79, **259**
    nigromarginatus, 80, **259**
Gymnura micrura, 66

H
Haemulon aurolineatum, 226, **291**
    flavolineatum, 227, **291**
    plumieri, 227, **291**
    sciurus, 228, **291**
    striatum, 229, **291**
Hairy blenny, 304, **307**
Hake, Gulf, 123
    luminous, 123
    southern, 124
    spotted, 124
Halfbeak, 138
    flying, 135
Halfbeaks, 132
Halichoeres bathyphilus, 269
    bivittatus, 269, **302**
    caudalis, 272
Halieutichthys aculeatus, 116, **263**
Hamlet, barred, 176, **274**
    yellowtail, 176, **274**
Hammerhead, great, 55
    scalloped, 55
    smooth, 57
    smalleye, 56
    sharks, 54
Harengula clupeola, 97
    humeralis, 97
    pensacolae, 98
harperi, Sphoeroides, 411
Harvestfish, 356
hastatus, Gobionellus, 326
Headfishes, 414
heidi, Uraspis, 212
Hemanthias vivanus, 175
Hemicaranx amblyrhynchus, 201
Hemipteronotus novacula, 272, **303**
HEMIRAMPHIDAE, 132
Hemiramphus balao, 136, **266**
    brasiliensis, 137
hentzi, Hypsoblennius, 316
hepsetus, Anchoa, 100
Herring, Atlantic thread, 98
    round, 96
    skipjack, 93
Herrings, 92
Heterandria formosa, 148, **267**
heterurus, Cypselurus, 135
heudeloti, Aluterus, 396
hians, Ablennes, 139
Highfin blenny, 309
hildebrandi, Syngnathus, 160
Hind, red, 171
    rock, 169
    speckled, 170
Hippocampus erectus, 156, **270**

hudsonius, 157
regulus, 158
zosterae, 157
hippos, Caranx, 198
hippurus, Coryphaena, 214
Hirundichthys affinis, 137
hispidus, Monacanthus, 404
Histrio gibba, 114
histrio, 114, **263**
histrio, Histrio, 114
Hogchoker, **315**, 389
Hogfish, 273, **303**
Holacanthus bermudensis, 256, **298**
ciliaris, 256, **299**
isabelita, 256
holbrooki, Diplodus, 234
holbrooki, Ophidion, 129
HOLOCENTRIDAE, 150
Holocentrus ascensionis, 151, **270**
bullisi, 151, **270**
vexillarius, 152, **270**
Horned searobin, 361
whiff, 374
Hoplunnis diomedianus, 81
macrurus, 81
tenuis, 81
Horse-eye jack, 198, **282**
Horsehair eel, 86
hudsonius, Hippocampus, 157
humeralis, Harengula, 97
Hunchback scorpionfish, 359
Hynnis cubanus, 196
Hyperoglyphe bythites, 353
Hypleurochilus geminatus, **307**, 313
Hypoplectrus chlorurus, 176, **274**
puella, 176, **274**
Hyporhamphus unifasciatus, 138
Hypsoblennius hentzi, 316
ionthas, 316
hystrix, Diodon, 414

I

impressa, Ariosoma, 81
inermis, Dermatolepis, 168
Inshore lizardfish, 104, **262**
intermedius, Synodus, 105
intertinctus, Mystriophis, 88
ioglossus calliurus, **311**, 331
ionthas, Hypsoblennius, 316
irretitus, Gordiichthys, 86
isabelita, Holacanthus, 256
isodon, Aprionodon, 45
ISTIOPHORIDAE, 348
Istiophorus platypterus, 348
Isurus oxyrinchus, 44
itaiara, Promicrops, 172
itajara, Epinephelus, 172

J

Jack, almaco, 207
bar, 199
black, 199
bluntnose, 201
cottonmouth, 211
crevalle, 198
horse-eye, 198
yellow, 197
Jackknife-fish, 239, **294**
Jacks, 195
jamaicensis, Urolophus, 67
Jambeau, 395
japonicus, Scomber, 341
Jawfish, mottled, 296
moustache, 293
swordtail, 293
Jawfishes, 292

jeannae, Lepophidium, 127
jenkinsi, Fundulus, 145
Jenny, silver, 223
Jewfish, 172, **271**
jocu, Lutjanus, 218
Jolthead porgy, 232, **291**

K

Kathetostoma albigutta, 301
Katsuwonus, 340
Keeltail needlefish, 140, **267**
Key worm eel, 85, **259**
Killifish, bayou, 146
diamond, 142
goldspotted, 143
Gulf, 145
least, 148
longnose, 146
marsh, 144
rainwater, 147
Killifishes, 142
King mackerel, 341
Kingfish, Gulf, 243
southern, 242
Knobbed porgy, 233, **294**
KYPHOSIDAE, 248
Kyphosus sectatrix, 248, **295**

L

LABRIDAE, 269
Labrisomus nuchipinnis, 304, **307**
Lachnolaimus maximus, 273, **303**
Lactophrys quadricornis, **318**, 407
tricornis, 407
trigonus, 407
Ladyfish, 75
laevigatus, Lagocephalus, 409
laevis, Ranzania, 416
Lagocephalus laevigatus, 409
Lagodon rhomboides, 235, **294**
LAMNIDAE, 43
LAMPRIDIFORMES, 153
lanceolata, Mola, 415
lanceolatus, Equetus, 239
lanceolatus, Microdesmus, 334
lanceolatus, Stellifer, 245
Lancer dragonet, **310**, 317
stargazer, 301
Lancetail wormfish, 334
Lane snapper, 219, **287**
Largescale lizardfish, 103
Largetooth sawfish, 59
Larimus fasciatus, 240
lathami, Trachurus, 211
laticeps, Benthoscopus, 301
latifrons, Prionotus scitulus, 368
latipinna, Poecilia, 149
latus, Caranx, 198
Least killifish, 148, **267**
puffer, 411
Leatherjacket, 202, **283**
lefroyi, Eucinostomus, 224
Leiostomus xanthurus, 241, **294**
Lemon shark, 53
lentiginosa, Raja, 62
lentiginosus, Rhinobatos, 59
Leopard searobin, 367
toadfish, 110
LEPISOSTEIDAE, 73
Lepisosteus spatula, 73, **259**
Lepophidium brevibarbe, 127
cervinum, 128
graellsi, 127
jeannae, 127, **266**
marmoratum, 128

profundorum, 128
lepturus, Trichiurus, 337
Lesser amberjack, 206
    electric ray, 60, **258**
Letharchus velifer, 87
lethostigma, Paralichthys, 382
leucas, Carcharhinus, 47
leucosteus, Calamus, 232
leucostictus, Eupomacentrus, 265
lewini, Sphyrna, 55
limbatus, Carcharhinus, 48
lindneri, Lonchopisthus, 293
lineata, Parahollardia, 395
lineatus, Achirus, 387
lineatus, Oostethus, 158
Lined seahorse, 156, **270**
    sole, 387
Liopropoma, 177
    mowbrayi, **274**
    rubre, **274**
Little tunny, 340
Littlehead porgy, 234
littoralis, Menticirrhus, 243
Livebearing killifishes, 147
Lizardfish, inshore, 104
    largescale, 103
    offshore, 105
    red, 106
    shortjaw, 104
    smallscale, 103
Lizardfishes, 102
Lobotes surinamensis, 222, **290**
LOBOTIDAE, 222
Lonchopisthus lindneri, 293
lonchurus, Opistognathus, 293
Longbill spearfish, 350
Longfin scorpionfish, 357
longimanus, Carcharhinus, 49
longipala, Gobiosoma, 328
longipenis, Gunterichthys, 126
longipinnis, Microdesmus, 334
Longnose anchovy, 101
    cusk-eel, 128
    killifish, 146
Longspine porgy, 236
Longtail tonguefish, 392
Lookdown, 203, **283**
LOPHIIFORMES, 112
louisianae, Syngnathus, 160
Lucania parva, 147
lugubris, Caranx, 199
Luminous hake, 123
Lutjanus analis, 215, **286**
    apodus, 215, **286**
    aya, 217
    blackfordi, 217
    buccanella, 216, **286**
    campechanus, 216, **286**
    cyanopterus, 217, **286**
    griseus, 217, **286**
    jocu, 218, **287**
    mahogoni, 218, **287**
    synagris, 219, **287**
    vivanus, 220, **287**
LUTJANIDAE, 214
lyolepis, Anchoa, 101
Lyosphaera, 413
Lyre goby, 324
lyricus, Evorthodus, 324

M

Mackerel, bullet, 339
    chub, 341
    king, 341
    sharks, 43

Spanish, 342
Mackerels, 338
macrops, Citharichthys, 375
macrosoma, Congrina, 83
macrurus, Hoplunnis, 81
maculatus, Apogon, 187
maculatus, Aulostomus, 154
maculatus, Canthidermis, 402
maculatus, Dormitator, 320
maculatus, Pseudupeneus, 247
maculatus, Scomberomorus, 342
maculatus, Trinectes, 389
maculipinnis, Carcharhinus, 49
Mahogany snapper, 218, **287**
mahogoni, Lutjanus, 218
Makaira nigricans, 349
Mako, shortfin, 44
Malacanthus plumieri, 190, **279**
Man-of-war fish, **314**, 354
Manta, Atlantic, 70
Manta birostris, 70
Mantas, 70
Marbled grouper, 168
    puffer, 410
Margate, black, 225
marginata, Rissola, 125
Margined flyingfish, 133
Margintail conger, 83
marina, Strongylura, 140
marinus, Bagre, 108
Marked goby, 327
Marlin, blue, 349
    white, 349
Marlinsucker, 194
marmoratum, Lepophidium, 128
marmoreus, Blennius, 308
Marsh killifish, 144
martinica, Membras, 149
martinicus, Mulloidichthys, 246
martis, Prionotus, 363
Masturus, 415
maxillosus, Opistognathus, 296
maximus, Lachnolaimus, 273
mcgintyi, Zalieutes, 121
Megalops atlantica, 75
melana, Centropristis, 167
melas, Gymnachirus, 388
Melichthys niger, **318**, 402
Membras martinica, 149
Menhaden, 92
    finescale, 93
    Gulf, 94
    yellowfin, 95
Menidia beryllina, 150
Menticirrhus americanus, 242
    focaliger, 242
    littoralis, 243
Mexican flounder, 376
    searobin, 365
MICRODESMIDAE, 333
Microdesmus lanceolatus, 334
    longipinnis, 334
Micrognathus crinigerus, 158, **270**
Microgobius carri, **311**, 331
    gulosus, 332
    thalassinus, 333
microlepis, Mycteroperca, 178
microlepis, Prionotus, 366
Micropogon undulatus, 243
microstomus, Etropus, 379
micrura, Gymnura, 66
micrurum, Syacium, 384
Midshipman, Atlantic, 110
milberti, Carcharhinus, 50
militaris, Bellator, 361

Minkfish, 242
minnow, sheepshead, 143
mitchilli, Anchoa, 101
MOBULIDAE, 70
Mojarra, mottled, 224
    spotfin, 223
    yellowfin, 224
Mojarras, 223
mokarran, Sphyrna, 55
Mola lanceolata, 415
Mola mola, **319**, 415
mola, Mola, 415
Mola, sharptail, 415
    slender, 416
MOLIDAE, 414
Mollienesia, 149
Molly miller, 308
Molly, sailfin, 149
MONACANTHIDAE, 395
Monacanthus ciliatus, **318**, 403
    hispidus, **318**, 404
    setifer, 404
monticola, Agonostomus, 284
Moonfish, Atlantic, 212
Moray, blackedge, 80
    spotted, 79
Morays, 79
mordax, Mystriophis, 89
moringa, Gymnothorax, 79
MORINGUIDAE, 78
morio, Epinephelus, 173
Morone saxatilis, 164
Mosquitofish, 148, **267**
Mottled cusk-eel, 127, **266**
    jawfish, 296
    mojarra, 224
Mountain mullet, 284
Moustache jawfish, 293, **307**
mucronatus, Neoconger, 79
Mugil cephalus, 285, **306**
    curema, 285, **306**
    trichodon, 288
MUGILIDAE, 284
Mullet, mountain, 284
    striped, 285
    white, 285
Mullets, 284
MULLIDAE, 246
Mulloidichthys martinicus, 246, **294**
Mullus auratus, 247
muraena, Callechelys, 86
MURAENESOCIDAE, 80
MURAENIDAE, 79
Mustelus canis, 52
Mustelus norrisi, 52
Mutton snapper, 215, **286**
Mycteroperca bonaci, 178, **275**
    microlepis, 178, **275**
    phenax, 179, **275**
    rubra, 179, **275**
    venenosa, 180, **275**
MYCTOPHIFORMES, 102
MYLIOBATIDAE, 68
Myliobatis freminvillei, 69
myops, Trachinocephalus, 107
Myrophis punctatus, 88, **262**
mystacinus, Gnathypops, 296
Mystriophis intertinctus, 88, **262**
    mordax, 89
    punctifer, 90

N

Naked goby, 328
    sole, 388
Narcine brasiliensis, 60, **258**
narinari, Aetobatus, 68

Nassau grouper, 175, **274**
nasuta, Anchoa, 101
Naucrates ductor, 202, **282**
naucrates, Echeneis, 193
nebulosus, Cynoscion, 238
Needlefish, Atlantic, 140
    flat, 139
    keeltail, 140
    redfin, 140
Needlefishes, 139
Negaprion brevirostris, 53
Neoconger mucronatus, 79
Neon goby, **310**, 329
nephelus, Sphoeroides, 410
nicholsi, Blennius, 309
nicholsi, Nodogymnus, 388
Nicholsina usta, 280
niger, Melichthys, 402
nigricans, Makaira, 349
nigritus, Epinephelus, 173
nigromarginatus, Gymnothorax, 80
niveatus, Epinephelus, 174
nobilis, Conodon, 226
Nodogymnus nicholsi, 388
    williamsoni, 388
nodosus, Calamus, 233
NOMEIDAE, 353
Nomeus gronovii, **314**, 354
normani, Saurida, 104
norrisi, Mustelus, 52
Northern pipefish, 159, **270**
    sennet, 289, **306**
notata, Strongylura, 140
novacula, Hemipteronotus, 272
Nurse shark, 39, **258**
nuttingi, Phrynelox, 114

O

Oarfish, 153
obesus, Thunnus, 345
obscurus, Carcharhinus, 50
obtusirostris, Exocoetus, 136
Ocean sunfish, **319**, 415
    triggerfish, **318**, 401
Oceanic two-wing flyingfish, 136
    whitetip shark, 49, **258**
oceanicus, Gobionellus, 326
oceanops, Gobiosoma, 329
ocellata, Sciaenops, 244
ocellata, Starksia, 305
Ocellated flounder, 372
    frogfish, 113, **263**
ocellatus, Antennarius, 113
ocellatus, Bothus, 373
ocellatus, Chaetodon, 252
ocellatus, Ophichthus, 91
octonemus, Polydactylus, 292
Ocyurus chrysurus, 220, **287**
ocyurus, Centropristis, 166
ODONTASPIDIDAE, 41
Odontaspis taurus, 41
Offshore lizardfish, 105, **262**
    tonguefish, 390
OGCOCEPHALIDAE, 115
Ogcocephalus parvus, 116
    radiatus, 117, **263**
    sp. A, 118, **263**
    sp. B, 120
oglinum, Opisthonema, 98
Oligoplites saurus, 202, **283**
olseni, Raja, 62
omostigmum, Otophidium, 130
Oostethus lineatus, 158
OPHICHTHIDAE, 84
Ophichthus gomesi, 90
    ocellatus, 91

OPHIDIIDAE, 125
Ophidion beani, 128
    grayi, 129
    holbrooki, 129, **266**
    welshi, 130
Ophioblennius atlanticus, **310**, 317
ophryas, Prionotus, 364
Opisthonema oglinum, 98
OPISTOGNATHIDAE, 292
Opistognathus lonchurus, 293, **307**
    maxillosus, 296
Opossum pipefish, 158
Opsanus beta, 109
    pardus, 110
Orange filefish, **315**, 396
Orangespotted filefish, **315**, 400
ORECTOLOBIDAE, 39
Orthopristis chrysoptera, 229
OSTEICHTHYES, 72
osteochir, Remora, 194
OSTRACIIDAE, 406
Otophidium omostigmum, 130
oxyrhynchus, Acipenser, 72
oxyrinchus, Isurus, 44

P

Pagrus sedecim, 235
Painted wrasse, 272
Palespot batfish, 118
Palespotted eel, 91
Palometa, 210
Pancake batfish, 116, **263**
papillosum, Syacium, 385
Paraclinus fasciatus, 305, **307**
Paraconger caudilimbatus, 83
Parahollardia lineata, 395
paralatus, Prionotus, 365
Paralichthys albigutta, 381
    lethostigma, 382
    squamilentus, 382
Paranthias furcifer, 180, **275**
pardus, Opsanus, 110
Parepinephelus acutirostris, 180
Parexocoetus brachypterus, 138
Parrotfish, bluelip, 277
    bucktooth, 281
    emerald, 280
    stoplight, 281
    striped, 280
Parrotfishes, 277
paru, Peprilus, 356
paru, Pomacanthus, 260
parva, Lucania, 147
parvus, Ogcocephalus, 116
parvus, Sphoeroides, 411
parvus, Symphurus, 392
parvus, Upeneus, 248
patronus, Brevoortia, 94
Pearlfish, 131, **266**
Pearly razorfish, 272, **303**
pectinata, Pristis, 58
pectoralis, Prionotus, 367
pelagicus, Syngnathus, 161
pelicanus, Symphurus, 392
pensacolae, Harengula, 98
Peprilus alepidotus, 356
    burti, 355
    paru, 356
Perch, dwarf sand, 168
    sand, 169
    silver, 237
PERCICHTHYIDAE, 164
PERCIFORMES, 163
perfasciata, Anchoviella, 102
PERISTEDIIDAE, 362

Peristedion, **314**, 361
Permit, 210, **283**
perotteti, Pristis, 59
petenense, Dorosoma, 96
Petrometopon cruentatum, 181, **275**
pfluegeri, Tetrapturus, 350
Phaeoptyx conklini, 189, **279**
phenax, Mycteroperca, 179
philadelphica, Centropristis, 166
phoebe, Serranus, 183
Phrynelox nuttingi, 114
Pigfish, 229
Pike congers, 80
Pikea, 178
Pilchard, false, 97
Pilotfish, 202, **282**
Pinfish, 235, **294**
    spottail, 234
Pink wormfish, 334
Pipefish, bull, 162
    chain, 160
    dusky, 159
    dwarf, 160
    fringed, 158
    Gulf, 161
    northern, 159
    opossum, 158
    sargassum, 161
    shortfin, 159
Pipefishes, 155
Pipehorse, 156
pisonis, Eleotris, 321
plagiusa, Symphurus, 393
Planehead filefish, **318**, 404
Platybelone argalus, 140, **267**
platypterus, Istiophorus, 348
PLECTOGNATHI, 394
PLEURONECTIFORMES, 370
plumieri, Haemulon, 227
plumieri, Malacanthus, 190
plumieri, Scorpaena, 359
Poecilia latipinna, 149, **267**
POECILIIDAE, 147
poeyi, Synodus, 105
Pogonias cromis, 244
Polka-dot batfish, 117, **263**
    cusk-eel, 130
Polydactylus octonemus, 292
POLYNEMIDAE, 292
Polynemus, 292
POMACANTHIDAE, 255
Pomacanthus arcuatus, 257, **299**
    paru, 260, **299**
POMACENTRIDAE, 261
Pomacentrus, 268
POMADASYIDAE, 225
Pomadasys crocro, 230
POMATOMIDAE, 191
Pomatomus saltatrix, 191
Pompano, African, 196
    Florida, 209
    dolphin, 213
Porcupinefish, **319**, 414
Porcupinefishes, 413
Porgy, grass, 231
    jolthead, 232
    knobbed, 233
    littlehead, 234
    longspine, 236
    red, 235
    whitebone, 232
Porgies, 230
Porichthys porosissimus, 110, **263**
Poronotus triacanthus, 356
porosissimus, Porichthys, 110

427

porosus, Carcharhinus, 51
PRIACANTHIDAE, 185
Priacanthus arenatus, 186, **278**
Prionace glauca, 53
Prionodes, 184
Prionotus alatus, 362
  martis, 363
  microlepis, 366
  ophryas, 364
  paralatus, 365
  pectoralis, 367
  roseus, 365
  rubio, 366
  salmonicolor, 367
  scitulus, 367
  stearnsi, 368
  tribulus, 369
PRISTIDAE, 58
Pristigenys alta, 186, **278**
Pristipomoides andersoni, 221
  aquilonaris, 221, **290**
Pristis pectinata, 58
  perotteti, 59
probatocephalus, Archosargus, 231
prochilos, Gobiosoma, 329
profundorum, Lepophidium, 128
Prognichthys gibbifrons, 138
Promicrops itaiara,.172
proridens, Calamus, 234
Psenes cyanophrys, 354
pseudomaculatus, Apogon, 188
Pseudupeneus maculatus, 247, **295**
Pseudopriacanthus, 186
psittacus, Xyrichthys, 273
puella, Hypoplectrus, 176
Puffer, bandtail, 411
  checkered, 412
  least, 411
  marbled, 410
  sharpnose, 408
  smooth, 409
  southern, 410
Puffers, 408
pullus, Cantherhines, 400
pulvereus, Fundulus, 146
pumilio, Serraniculus, 182
punctatus, Decapterus, 200
punctatus, Myrophis, 88
punctifer, Mystriophis, 90
punctulatus, Gobiesox, 111
Purple reeffish, 264, **302**
Pygmy filefish, 404
  sea bass, 182
  tonguefish, 392

Q

quadricornis, Lactophrys, 407
quadrocellata, Ancylopsetta, 372
Queen angelfish, 256, **299**
  triggerfish, **315**, 399

R

RACHYCENTRIDAE, 192
Rachycentron canadum, 192, **279**
radians, Sparisoma, 281
radiatus, Ogcocephalus, 117
Ragged goby, 323
Rainbow runner, 201, **282**
Rainwater killifish, 147
Raja eglanteria, 61
  lentiginosa, 62
  olseni, 62
  texana, 63
RAJIDAE, 61
RAJIFORMES, 58
randalli, Acanthurus, 336

Ranzania laevis, 416
  truncata, 416
Ray, bullnose, 69
  cownose, 70
  eagle, 68
  lesser electric, 60
  smooth butterfly, 66
  spotted eagle, 68
Razorfish, pearly, 272
Red barbier, 175
  drum, 244
  goatfish, 247
  grouper, 173, **274**
  hind, 171, **271**
  lizardfish, 106, **262**
  porgy, 235
  snapper, 216, **286**
Redear sardine, 97
Redfin needlefish, 140, **267**
Redlip blenny, **310**, 317
Reef butterflyfish, 253, **298**
Reeffish, purple, 264
  yellowtail, 264
REGALECIDAE, 153
Regalecus glesne, 153
regalis, Scomberomorus, 343
regius, Urophycis, 124
regulus, Ariomma, 352
regulus, Hippocampus, 158
Remora, 194
  spearfish, 194
Remora australis, 193
  brachyptera, 194
  osteochir, 194
  remora, 194
remora, Remora, 194
Remoras, 192
Requiem sharks, 45
Rhincodon typus, 40
RHINCODONTIDAE, 40
RHINOBATIDAE, 59
Rhinobatos lentiginosus, 59
Rhinoptera bonasus, 70
Rhizoprionodon terraenovae, 54
rhomboides, Lagodon, 235
Rhomboplites aurorubens, 221, **290**
rimator, Bathystoma, 227
rimosus, Etropus, 380
ringens, Xanthichthys, 405
Rissola marginata, 125
rivoliana, Seriola, 207
robustum, Gobiosoma, 330
rochei, Auxis, 339
Rock hind, 169, **271**
  sea bass, 166
roseus, Cryptotomus, 277
roseus, Prionotus, 365
rostrata, Anguilla, 78
rostrata, Canthigaster, 408
Rough scad, 211
  silverside, 149
Roughback batfish, 116
Round herring, 96
  scad, 200, **282**
Roundel skate, 63
ruber, Caranx, 199
rubio, Prionotus. 366
rubra, Mycteroperca, 179
Rudderfish, banded, 208
Ruffs, 352
Runner, blue, 197
  rainbow, 201
Rypticus saponaceus, 185, **278**

S

sabina, Dasyatis, 65

saburrae, *Chasmodes*, 313
Sailfin eel, 87
   flyingfish, 138
   molly, 149, **267**
Sailfish, 348
salmonicolor, *Prionotus*, 367
saltatrix, *Pomatomus*, 191
Saltmarsh topminnow, 145
Sand diver, 105, **262**
   drum, 246
   perch, 169, **271**
   seatrout, 238
   stargazer, 296
   tiger, 41
   tilefish, 190, **279**
Sandbar shark, 50
Sandfish, belted, 184
saponaceus, *Rypticus*, 185
Sarda sarda, 341
sarda, *Sarda*, 341
Sardine, redear, 97
   scaled, 98
   Spanish, 99
Sardinella anchovia, 99
Sargassum pipefish, 161
   triggerfish, **318**, 405
Sargassumfish, 114, **263**
Sash flounder, 386
Saurida brasiliensis, 103
   caribbaea, 103
   normani, 104, **262**
saurus, *Elops*, 75
saurus, *Oligoplites*, 202
Sawfish, largetooth, 59
   smalltooth, 58
Sawfishes, 58
saxatilis, *Abudefduf*, 261
saxatilis, *Morone*, 164
saxicola, *Gymnothorax nigromarginatus*, 80
sayi, *Dasyatis*, 65
scaber, *Antennarius*, 114
Scad, bigeye, 203
   rough, 211
   round, 200
Scaled sardine, 98
Scalloped hammerhead, 55, **258**
Scamp, 179, **275**
SCARIDAE, 277
Scarus croicensis, 280, **303**
schoepfi, *Aluterus*, 396
schoepfi, *Chilomycterus*, 413
Schoolmaster, 215, **286**
SCIAENIDAE, 237
Sciaenops ocellata, 244
scitulus, *Prionotus*, 367
sciurus, *Haemulon*, 228
Scomber japonicus, **311**, 341
Scomberomorus cavalla, 341
   maculatus, 342
   regalis, **311**, 343
SCOMBRIDAE, 338
Scorpaena agassizi, 357
   atlantica, 359
   brasiliensis, **314**, 358
   calcarata, **314**, 358
   colesi, 358
   dispar, 359
   ginsburgi, 360
   plumieri, **314**, 359
   similis, 359
   stearnsi, 358
SCORPAENIDAE, 357
Scorpionfish, hunchback, 359
   longfin, 357
   smoothhead, 358
   spotted, 359
Scorpionfishes, 357
scotti, *Chromis*, 264
scovelli, *Syngnathus*, 161
Scrawled cowfish, **318**, 407
   filefish, **315**, 397
scriptus, *Aluterus*, 397
scuticaris, *Bascanichthys*, 85
Sea catfish, 108
Seahorse, dwarf, 157
   lined, 156
Seahorses, 155
Searobin, armored, 361
   bandtail, 364
   barred, 363
   bighead, 369
   blackfin, 366
   blackwing, 367
   bluespotted, 365
   horned, 361
   leopard, 367
   Mexican, 365
   shortwing, 368
   spiny, 362
Searobins, 360
Seatrout, sand, 238
   silver, 239
   spotted, 238
Seatrouts, 237
Seaweed blenny, **307**, 308
sectatrix, *Kyphosus*, 248
secunda, *Uraspis*, 211
sedecim, *Pagrus*, 235
sedentarius, *Chaetodon*, 253
Selar crumenophthalmus, 203, **283**
Selene vomer, 203, **283**
Seminole goby, **311**, 331
SEMIONOTIFORMES, 73
Sennet, northern, 289
senta, *Engyophrys*, 378
Sergeant major, 261, **299**
Seriola dumerili, 205, **283**
   fasciata, 206
   rivoliana, 207, **283**
   zonata, 208
Serraniculus pumilio, 182
SERRANIDAE, 165
Serranus atrobranchus, 183
   phoebe, 183, **275**
   subligarius, 184
setapinnis, *Vomer*, 212
setifer, *Monacanthus*, 404
Shad, Alabama, 92
   gizzard, 95
   threadfin, 96
Shark, Atlantic angel, 57
   Atlantic sharpnose, 54
   blacknose, 46
   blacktip, 48
   blue, 53
   bull, 47
   dusky, 50
   finetooth, 45
   lemon, 53
   mackerel, 43
   nurse, 39
   oceanic whitetip, 49
   sandbar, 50
   silky, 47
   smalltail, 51
   spinner, 49
   thresher, 43
   tiger, 51
   whale, 40
   white, 43

Sharks, angel, 57
    carpet, 39
    hammerhead, 54
    requiem, 45
    thresher, 42
Sharksucker, 193, **279**
Sharpnose puffer, **319**, 408
Sharptail goby, 326
    mola, 415
Sheepshead, 231, **291**
    minnow, 143, **267**
Shoal flounder, 383
Short bigeye, 186, **278**
Shortbelly eel, 91
Shortfin mako, 44
    pipefish, 159
Shortjaw lizardfish, 104, **262**
Shortwing searobin, 368
Shrimp eel, 90
    flounder, 380
shufeldti, Gobionellus, 327
Silk snapper, 220, **287**
Silky shark, 47
SILURIFORMES, 107
Silver conger, 81
    jenny, 223, **290**
    perch, 237
    seatrout, 239
Silverside, rough, 149
    tidewater, 150
Silversides, 149
similis, Fundulus, 146
similis, Scorpaena, 359
Singlespot frogfish, 113
Skate, clearnose, 61
    freckled, 62
    roundel, 63
    spreadfin, 62
Skates, 61
Skilletfish, 112, **263**
Skipjack herring, 93
    tuna, **311**, 340
Sleeper, bigmouth, 322
    emerald, 321
    fat, 320
    spinycheek, 321
Sleepers, 320
Slender mola, 416
    pike eel, 79
    suckerfish, 193
Slippery dick, 269, **302**
Smalleye hammerhead, 56
Smallmouth flounder, 379
Smallscale lizardfish, 103
Smalltail shark, 51
Smalltooth sawfish, 58
smaragdus, Erotelis, 321
smithi, Brevoortia, 95
Smooth butterfly ray, 66
    dogfish, 52
    hammerhead, 57
    puffer, 409
Smoothhead scorpionfish, **314**, 358
Smoothhound, Florida, 52
Snake eels, 84
Snakefish, 107, **262**
Snapper, blackfin, 216
    cubera, 217
    dog, 218
    gray, 217
    lane, 219
    mahogany, 218
    mutton, 215
    red, 216
    silk, 220

    vermilion, 221
    yellowtail, 220
Snapper eel, 89
Snappers, 214
Snook, 163, **271**
Snowy grouper, 174, **274**
Soapfish, greater, 185
sobaco, Canthidermis, 402
solanderi, Acanthocybium, 339
Sole, fringed, 388
    lined, 387
    naked, 388
SOLEIDAE, 387
Soles, 387
Sooty eel, 86
soporator, Bathygobius, 323
Southern flounder, 382
    hake, 124
    kingfish, 242
    puffer, 410
    stargazer, 297
    stingray, 64
Spadefish, Atlantic, 249
Spaghetti eels, 78
Spanish mackerel, 342
    sardine, 99
SPARIDAE, 230
Sparisoma radians, 281, **306**
    viride, 281, **306**
spatula, Lepisosteus, 73
Spearfish, longbill, 350
    remora, 194
Speckled hind, 170
    worm eel, 88, **262**
spengleri, Sphoeroides, 411
Sphoeroides dorsalis, 410
    harperi, 411
    nephelus, 410
    parvus, 411
    spengleri, **319**, 411
    testudineus, **319**, 412
Sphyraena barracuda, 288, **306**
    borealis, 289, **306**
    guachancho, 289
SPHYRAENIDAE, 288
Sphyrna bigelowi, 54
    diplana, 54
    lewini, 55, **258**
    mokarran, 55
    tiburo, 56
    tudes, 56
    zygaena, 57
SPHYRNIDAE, 54
Spikefishes, 394
spilopterus, Citharichthys, 376
Spinner shark, 49
Spiny flounder, 378
    searobin, 362
Spinycheek sleeper, **310**, 321
Splitlure frogfish, 114, **263**
Sponge goby, 324
spongicola, Evermannichthys, 324
Spot, 241, **294**
Spotfin butterflyfish, 252, **298**
    flounder, 377
    flyingfish, 134
    mojarra, 223, **290**
Spottail pinfish, 234
    tonguefish, 393
Spotted driftfish, 352
    eagle ray, 68, **258**
    goatfish, 247, **295**
    hake, 124
    moray, 79, **259**
    scorpionfish, **314**, 359

seatrout, 238
spoon-nose eel, 88, **262**
whiff, 375
Spottedfin tonguefish, 391
Spreadfin skate, 62
springeri, Gordiichthys, 87
springeri, Syngnathus, 162
SQUALIFORMES, 39
squamilentus, Paralichthys, 382
Squatina dumerili, 57
SQUATINIDAE, 57
Squirrelfish, 151, **270**
    deepwater, 151
    dusky, 152
Squirrelfishes, 150
Star drum, 245
Stargazer, freckled, 300
    lancer, 301
    sand, 296
    southern, 297
Stargazers, 297
Starksia ocellata, 305, **307**
stearnsi, Blennius, 309
stearnsi, Prionotus, 368
stearnsi, Scorpaena, 358
Steindachneria argentea, 123
Stellifer lanceolatus, 245
Stenotomus caprinus, 236
Stephanolepis, 405
stigmaticus, Gobionellus, 327
Stingray, Atlantic, 65
    bluntnose, 65
    southern, 64
    yellow, 67
Stingrays, 64
Stippled clingfish, 111
    spoon-nose eel, 90
Stoplight parrotfish, 281, **306**
striata, Centropristis, 167
striatum, Haemulon, 229
striatus, Chaetodon, 254
striatus, Epinephelus, 175
Striped anchovy, 100
    bass, 164
    blenny, 312
    burrfish, **319**, 413
    grunt, 229, **291**
    mullet, 285, **306**
    parrotfish, 280, **303**
STROMATEIDAE, 355
STROMATEOIDEI, 351
Strongylura marina, 140
    notata, 140, **267**
    timucu, 141
strumosus, Gobiesox, 112
Sturgeon, Atlantic, 72
Sturgeons, 72
subligarius, Serranus, 184
Suckerfish, slender, 193
sufflamen, Canthidermis, 401
Sunfish, ocean, 415
superciliosus, Alopias, 42
Surgeonfish, Gulf, 336
Surgeonfishes, 335
surinamensis, Anisotremus, 225
surinamensis, Lobotes, 222
Swordfish, 347
Swordtail jawfish, 293
Syacium gunteri, 383
    micrurum, 384
    papillosum, 385
Symphurus civitatus, 390
    diomedianus, 391
    parvus, 392
    pelicanus, 392

plagiusa, **315**, 393
urospilus, 393
synagris, Lutjanus, 219
SYNGNATHIDAE, 155
Syngnathus elucens, 159
    floridae, 159
    fuscus, 159, **270**
    hildebrandi, 160
    louisianae, 160
    pelagicus, 161
    scovelli, 161
    springeri, 162
SYNODONTIDAE, 102
Synodus foetens, 104, **262**
    intermedius, 105, **262**
    poeyi, 105, **262**
    synodus, 106, **262**
synodus, Synodus, 106
syringinus, Uroconger, 84

T

tabacaria, Fistularia, 155
Tang, blue, 336
Tarpon, 75
Tarpon, 76
Tattler, 183, **275**
taurus, Carcharhias, 42
taurus, Odontaspis, 41
tenuis, Hoplunnis, 81
teres, Bascanichthys, 86
teres, Etrumeus, 96
terraenovae, Rhizoprionodon, 54
testudineus, Sphoeroides, 412
TETRAODONTIDAE, 408
TETRAODONTIFORMES, 394
Tetrapturus albidus, 349
    pfluegeri, 350
texae, Gymnachirus, 388
texana, Raja, 63
thalassinus, Microgobius, 333
Thalassoma bifasciatum, 276, **303**
thazard, Auxis, 339
Thick-tail batfish, 120
Thread eel, 87
Threadfin, Atlantic, 292
    shad, 96
Threadtail conger, 84
Three-eye flounder, **314**, 371
Thresher, bigeye, 42
    shark, 43
Thunnus alalunga, 343
    albacares, 344
    atlanticus, 344
    obesus, 345
    thynnus, 345
thynnus, Thunnus, 345
tiburo, Sphyrna, 56
Tidewater silverside, 150
Tiger shark, 51
Tilefish, blackline, 190
    sand, 190
Timucu, 141
timucu, Strongylura, 141
Toadfish, Gulf, 109
    leopard, 110
Tomtate, 226, **291**
Tonguefish, blackcheek, 393
    longtail, 392
    offshore, 390
    pygmy, 392
    spottail, 393
    spottedfin, 391
Tonguefishes, 390
Topminnow, saltmarsh, 145
TORPEDINIDAE, 60

townsendi, Angelichthys, 257
Trachinocephalus myops, 107, **262**
Trachinotus carolinus, 209, **283**
    falcatus, 210, **283**
    goodei, 210
Trachurus lathami, 211 .
TRIACANTHODIDAE, 394
triacanthus, Poronotus, 356
tribulus, Prionotus, 369
TRICHIURIDAE, 337
Trichiurus lepturus, 337
trichodon, Mugil, 288
Trichopsetta ventralis, 386
Tricorn batfish, 121
tricornis, Lactophrys, 407
tridigitatus, Dactyloscopus, 296
Triggerfish, gray, 398
    ocean, 401
    queen, 399
    sargassum, 405
Triggerfishes, 395
TRIGLIDAE, 360
trigonus, Lactophrys, 407
Trinectes maculatus, **314**, 389
Tripletail, 222, **290**
Trumpetfish, 154, **270**
truncata, Ranzania, 416
Trunkfish, 407
tudes, Sphyrna, 56
Tuna, bigeye, 345
    blackfin, 344
    bluefin, 345
    skipjack, 340
    yellowfin, 344
Tunas, 338
Tunny, little, 340
Twoscale goby, 328
Twospot cardinalfish, 188, **278**
Tylosurus acus, 141, **267**
typus, Rhincodon, 40

U

Ulaema, 224
Umbrina coroides, 246
umbrosus, Equetus, 240
undecimalis, Centropomus, 163
undulatus, Micropogon, 243
unifasciatus, Hyporhamphus, 138
Upeneus parvus, 248
URANOSCOPIDAE, 297
Uraspis heidi, 212
    secunda, 211
Uroconger syringinus, 84
UROLOPHIDAE, 68
Urolophus jamaicensis, 67, **258**
Urophycis cirratus, 123
    floridanus, 124
    regius, 124
urospilus, Symphurus, 393
usta, Nicholsina, 280

V

variabilis, Eupomacentrus, 268
variegatus, Cyprinodon, 143
velifer, Letharchus, 87
velox, Euleptorhamphus, 135
venenosa, Mycteroperca, 180
ventralis, Aluterus, 396

ventralis, Trichopsetta, 386
Vermilion snapper, 221, **290**
vetula, Balistes, 399
vexillarius, Holocentrus, 152
Violet goby, 325
viride, Sparisoma, 281
vivanus, Hemanthias, 175
vivanus, Lutjanus, 220
volitans, Dactylopterus, 370
vomer, Selene, 203
Vomer setapinnis, 212
vulpes, Albula, 76
vulpinus, Alopias, 43

W

Wahoo, 339
Warsaw grouper, 173
welshi, Ophidion, 130
Wenchman, 221, **290**
Whale shark, 40
Whalesucker, 193
Whiff, bay, 376
    horned, 374
    spotted, 375
Whip eel, 85
White grunt, 227, **291**
    marlin, 349
    mullet, 285, **306**
    shark, 43
Whitebone porgy, 232
Whiteline goby, **310**, 329
williamsoni, Nodogymnus, **388**
Worm eels, 84
Wormfish, lancetail, **334**
    pink, 334
Wrasse, greenband, 269
    painted, 272
Wrasses, 269

X

Xanthichthys ringens, **318**, 405
xanthurus, Leiostomus, 241
xenica, Adinia, 142
Xiphias gladius, 347
XIPHIIDAE, 347
Xyrichthys psittacus, 273

Y

Yellow conger, 82
    goatfish, 246, **294**
    jack, 197, **279**
    stingray, 67, **258**
Yellowedge grouper, 170
Yellowfin grouper, 180, **275**
    menhaden, 95
    mojarra, 224, **290**
    tuna, 344
Yellowtail hamlet, 176, **274**
    reeffish, 264, **302**
    snapper, 220, **287**
ygraecum, Astroscopus, 297

Z

Zalieutes mcgintyi, 121
ZEIFORMES, 152
zonata, Seriola, 208
zosterae, Hippocampus, 157
zygaena, Sphyrna, 57

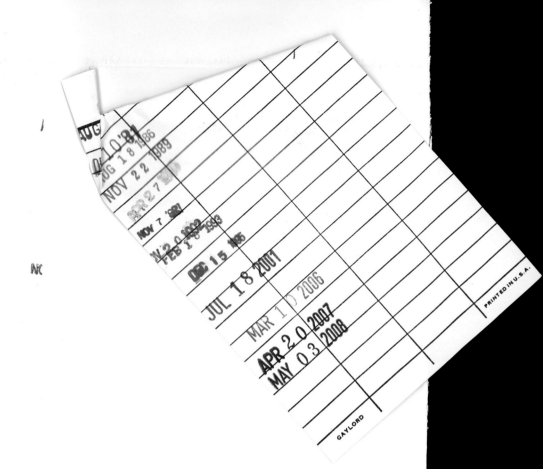